FRIDAY, SATURDAY, SUNDAY IN TEXAS

FRIDAY, SATURDAY, SUNDAY IN TEXAS

A Year in the Life of Lone Star
Football, from High School to
College to the Cowboys

NICK EATMAN

DEY ST.
AN IMPRINT OF WILLIAM MORROW *PUBLISHERS*

DEY ST.

HarperCollins books may be purchased for educational, business, or sales promotional use. For information, please email the Special Markets Department at SPsales@harpercollins.com.

FIRST EDITION

Composed by North Market Street Graphics, Lancaster, PA

Library of Congress Cataloging-in-Publication Data has been applied for.

ISBN 978-0-06-243331-2

16   17   18   19   20   NMSG/RRD   10   9   8   7   6   5   4   3   2   1

This book is dedicated to every raised eyebrow,
every optimistic grin, and for anyone and everyone who told me
this book "was a great idea" or something they "couldn't wait to read."
There were many long nights, bumps in the road from start to finish,
but those encouraging words along the way from colleagues, friends,
and certainly my family helped me push through to the end.

CONTENTS

INTRODUCTION

In football, at any level, you never know what is going to happen. It doesn't matter if it's high school, college, or the NFL, that's the beauty of the game, the frustration of it, and sometimes both at the same time.

Unpredictability is why we watch football; why we, as fans, stick around even when all signs point to the game being over. It's what happens just when you think you know the end of the story. It's what happens even when you think the end has already been written.

My unpredictable journey writing this book began long before the 2015 football season. The idea first began in the fall of 2013. I had just published a biography of Art Briles called *Looking Up* and was working on a collection of Dallas Cowboys stories titled *If These Walls Could Talk*, when my thoughts shifted to a possible third book.

But time was limited, especially since I was traveling around to promote the Baylor book in Waco on Saturday; attending every Cowboys game on Sunday, home and away; and then trying to squeeze in some Friday night high school action with the Plano Wildcats, a team I had followed over the years thanks to a couple of friends on the coaching staff.

One night around 11 p.m., though, while flipping through the channels on television, I found some unexpected inspiration. The show *Modern Family* has been one of my favorites, and I have seen dozens of episodes. But on this night, as I watched the episode bounce back and forth between three different families and three different sets of issues, yet all seemingly wanting the same goal for each other . . . it hit me.

Right then and there is where this idea first popped into my head: I wanted to write a book on the three levels of football in Texas, showing just how different, yet similar, the sport can be when it's played for the most passionate football fans in the country. Whether it's the high schooler preparing for his SAT test, the college kid studying for his next trigonometry exam, or a rookie linebacker for the Cowboys digging into his playbook for an upcoming game against the Washington Redskins, there are parallels, problems, and plays that speak to every level of the game.

Obviously, the interest in high school, college, and pro football is vastly different. Only a handful of high school games are ever televised during the regular season. Conversely, just a few games in big-time college football are played without TV exposure, and in the NFL, fans now have the ability to watch every game coast to coast.

Still, no matter the day, no matter the place, and no matter the amount of media attention, the goal, especially in Texas, remains the same: win. Once the shoulder pads come on, the helmets gets strapped tight, and the scoreboards light up, it doesn't matter if it's the Cowboys' Tony Romo, the Bears' Seth Russell, or even the Wildcats' Matt Keys; they're all just playing quarterback in a kid's game that has now become America's favorite sport.

And in Texas, it's a way of life.

And so that became the goal for this book: chronicle an entire football season from the inside out, from start to finish.

As I settled in to write about the 2015 football season in Texas, I honestly had no idea what to expect from any of these three programs. I've been covering football for over 20 years and the thing that never ceases to amaze me is what the beginning of each season feels like—that blank slate when it seems almost anything can happen. You might think you know your team and what they're capable of (or not capable of), but until that first snap, there's still a part of you that thinks: anything is possible.

I'd be lying if I didn't say I was hopeful about the stories I would get entering the 2015 season. Each of these teams had strong showings the previous year. Each seemed, at least on paper, to have the tools to do it again. Would teams make the playoffs? Would they go all the way? Would there be injuries? Would the coaches keep their jobs?

The thing about football stories is that, as unpredictable as they are, if you're a fan who's been around, you think you know all the different ways they can end. You've seen the seasons when success comes out of nowhere. The places when expectations override talent. The times when everything is there on paper, but for some reason it never translates to the actual game. Sure, things might be unpredictable, but watch football long enough, and even the unpredictability has a pattern to it.

Perhaps that's where the 2015 season, or to be more specific, Baylor's 2015 season, became a different story altogether. For a team hopeful of winning the school's first-ever national title, losing three quarterbacks throughout the season should've been the biggest hurdle to overcome. But that was just a puddle of water compared to the deluge of problems the Bears would eventually face, problems that would shake not only Baylor's football program but also the university and the world of college football as a whole. While this is a story that continues to unfold even as I write this, I've done my best to capture the story as it currently stands, even as much about the facts and the decisions that surround them remains shrouded in mystery.

Ultimately, the events at Baylor highlight the reality of playing in football's biggest state: whether it's Plano, Baylor, or the Cowboys, football seasons rarely just end. Sure, the games finish around November and December, with a few more played in January, but football is a 365-day-a-year sport that never comes to a complete stop, particularly in the Lone Star State. Football doesn't stop when the teams leave the field. It doesn't stop when hope for the playoffs is lost. It doesn't stop when players realize that their time wearing the team's jersey is ending. And because it never stops, the problems that follow teams and players onto the field aren't always easy to separate from the problems that follow them off.

In Texas, football truly is a way of life. While each level of the game has its fans, football is far greater than any one day of the week. Here, game day lives three days a week—Friday, Saturday, Sunday—which means the players, the coaches, and the fans have to be ready for whatever comes their way, all season long.

PROLOGUE: EXPECTING THE BEST

Friday

Starting in late August, Plano, Texas gets a bit quiet on Friday evenings. The family-owned diners, the antique shops, and even the popular Dairy Queen all have one thing in common: they flip their signs over to Closed, so that everyone can make it to the stadium to watch the game. And if their team is on the road, the town shuts down even earlier, so that the caravan of polished cars can make the trek to the nearby rival.

In truth, Plano isn't that unique in that regard. High school football is a way of life for just about every town in Texas, although make no mistake, the population doesn't have to be less than six digits to carry out this tradition. Plano, a northern suburb of Dallas that was once considered in the country, is now anything but rural. In fact, Plano's population in 2014 was more than 275,000, making it the ninth-largest city in the state. And in terms of enrollment, three of the largest schools in Texas all reside in the Plano Independent School District. Even as late as 1970, Plano's population was under 20,000, but by 1980, thanks to at least one hundred new businesses sprouting up in the area, Plano had exploded to more than 72,000 people.

More families mean more kids. More kids mean a bigger pool of players from which to choose and that typically results in better football teams. And while Plano Senior High did win two championships in the 1960s as a small 2A school, the Wildcats quickly became one of the biggest and best programs in Texas, winning seven state titles overall by 1994, including three at the 5A level.

Serving as a first-year assistant coach on that 1994 squad was an ultra-intense go-getter named Jaydon McCullough, who didn't need to be sold on the school's tradition. He had been a standout player for the Wildcats in 1979 and 1980 with hopes of coaching at Plano one day. And in his very first year on staff, he not only picked up one state championship ring in football; he earned another as an assistant on the boys' soccer team, which also claimed a title that spring.

One school year, two state championship rings? This coaching thing wasn't so bad, huh?

Fast-forward two decades and McCullough was still chasing that third ring. And the chase seemed to get more intense with every passing year, especially since 2008 when McCullough was promoted to head coach. On the surface, McCullough wasn't just the shortest coach on the staff; his 5–7 stature probably had him under many of his varsity players. But McCullough more than made up for what he lacked in sheer height with extreme intensity. And he was a big believer in physical fitness, biding by his own rule that "working out every day helps me both mentally and physically." At fifty-three years old, he filled out his shirt with a stronger upper body. Full of dark, curly hair, McCullough had an infectious smile, but it was rarely shown on the football fields, either in a game or practice.

For McCullough, winning was truly the only thing that matters. And his teams had still done well, making the playoffs six times through his first seven seasons as head coach for an overall record of 45–33. But what might be successful to some programs only whetted the appetite of the folks at Plano.

No one understood that more than McCullough, who not only felt the pressure to win, but seemed to welcome it. He had a photo hanging above the desk in his office of three former head coaches at Plano—John

Clark, Tom Kimbrough, and Gerald Brence—who all earned at least one state title.

Plano's main home stadium was aptly named John Clark Field for the legendary coach who won two state championships. With two other high schools in the Plano Independent School District, there was now a high demand for the facility. So the Wildcats occasionally also played home games at nearby Tom Kimbrough Stadium, which is named after the coach for whom McCullough played during his high school days and who won three state crowns. And the man who promoted McCullough to be Plano's varsity coach was Gerald Brence, winner of the 1994 title and now the district's athletic director. All three still stayed visible in the program, despite Clark and Kimbrough officially being retired.

As McCullough entered his thirtieth season in coaching, this was exactly where he wanted to be—as it always had been. A few years into his career, McCullough had scribbled words down on a piece of paper that he still kept to this day:

My goal is to one day become the head coach of the Plano Wildcats.

But while he was living his dream, he knew there was unfinished business ahead. At some schools, postseason appearances or playoff victories were the measure. At Plano, the goal was to win championships, a reality that McCullough and his coaching assistants were reminded of daily when they walked past the school's trophy case. For many of the school's fans, rooting for the team went beyond just watching the current crop of Wildcats, and instead it was an opportunity for them to relive some of the glory years when they themselves were either playing on the same field or cheering from the sidelines or even participating in the drill team or marching band. And that trophy case, like the fans themselves, was a direct link to the program's past glory.

And because the goal never changed, the expectations never wavered either. Regardless if the crop of returning players appeared to be promising with several experienced seniors or if the cupboard looked bare, the ultimate objective was to win a ring. That pressure was both exciting and daunting. The same thing that kept McCullough up at night was the same thing that got him up in the morning.

Heading into the 2015 campaign, McCullough's spirits were higher than ever, especially coming off a 7–4 season that saw the Wildcats return to the playoffs, albeit for another first-round exit. Just winning seven games was quite a feat in itself, though, considering Plano was placed in a nine-team district, the largest in Class 6A. Not only did it include neighboring Allen High School, which won its third straight state title in 2014, but always formidable teams such as Flower Mound Marcus, McKinney Boyd, Hebron, Lewisville, and, of course, the two crosstown rivals, Plano East and Plano West.

Eight district games on the schedule meant Plano had only two non-district contests to work out the kinks. In the past, teams would have as many as three, sometimes four or five, opportunities to fully get prepared for the games that really counted, the district play.

But with only two non-district games, including an opener against traditional power John Tyler High School out of Tyler, Texas, Plano put even more emphasis on a scrimmage with Mesquite High School, located in the east Dallas suburb of the same name.

These controlled scrimmages had no real scoreboard and were designed to give both teams a chance to evaluate themselves against comparable competition. The goal was to execute and stay healthy—and not necessarily in that order. A year ago, the Wildcats had lost their backup quarterback, Matt Keys, to a broken collarbone in this scrimmage with Mesquite. And it's likely Keys would've played considerable time after starter Brooks Panhans broke his foot in the 2014 season opener, forcing Plano to call up a junior varsity quarterback to run the show for most of the 2014 season.

This time around, Plano entered its workout with Mesquite still unclear about the quarterback position. Keys, a senior who looked the part at 6–4, didn't have the most accurate arm or the greatest athletic ability, but he offset both with toughness. He was competing in practice with junior Aaron Regas, a cornerback the last two years who provided more quickness but with a lesser arm.

After the scrimmage, neither of the two wowed the coaches with impressive plays, but each also really didn't do anything to lose the job. For Plano, the decision came down to common sense more than anything. McCullough knew the defense lacked depth. Moving Regas to quarterback only thinned out the unit even more. It's not like Keys was going to switch over to the other side of the ball. Starting Keys and keeping Regas on defense not only satisfied the defensive coaches; the move also seemed best for the offense as well. Quarterback, after all, would take a backseat to the running attack.

At the center of that attack was Brandon Stephens, a three-year letterman who had been a contributor since his freshman year. One of the nation's top recruits, Stephens entered fall practices with a list of schools in the hunt for furthering his education, including Alabama, Texas A&M, Oklahoma, and Stanford. Stephens looked a bit tall for a traditional running back, standing a little over six feet, but he'd proven he could get low and break tackles while also using long strides for breakaway runs. He was a first-team "Super Team" selection in *Dave Campbell's Texas Football,* a magazine that is the "bible" for everything football in Texas.

So how much was it worth to have one of the best running backs in the state? Plano, with its lack of experience at quarterback, lack of playmakers at wide receiver, lack of size on the offensive line, and lack of depth on defense, was about to find out.

Saturday

On a steamy Texas evening in mid-July 2009, Art Briles sat in a popular barbecue spot near Austin. He was supposed to be on vacation, as the football season was still about six weeks away.

After just one year as the new head coach at Baylor University, a season that ended with a 4–8 record but included more hard-fought games than the program had seen in some time, the arrow was pointing up for

Briles and his team. So while the rest of his family was focused on the brisket and ribs, he had other thoughts on his mind.

"You know, I really think Robert can win the Heisman. He's that good," Briles said of his soon-to-be sophomore quarterback, Robert Griffin III. "If we can win some games, he'll have a chance when he's a junior or senior. If he does that, we'll be in good shape and can get a lot of good kids in here. Man, what we need to do is get a new stadium someday and bring football back to the campus. That's what I'm really trying to do."

Fast-forward six years to another afternoon of sweltering heat in Waco. It's mid-August and all of those dreams Briles had shared back in that restaurant had come to fruition.

He was 100 percent right about Griffin, who brought home the Heisman Trophy in 2011, a season in which he guided Baylor to a 10–3 record. And Briles was certainly spot-on about turning the program around, as the Bears went to five straight bowl games from 2010 to 2014, also winning the school's first Big 12 title in 2013, which earned the team a BSC berth in the Fiesta Bowl.

Not only had that on-campus stadium he envisioned more than a half-decade earlier opened in 2014, with Griffin's statue nestled in between the east end zone and the Brazos River; but Baylor finished 11–2 en route to defending its Big 12 title and just missing inclusion in college football's first-ever four-team playoff.

Having enjoyed a magical rise from perennial doormat to one of the nation's most attractive programs, the Bears now showcased a fast-paced, high-scoring offense while often wearing cool chrome helmets and all-black uniforms. This certainly wasn't the Baylor University most of the country remembered . . . and that's exactly the way Briles wanted it.

Or so he thought. During seven full seasons in Waco, there had been only a handful of controversial issues that had come up, the most severe of which was a rape charge against one of Briles' former players in 2012. In addition, there had been some drug-related suspensions on the team, which included dismissing Josh Gordon, who then went on to become a star receiver in the NFL before more failed marijuana tests derailed his pro career as well. Still, despite these mistakes for the program, there wasn't a public perception of any problems in the way Briles was running things. In Texas, success on the field has a way of overshadowing everything, especially if it's newfound success.

The tide had certainly changed for Briles and his program. And he was no stranger to this shift in perception. It had also happened at his previous head coaching position with the University of Houston, which actually had considered dropping the football program in the early 2000s for financial reasons. But when Briles showed up as one of the lowest-paid coaches in Division I, he quickly turned the Cougars into a respectable team that went to four bowl games in five seasons from 2003 to 2007.

Prior to that, an even greater transformation occurred at Stephenville High School, where Briles took over a mediocre program in 1988 and went on to become a legendary coach in the high school ranks. The Yellow Jackets grew into a state powerhouse, winning four titles in the 1990s, the last of which came in 1999 with his son, Kendal, as the starting quarterback.

Just like at Stephenville and then Houston, Briles was now feeling the effects of what he called "going from hunters to the hunted." Winning forty games in four years at Baylor will do that. To put those numbers in perspective, when Briles took over the program in 2008, the last forty victories spanned thirteen seasons and four different head coaches.

In those four years from 2011 to 2014, Baylor enjoyed three seasons of at least ten wins. Only once before in school history (1980) had the Bears reached the ten-win plateau. That team was led by longtime coach, Grant Teaff, who has a statue outside of Baylor's McLane Stadium. Needless to say, in his relatively short tenure, Briles had already far exceeded the success of Teaff or any other coach in school history.

Ironically enough, the off-season following that 2014 campaign was arguably the first time since Briles' first year at Baylor that his phone didn't ring too often from other schools looking to pry him away from his Waco nest.

There were two different times when he had to turn down Texas Tech University; most Baylor fans never knew the difficulty of his decisions. Briles not only grew up in Rule, Texas, a small town only about two hours away from Lubbock, but he actually graduated from Texas Tech with his girlfriend, Jan, who became his wife in 1978. But despite those calls from the Red Raiders and some interest from schools such as Auburn that he didn't really consider, there was only one university that even Briles wasn't sure he could ever deny, and it had come to the forefront the year before.

The worst-kept secret in the state during the 2013 season was that University of Texas head coach, Mack Brown, was going to be replaced. Had Baylor not dusted off Texas in the regular-season finale to win the conference, the Longhorns would have claimed the Big 12 title and headed to a BCS bowl game. Maybe then Brown would've saved his job for another year, although it was clear that the fan base in Austin wanted a change. They wanted something new and exciting. They wanted Briles.

For a born-and-raised Texan who has never lived outside of the state, being considered for the job certainly would have been flattering for Briles—if it were ever offered. All season long his name was linked to a position that wasn't even open yet. And when it finally became available in mid-December, as Briles was trying to prepare his team for the Fiesta Bowl, the rumors and speculation started to become overwhelming.

Briles was contacted by the Longhorns during the weeks leading up to the bowl game and was asked to interview. Trying to maintain his focus for the game, he declined the opportunity with Texas' search committee. If the job would've been flat-out offered to Briles, who knows what color ball cap he might be wearing today? But, it never was. Only a chance to interview was given. And while Briles is as humble as they come, flirting with another job—even one as prestigious as Texas—for the *chance* to interview was too risky. He didn't just have a good thing going in Waco. He had a great thing.

And with that, he announced he would be staying put at Baylor, the only place he really wanted to be.

Once Briles turned down the University of Texas, it was hard to assume anyone else could get him to leave what was now a powerhouse in Waco. Baylor was entering the 2015 season as one of the "most hunted," picked to finish among the final four teams in the College Football Playoff.

Wait, Baylor in the final four—for the entire nation?

It wasn't too long again when Baylor fans would've settled for a top-four finish in the now-defunct Big 12 South, which housed only six teams. Now, Baylor had not only won the ten-team conference the last two seasons, but had its sights set on the bigger prize.

For the Baylor fandom, this reversal of fortunes was being celebrated by fans of all ages. Entering 2015, the Bears were coming off a pair of eleven-win seasons. To put those twenty-two victories in the proper perspective, Baylor joined the Big 12 conference in 1996 after the old Southwest Conference folded the year before. But joining the big boys of college football such as Oklahoma, Nebraska, Texas, and Texas A&M had its early troubles for Baylor, which needed nine seasons after joining the Big 12 to finally accumulate more than twenty-two wins.

Once the doormats of college football, Baylor fans had reason to stick their chests out even farther these days. The older generation of Baylor fans that remembered the Grant Teaff era (1972–1992) still hadn't seen five straight bowl games like this team had currently achieved. Even the more recent alumni, the middle-aged fans who saw this school collect eleven conference wins in twelve seasons before Briles' arrival, now had reason to gloat throughout Texas, especially after consecutive 8–1 conference records.

It was possible that the current Baylor students had no clue their program was once considered the laughingstock of football. Even a fifth-year senior entering the 2015 season had already seen forty wins in their first four seasons in Waco, a town that until recently didn't have many apparel shops off campus that carried Baylor merchandise. The sporting goods stores were filled with Texas and Texas A&M gear but only specialty stores would sell the Green & Gold. Now, anything from shirts, polos, caps, socks, and ties to even apparel for pets could be found with Baylor's logo and colors on it.

That change occurred in Waco around 2010, when Baylor made its first bowl game in fifteen years. Now, around the entire state, Baylor merchandise was prominently found, especially up in the Dallas-Fort Worth area, where Texas, Texas A&M, Oklahoma, Texas Tech, and later TCU had hogged most of the clothing racks.

Fans were back on the Baylor bandwagon not just for the recent success the school had experienced, but for a bigger prize that perhaps awaited them.

What made the lofty expectations so remarkable was the lack of experience quarterback Seth Russell brought to the table. Yes, as the backup to Bryce Petty the last two years, Russell had seen some action, even starting one game in 2014 against Northwestern when he threw five touchdown passes. He also relieved an injured Petty that same season against Texas Tech with the Bears up comfortably in the third quarter, but they had to hold on for a two-point win.

But Russell was really the only unknown about a Baylor team that brought back four seniors on the offensive line, including left tackle Spencer Drango, who even surprised most of the coaching staff with his decision in the spring to return to school and not enter the NFL Draft. On the other side of the line, the Bears were also pleasantly surprised that defensive end Shawn Oakman, the massive specimen that looked more like a WWE superstar than a football player, returned for his final year. A transfer from Penn State, Oakman made his way down to Waco after a tumultuous two seasons that included some off-the-field mishaps, including a reported incident in which Oakman forcefully grabbed a store clerk's hand after she accused him of stealing a sandwich. Oakman was dismissed by then-PSU head coach Bill O'Brien, and he wound up at Baylor, where Briles had already successfully welcomed defensive end Phil Taylor from Penn State and helped him blossom into a first-round draft pick in 2011. Heading into the 2015 season, Oakman had no reported incidents at Baylor and returned to not only help his stock for the

NFL Draft and become Baylor's all-time sack leader but also to graduate with a health degree. By pairing Oakman with NFL-ready defensive tackle, Andrew Billings, Baylor looked to have its best defense in years.

And to think, defense had always been the issue for Briles-coached teams, while the offense never seemed to have a problem putting up points.

So Art Briles had a defense. He had a star-studded offense with a quarterback that *he* believed in, even if the rest of the country wasn't so sure. He had the new-look uniforms that today's players love to wear, and he now had the stadium—on campus—to house them and the excited fan base.

This team was primed to beat anyone on the field. Little did Briles know, what would ultimately become the team's and his greatest challenge, both during and after the season, would have nothing to do with the playing field.

Sunday

Did he catch it? Or did the NFL officially, painfully get this one right?

Either way, the 2014 season, as magical as it was for the Dallas Cowboys at times, couldn't have ended in a more disappointing fashion. For an entire off-season, the Cowboys, including players, coaches, front-office personnel, and, of course, fans, were left with nothing but what-ifs. What if the NFL's instant replay officials had stuck with the call on the field in Green Bay and awarded Dez Bryant a catch at the Packers' 1-yard line late in the fourth quarter?

What if the Cowboys had scored a touchdown there to take the lead? What if they found a way to stop Green Bay quarterback Aaron Rodgers one more time and advance to the NFC Championship Game?

What if they had gone back to Seattle the following week and what if they defeated the Seahawks just like they did a few months earlier to put themselves on the proverbial NFL map as a team to beat?

What if? What if? What if?

But no matter how many Twitter handles were changed to "Dez Caught It" or T-shirts and bumper stickers were printed with similar messages, one fact still remained the same heading into the 2015 season: the Cowboys were back to 0–0 once again. The 12–4 season from 2014 that included their first NFC East title under head coach Jason Garrett, who then also collected his first career playoff win, was all in the rearview mirror.

And that process actually began just a week after the unfortunate loss to the Packers. The Cowboys' coaching staff worked the Pro Bowl in Arizona, and it was there that veteran defensive coordinator Rod Marinelli dismissed any talk of the "B" word.

"You don't build on anything in this league," the seventy-one-year-old said to a few surprised reporters who thought they had delivered a layup question. "No, we're not going to build. You tear it all down, and you start over. If you don't have that mindset, you get lazy. We won't be lazy. Just like last year, we're going to start over."

If there was one major carryover, it occurred immediately after the Green Bay loss as owner and general manager, Jerry Jones, locked up Garrett with a five-year contract extension worth $30 million, proving the point that players aren't the only ones who can succeed in a "contract year." Garrett spent 2014 in the final year of his deal, after Jones had stood by his coach despite three 8–8 seasons. He'd nearly pulled the plug on Garrett's tenure as head coach at the end of 2013, and sources in the front office say Jones probably would have if quarterback Tony Romo had not suffered a back injury that kept him out of the season finale against the Eagles with the division title on the line. The Cowboys lost the game with their backup, Kyle Orton, behind center—an ugly case of foreshadowing that would be revisited more than the team could have ever imagined—and finished with a .500 record for the third straight year, dropping the last game of the season all three times.

But Garrett was Jones' guy from the start. He had handpicked him to be the offensive coordinator in 2007, even before he hired Wade Phillips to become head coach. Jones wanted Garrett, the former Princeton standout who served as the Cowboys' primary backup behind quarter-back Troy Aikman during the 1990s, to eventually become the head coach long before he was even ready.

That's why Garrett got the interim job in 2010 when the Cowboys were 1–7 under Phillips. That's why, after then finishing 5–3 over the second half of the schedule, Garrett was officially named head coach the following off-season. And that's why Jones never decided to remove him despite repeated losses in the final game of the season when the playoffs were within reach.

The billionaire in Jones isn't afraid to spend money, but there likely wasn't another $30 million purchase he was more excited about that year than this extension for Garrett.

It's often been said around the Cowboys' headquarters in Valley Ranch, a northern neighborhood in the Dallas suburb of Irving, Texas, that while Jones wants to win, he wants to win *his way*. His way was with Garrett leading the charge, and he couldn't have been happier to extend his contract and prove that his guy was the right guy.

Garrett, always calculated in his words and demeanor, is as business-like as they come, and he has gotten used to the "splash" moves the Cowboys seem to make every off-season. And 2015 was no different, if not for being a little extreme.

Most teams would roll out the red carpet for a player who not only won the Associated Press Offensive Player of the Year Award, but also set a franchise record with 1,845 rushing yards, surpassing a nineteen-year-old mark set by Hall of Famer Emmitt Smith. The only red DeMarco Murray saw, however, was the exit sign as he left—for the rival Philadelphia Eagles to boot.

Now, it's not as if the Cowboys didn't want their starting tailback to return, but after watching him develop over four seasons, many in the organization feared he was only "a good back," not special. Maybe it wasn't so much Murray, but an offensive line that featured three first-round picks, not to mention the greatness of Romo, along with Jason Witten and Dez Bryant, that made the 2014 offense click so well.

The Cowboys had a ceiling of about $6.5 million per season for Murray at the start of free agency. And had they proposed the same deal the previous October instead of the four-year, $16 million contract they offered, it's likely Murray would've remained a Cowboy. Instead, he tested the market and found a lot more green—figuratively and literally.

Murray's $42 million deal, worth more than $8 million a year, was too rich to pass up, even if it meant he had to join the hated Eagles. Business is business, and while the Cowboys' fan base seemed to be split on losing such an accomplished player, the blow was softened just a day later when Dallas signed running back Darren McFadden, a former first-round pick, fourth overall, of the Oakland Raiders in 2008. While he had never been healthy enough to meet the lofty expectations of being such a high selection, McFadden still had enough name power to generate some excitement.

And then there was Greg Hardy. Talk about name recognition. The Cowboys stirred the pot when they inked him on March 18 to a one-year, incentive-based deal that could've paid him more than $13 million, depending on his availability with the league. At the time of the signing, Hardy was awaiting word from NFL Commissioner Roger Goodell on a possible suspension stemming from a domestic violence charge that was later dismissed.

Hardy was accused and found guilty of assaulting his girlfriend in July 2014, and was thus placed on the Exempt/Commissioner's Permission List, which required him to sit out fifteen games that season with the Panthers, who eventually waived him. But after Hardy appealed the judge's decision to a trial jury, the alleged victim failed to show up in the courtroom to testify. Whether or not the two reached a civil settlement was never determined, but the charges on Hardy were dropped, and he was free to sign with any club.

Regardless of the legal system's outcome, though, Hardy still faced a suspension from the NFL for conduct detrimental to the league. The Cowboys signed him hoping for a two- to four-game suspension, although reports from the commissioner's office suggested something in the range of eight to ten games. Of course, Hardy's case wasn't front and center on Goodell's mind at the time, as he was trying to make a decision on the Deflategate saga involving Tom Brady and the New England Patriots.

And that was all before April's draft.

Dallas then found a way to make yet another splash despite picking twenty-seventh overall. Getting athletic University of Connecticut cornerback Byron Jones in the first round was a safe, smart pick; but even with Hardy already in the fold, the Cowboys still showed they weren't afraid of adding a little more controversy.

Thanks to having failed a drug test at the annual NFL Scouting Combine in late February, University of Nebraska defensive end Randy Gregory fell right to the Cowboys at number sixty overall. And then after the draft, the salesman in Jones rounded up Romo, Witten, and some of his talented offensive linemen to help recruit rookie free agent La'el Collins, who had to leave the NFL Draft in Chicago to meet with police investigators back in Louisiana for a possible involvement with the murder of his ex-girlfriend. The untimely circumstance cost Collins, who was considered one of the top linemen in the draft, millions of dollars, as he not only fell out of the first round but also went undrafted.

Once the police cleared Collins of any involvement or wrongdoing, he was free to sign with the team of his choosing, and so the rich got richer as the Cowboys added him to their already talented stable of linemen.

By July, the only major concern the Cowboys still had was re-signing Bryant, who was given the franchise tag. He had threatened to sit out the season opener against the New York Giants if a new contract wasn't in place—a move that would've cost him $750,000 per game and didn't seem all that practical for the wide receiver. Still, the Cowboys didn't let it get that far, signing their superstar to a five-year, $70 million contract that paid him $32 million guaranteed.

For the most part, things were shaping into form for these Cowboys, a trendy Super Bowl pick by the oddsmakers, who figured even the loss of Murray would be offset by dynamic defenders like Hardy and Gregory, as well as the talented group of core offensive players surrounding Romo.

Could this finally be the year the Cowboys got back to the glory days? Their success-starved fan base could only hope so, as they had now waited over twenty years since the last Super Bowl title. And last year, many of them felt robbed by the "catch that wasn't" in Green Bay.

But that controversial play had only fueled the burning fire inside of these fans heading into 2015. With a nickname like America's Team, the Cowboys were used to the hype. Expectations to win a sixth Super Bowl always existed, no matter the level of talent Jones had assembled.

But this 2015 team seemed to be as can't-miss as they could get, even in the parody-stricken NFL that sees teams go from worst to first and vice versa quicker than any other sport. These Cowboys were ready to roll.

Now all they needed was the "breaks" to go their way.

Chapter 1

PREP WORK

Friday

A state as big as Texas makes for some pretty long bus rides, and in 2014, Plano went on one of the farthest treks head coach, Jaydon McCullough, could ever recall, especially for a regular-season game. After traveling 111 miles to John Tyler High School in Tyler, Texas, the Wildcats dropped a hard-fought battle that looked a lot worse on the final scoreboard—Tyler 30, Plano 12. And if you think the ride there was long, try the ride home after a loss like that.

Needless to say, with John Tyler traveling to Plano this year for the 2015 opener, the Wildcats were out to avenge that loss, but more importantly get the season off on the right foot.

With a 7:30 p.m. start, the standard time for all high school games on Friday nights across the state, it was a long afternoon for the players. At Plano, the team members wore game-day polos with their jersey numbers sewn on the sleeves at school during the day, giving students and faculty a chance to not only put faces and numbers together, but perhaps increase the excitement of game day even more in an effort to fill as many seats as possible. Every time you saw those polos in the hall, you remembered what was starting at 7:30.

On this day, Matt Keys couldn't stop looking at the time. Whether it was his watch, his cell phone, or the clocks on the wall in the classroom, the senior was having the hardest time paying any attention in his World Ideas philosophy class. It was the longest day ever because, to him, it was a prelude to what might be the most important night of his life. At least that was how it felt as the seconds and minutes dragged by while he anxiously awaited his first start as the quarterback of Plano Senior High.

Keys didn't really need to wear the game-day polo or even a football uniform to look the part. He stood out, even on a football team, at 6–5 and 225 pounds. But more than just his broad shoulders and towering height, Keys always carried a confident look about him, keeping a steady grin that matched his generally easygoing nature.

But during sixth-period English, the last class before he would join his teammates, Keys wasn't feeling so easy on the inside and was absolutely tuning out what was occurring in the classroom. His mind continued to race. Then he looked at his phone and saw a group text from one of his friends, also on the team, showing an old picture of a packed John Clark Stadium, giving them all a taste of what they would see tonight.

The text read, "Look at all these people we have to disappoint." It was supposed to be a joke, and Keys laughed it off. But inside, it started to hit home.

"That's when it really got real. This was really happening."

The buses pulled right up to the gate, just about twenty yards from the locker room doors. It was not a long walk at all for the players, who had arrived with half of their uniforms on. From the waist down, the players looked ready, donning their football pants—complete with thigh-, hip-, and kneepads—along with taped ankles and game cleats.

But even the short walk to the locker room didn't escape a few early-bird parents and tailgating fans who had lined up on two sides to cheer on their beloved Wildcats.

"Let's go Plano. It's our year!" shouted a mother wearing a button with her son's picture on it.

"Here we go. Let's go, boys. Let's get after 'em tonight," another proud father said, waving a Plano T-shirt he just purchased from the souvenir stand.

Inside the locker room, the mood was a little more subdued than for other games. Make no mistake, the quietness was related more to nerves than to a laid-back approach. Even a senior such as Brandon Stephens, who played in the 2012 season opener as a freshman, had butterflies swarming inside his stomach just minutes before his final year was set to begin.

On every level, Stephens was a high school senior and then some. Throughout his time at Plano, Stephens hadn't just acted more mature for his age but looked older as well. When his ear-to-ear smile wasn't lighting up the room, Stephens had a determined look that could be mistaken for a scowl. Stephens sported one of the more popular hairstyles, going with a tapered-fro, which was nice and neat but showed some length at the top and back of his head.

This really wasn't the time for pep talks, at least not for the players. That was taken care of Thursday before the first game when the team had held its annual preseason squad meeting at the school. There were no set rules or an agenda for who stood up and addressed the team. Usually it was the captains, but other seniors with something to add were more than welcome.

Established seniors such as Keys and Stephens addressed the team, as did Kadarius Smith and T.J. Lee. But there might have been some players who were surprised to hear Darion Foster, wearing 35, speak. Here was a senior defensive lineman who was about to make his varsity debut. Typically, juniors who remained on junior varsity for that long had a hard time making contributions as seniors, but Darion was proving to be an exception to the rule—in more ways than one.

Darion wasn't like most of the other kids on the team. To go home from practice, he didn't get picked up by his parents like some of the underclassmen. Before he finally got his own car, Darion would get a ride home with assistant coach Chris Fisher, the team's longtime assistant defensive coordinator and defensive backs coach. Chris also happened to be Darion's live-in uncle, who had looked after him for the past seven years.

Yes, technically, Darion was his nephew, but for the father of three daughters as well as for his wife, Janna, Darion was the son they never had; and he got treated at home in the same way as their biological kids. Considering that Darion was half African-American, a quarter Hispanic, and a quarter white, while Chris was half Hispanic, you could find families with less diversity, but you couldn't find many with more love.

Athletically, Darion was what you'd call a late bloomer, which is why it took so long for him to make the varsity squad. Truth be told, had he not suffered a broken hand in his first JV game as a junior, he might have been called up during the previous year.

"But only if he's good enough," Chris said prior to the season, making sure that there would never be a hint of bias or favoritism displayed at his expense. "When he's ready, he'll play on varsity. But that doesn't help anyone to put him up just because he's my nephew."

By now, Darion was more than ready. Better yet, he was about to start for the Wildcats at defensive tackle. While it might have been his first game on Friday night, it certainly wasn't his first time on the sidelines. For five years, beginning when he was about ten, Darion was a Plano ball boy, hustling after overthrown passes and fielding balls in the end zone after field goals and extra points. He showed some speed and quickness to dodge the big boys when the plays went out-of-bounds as well.

Now, his job was to be right in the middle of the action. And the once-shy kid, who at first couldn't even look McCullough in the eyes because he was so intimidated, stood up in front of his peers.

"Like everyone else, I'm just excited to be able to start a season with them. I know we can have a great year if we just stick together. For the last seven years, Plano has been part of my family, starting when I was a ball boy on the sidelines. Now I'm about to start my senior year. I've seen a lot of great players and know how this thing is supposed to go. So let's go get the job done."

Without a single varsity snap under his belt, Darion instantly became one of the leaders.

Minutes before kickoff, Chris ran out of the locker room and uttered the first three words that came to his mind.

"Man, it's hot!" he said as he located about two-dozen family members who had made the drive from Amarillo, Texas. That was not only where Chris grew up and was a star defensive back for Palo Duro High School, but it was also where Darion's mother, Heather, still resided. She wasn't about to miss this game.

Chris, or "Coach Fish" to the players and coaches, made a point to high-five all of his defensive backs as they ran onto the field. Seconds after the national anthem was played by Plano's marching band, he turned to a few spectators fortunate enough to garner a sideline pass and said, "There's no place I'd rather be than right here."

Despite the near triple-digit temperatures around kickoff, that sentiment was shared by thousands of Plano residents who packed John Clark Field, waving their glossy "Wildcat" paws in unison.

With John Tyler getting the ball first, one of the biggest fears Plano's coaching staff had coming into the game was just how they'd compete in the trenches against a team with so much size. It didn't take long for the Wildcats to ease those concerns, though, as they forced the Lions into a three-and-out and a punt.

Finally, the wait was over for Keys. His time was now as he took the field donning jersey 28. (Jerseys in the 20s for quarterbacks were a Plano tradition.) And all eyes in the stands were fixed on Stephens, the do-it-all tailback who was considered by many to be one of the best in Texas.

So who got the first carry of this much-anticipated season? Well, that'd be Lopaka Yoro, of course. The five-foot, 160-pound runner was one of the smallest players Plano had ever put on the field, but he might have also been one of the toughest. Yoro had great quickness and power, and frankly, had a way of hiding behind blockers just long enough to break a big run.

But Yoro's first carry went for just four yards. Keys then ran the next play for no gain and took a big hit from John Tyler's best defensive tackle, who stayed in the quarterback's ear, telling him he would be hitting him like this all night.

Keys shrugged it off, and even told him, "Dude, you're not a big deal. We're fine."

So with his first hit out of the way, now it was on to his first pass, which he completed for a first down to Tarence Raymond.

This is where the public address announcer, Matt Cone, went to work, allowing the fans to participate.

"Catch by Raymond for seven yards is enough for a Plano . . ."

"FIRST DOWN!" the fans scream with a little more juice, considering it's the first of the season.

But what most were probably thinking was: When is Stephens going to get the ball?

The star running back finally got his chance on Plano's fourth play from scrimmage. The fifth play was an extra point.

That's right, Stephens showed everyone why there was so much hype around him, as he took a pitch to the right and darted around the corner untouched, cruising into the end zone thanks to a pancake block down the field by receiver Carson Williams.

One carry, one touchdown for Stephens. His senior year was already off to a great start.

Stephens was about as cool as they come for high school players, especially ones with so much talent. He smiled on his way off the field despite all of the attention his teammates were giving him. But the offensive linemen, they weren't as cool. All five of the starters were jumping around like kids on Christmas morning. They had been challenged all week by their coaches, having been told just how big and tough these Lions were up front. They had reason to celebrate.

Coach McCullough never lost his intensity, and he was not afraid to get after any kid at any moment. But he'd offer just as much praise as well, especially to the O-line, which he also oversaw along with his head-coaching duties.

"That's how you do it, guys!" he screamed at all of them with a snarl on his face that wouldn't be perceived as a compliment from any on-looker in the stands. "Great job! But get ready to do it again."

And that's what they did. On the next drive, Keys got himself out of a blitz and then found Stephens on a dump-off pass at the last minute. Stephens did the rest, running for thirty-nine yards to set up his second touchdown of the game just a few plays later.

But John Tyler had too many athletes, especially at quarterback, to go quietly. Quarterback Bryson Smith made about six Wildcats miss on a 67-yard touchdown run on the Lions' next possession to cut into the lead. Smith even led his team to a game-tying touchdown in the second quarter, but the visitor's momentum was stopped thanks to an intercep-tion by Aaron Ragas, who after nearly winning the quarterback job a few weeks ago, had shown why the coaches kept him at his more natural safety position.

That pick allowed Keys to find the end zone soon thereafter. With all of the defense's attention on Stephens, Keys kept a read option and cut it back up the field for a touchdown run and a 21–14 lead, where it remained heading into halftime.

Coming off the field, Keys was met by his quarterbacks coach, Carson Meger, who couldn't help but have his own flashbacks.

"Man, you look like me out there," said Meger, who not only quar-terbacked Plano to success in the 2007 and 2008 seasons, but also wore Keys' 28 jersey as well.

Meger's journey from Plano quarterback to quarterback coach went full circle rather quickly. After spending four seasons at University of Texas El Paso, where he played seventeen games, including three starts, Meger decided not to play a fifth season in El Paso so he could get a jump-start on his coaching career. Naturally, he went back to Plano, where he was hired as a middle school coach for one season before a spot opened up on the varsity staff. Just two years removed from playing college ball and six years after he was a star quarterback for the Wildcats, now Meger was back on the headsets, coaching his successors. A former player returning to his alma mater to coach isn't unique in Texas. Doing that in a six-year span is a quicker transition than most, but it just worked out that way—both for Meger and the Wildcats.

Following the thirty-minute break, which in high school allows both marching bands to perform, the Wildcats padded their lead in the third quarter with Stephens' third rushing touchdown of the night.

Shortly after, junior safety Nic Melson was forced into duty because of an injury. Nic always had his biggest fan rather close to him on the field. His father, Marty Melson, was a standout for the Wildcats back in the late 1970s and currently was serving as a freshman coach at one of Plano's feeder high schools. Marty's game-day duties weren't quite as intense as the varsity coaches', but he would keep an eye on the opposing offensive and defensive formations and might offer up a different perspective if needed. But when his son was in, even though the soft-spoken Marty had no problems staying in coach mode, he always kept the closest eye on his son, perhaps thinking every now and then about the fact that two generations of Melsons had donned Wildcat jerseys.

Immediately after hustling out onto the field, Nic made a tackle for a loss on second down. Then on fourth down, he didn't know where to be on the punt return unit. He was in the middle of the field, then went back toward the punt returners, who then pointed him to the left defensive end spot, where senior Byron Tate told him where to line up. Somewhat unsure of his duties, Melson just rushed up the field at the punter. Only the punter didn't get the snap; the ball sailed over his head and into the end zone, where the quick-footed junior pounced on the prize for a touchdown.

If that wasn't enough, he also was the backup holder and needed to be in the game for the extra point.

"Atta boy, Niiic!" Coach Fisher screamed into the earhole of Melson's helmet on his way off the field. "Look at you, son!"

Melson received a helmet slap or fifty in a matter of minutes. The bench was erupting, and not just because a guy who looks more like an athletic trainer had just scored a touchdown. It was also becoming very clear that Plano would win the game and avenge last year's 18-point loss to the Lions.

This time it was Plano turning the tables, pulling away by the same margin for a 35–17 win.

And now, McCullough could finally crack a smile. After hours of a permanent scowl, the head coach sought out his wife, Kathy, for a big hug and kiss. The other assistant coaches did the same with their wives and families, a Plano tradition after every game, no matter the outcome.

In the locker room, McCullough calmed down his elated group, which had its own victory chant with Stephens and the other seniors shouting at the highest of decibel levels.

"Men, that was a really good football team you beat tonight," McCullough said as he tried to look them all in the eye. "You went out there and won the game with offense and defense and special teams. That was a true team win."

And in typical coach-speak fashion, he made sure his players stayed hungry.

"Is that the best we can play?"

"Nooooo!" the players all yelled, seemingly as one.

"That's right. We can get better. And we're going to get better. But for this first game, it was hot, it wasn't easy, but we made the plays together. I'm really proud of all of you. Let's enjoy it. But remember, we've got a short week this week getting ready for Irving Mac."

And with that, some thirteen minutes after the final gun, the head coach had already mentioned the name of his team's next opponent. The coaches were going to enjoy the win, but only for tonight. That's all they could afford to, considering only fifteen hours later they would be back in the field house, breaking down the tape and getting ready to do it all over again.

Saturday

College preseason in Texas can be a brutal thing. Whereas the NFL teams travel to more hospitable locations, and high schools are limited by rules governing how early in the summer the teams can start playing together, the college programs start earlier and have to stay home. For many, including Baylor, this meant that the full force of preseason occurred under the intensity of the bright Texas summer sun.

And for weeks now, Art Briles had been putting the squeeze on his team. With the sprinklers working the practice facilities around the clock to prevent the grass from turning brown, the players had to work twice as hard to survive one of the most brutal parts of every season. His approach to conditioning was rooted in the experiences and philosophy that he'd cultivated going all the way back to his time as a high school coach. Preseason was a time of focus. Without the pressures of classes or the distraction of other students, this was a moment to concentrate solely on the team.

When Briles woke up early Friday morning on August 21, he did just that, his mind immediately homing in on the football team's being exactly two weeks away from start of the regular season. The Bears were not only attempting to win a third straight Big 12 title; they also had serious national championship aspirations as well. Going into the season, they were ranked in the top ten by all the major polls, and while Briles never put too much stock in any of those, he knew how helpful that kind of buzz was for helping to create a sense of responsibility and ownership for the team's players over the season. Now he just had to get them expecting to win without getting arrogant.

And so far, it didn't look like that would be a problem—this was a Baylor team that was prepared to live up to every bit of the hype. The preseason had gone well, almost too well at times. Quarterback Seth Russell had been showing himself to be every bit as skilled as he was in the spring when he'd won the starting job. The defense, which he'd known for the last nine months to look great on paper, was proving to be every bit as good as hyped.

By the middle of the morning on August 21, though, the upcoming matchup against Southern Methodist University in Dallas—and every other game to follow, for that matter—became an immediate afterthought.

The night before, Briles was informed that Sam Ukwuachu, a former member of the football program who had never actually suited up for the team, had been found guilty by a Waco jury for sexual assault. He faced a prison sentence of up to twenty years for an October 2013 incident involving a Baylor women's soccer player.

But facts that came out during the trial rapidly turned into intense criticism and speculation about Briles' integrity. During the proceedings, the prosecution put Ukwuachu's ex-girlfriend on the stand to tell the courtroom about a violent incident between the two that occurred when they were both attending Boise State. That soon prompted questions about Baylor's and Briles' reasoning for bringing Ukwuachu on campus in the first place.

A star defensive end from Pearland, Texas, Ukwuachu was originally recruited by Boise State, and in his first season with the Broncos earned 2012 Freshman All-America honors. But by the spring of 2013, he had been dismissed from the team for undisclosed reasons, and later that same fall began taking classes at Baylor, although he was ineligible to play for the Bears due to the NCAA's transfer rules.

On paper at least, Ukwuachu was the type of player Briles and his staff often coveted, which stemmed from a belief in their own support system and their ability to help players who needed to switch programs. Over the years, Briles had brought in many transfer students from other schools—Shawn Oakman and Phil Taylor, both from Penn State, were just two examples. Players that needed a change of scenery, new surroundings, or simply a fresh start were something the Baylor coaching staff never shied away from—especially Briles, who wrote in his second published biography that coaches are in the "kid-saving business."

He added in the book, "We wanted mavericks. We wanted guys with no sheet on their bed rather than silk sheets. I wanted tough guys. Guys that just had to fight and grind and work for everything that they ever earned. Someone who had to earn their respect. If they do falter or make a mistake, then we need to save them and give them a chance to get back on the right path."

When Briles went out that Friday before the first practice, he met a group of reporters—mostly the usual local group of writers and TV reporters from the Waco area. However, the story was picking up some national steam, prompting a few Dallas-Fort Worth media members to make the nearly two-hour drive down to Waco. Briles was immediately asked to comment on whether then–Boise State head coach Chris Petersen, who had since moved on to the University of Washington, had relayed any information to him regarding Ukwuachu's violent past.

"Lord, no," Briles said about having prior knowledge of any specific incidents. "There's no truth to that. Find out who informed us and talk to them please."

Briles patiently answered questions regarding the case, but his agitation was growing. At the end of the media session, he asked if "anyone had a football question" as he and his team were "trying to get ready for SMU." He went on to practice, but by the time the two-hour workout ended, things had taken another sour turn for his program and, again, his national perception.

More than 2,200 miles away in the Pacific Northwest, Petersen was getting his Washington team ready for the season when an ESPN reporter reached out for a comment regarding the situation at Baylor. Petersen issued a response that seemingly put an even darker cloud over Briles' head—justifiably or not.

Petersen's statement read:

"After Sam Ukwuachu was dismissed from the Boise State football program and expressed an interest in transferring to Baylor, I initiated a call with coach Art Briles. In that conversation, I thoroughly apprised Coach Briles of the circumstances surrounding Sam's disciplinary record and dismissal."

And just like that, a social media firestorm against Briles and Baylor was sparked. Briles was disappointed in the words from Petersen, whom he had met over the years at coaching clinics and retreats. To Briles, what Petersen said wasn't exactly inaccurate. However, what was getting lost in the translation was the assumption that Petersen indeed knew all of the facts.

Yes, he might have "thoroughly apprised" Briles of the circumstances that led to Ukwuachu's decision to transfer, but as it later was revealed, Petersen and other Boise State officials weren't aware of the incidents that later came out in the Waco trial.

And that's when Baylor went on the offensive, releasing Ukwuachu's official transfer papers from Boise State to Baylor. The school's findings included a printed document from BSU, which stated that Ukwuachu was indeed eligible to return to the school and was not removed by the team for disciplinary reasons.

Baylor also provided an email from November 2013 in which Boise State's dean of students informed Baylor that there were "no student conduct records for Samuel and that he is in good standing with Boise State."

To say Friday was a long day for Briles would be a gigantic understatement. With his character being attacked for the first time, he went home that afternoon with a feeling inside that was absolutely unfamiliar territory.

No stranger to adversity, Briles considered himself stronger than most when it came to hardship. On October 16, 1976, at the age of twenty, Briles knew something wasn't right when he couldn't locate his parents and aunt in the Cotton Bowl stands while playing wide receiver for the University of Houston. When he walked up the tunnel to join his victorious teammates after the game, longtime Cougars head coach, Bill Yeoman, pulled Briles aside and informed him of a tragic car accident on Highway 380 that killed all three passengers who were coming from Rule, Texas, to Dallas.

"The worst day of my life," Briles said. "It's something that has never gone away and never will."

Still filled with guilt about his parents being on the road simply to watch him play, Briles didn't let a day go by without honoring Dennis and Wanda Briles, as well as his Aunt Elsie, who raised him like a grandmother.

On the optimistic side, Briles also referred to that moment as a turning point in his life. His girlfriend at the time, Jan Allison, was set to travel with his family that day, but at the last minute, she stayed back to help with a bridal shower being held at her house. Two years later, Art and Jan were married, starting a family that included three children and then four grandkids.

Briles also said that day had helped him become a "fearless coach" as well.

"I've had my face on the floor and I've had people standing on me and not letting me breathe," he said. "Next thing you know, I was standing up and I'm alive. So, I'm not scared to go back. I've been there. I've made it."

And some thirty-nine years later, Briles would need every bit of the strength he gained from that tragic day.

His initial thought was that the backlash regarding the recent accusations would eventually blow over. But headlines all across the country were popping up left and right. Some suggested that Briles knew of Ukwuachu's violent history and should be fired or ought to resign from his post. For a coach whose season opener was less than two weeks away, football was now an afterthought.

A headline from one *USA Today* online article simply read, "Baylor Coach Art Briles Ignored Responsibility in Admitting Sam Ukwuachu." Another stated, "Baylor Coach Art Briles Is in Trouble." Even a columnist from the *Fort-Worth Star Telegram*, the hometown paper of the Bears' rival, Texas Christian University, weighed in, trying to assume the stance of his readership audience: "Like you, I believe Chris Petersen."

When Briles got home that afternoon after multiple conversations with Baylor's athletic director, Ian McCaw, President Ken Starr, and associate athletic director of communications, Heath Nielsen, Briles turned to another source for guidance—someone who had nearly ten years of public relations experience for a successful sports franchise.

This consultant also just so happened to be his daughter Jancy, the oldest of his three children, who found herself in the middle of family conversations and decision-making as early as her teenage years. Art and Jan Briles had always trusted her opinion, as they did with son Kendal and daughter Staley.

On this day, Jancy dipped into her experience as a media relations coordinator for the Dallas Cowboys to help advise her father on his next move. The coach was leaning toward not making any other statements on the matter until Jancy weighed in.

"Nobody is saying this is bad for Baylor or this is bad for the football team," she said. "They're saying this is bad for you. People are attacking your character."

Later that evening, the school issued another detailed statement from Briles, again declaring his lack of knowledge of any prior incident involving Ukwuachu:

> *"I was contacted by Coach Petersen at Boise State in spring 2013 and he told me he had a player from Texas who needed to get closer to home and that he thought our program would be a good spot for him. I know and respect Coach Petersen and he would never recommend a student-athlete to Baylor that he didn't believe in. In our discussion, he did not disclose that there had been violence toward women, but he did tell me of a rocky relationship with his girlfriend which contributed to his depression. The only disciplinary action I was aware of were team-related issues, insubordination of coaches and missing practice. In addition, I talked with Tony Heath, his high school coach, who gave us a great recommendation.*
>
> *As required with any transfer to Baylor, Boise State acknowledged that he was not suspended due to any institutional disciplinary reasons and further that he was eligible for competition if he chose to return to Boise State."*

Luckily for Briles, those statements alone started to sway the tide back in his favor somewhat. If nothing else, it gave the Baylor coach the benefit of the doubt he had earned throughout his coaching career.

His reputation was then helped even more when on the following Tuesday, August 25, Boise State released a statement that Ukwuachu's dismissal was unrelated to any allegations of violence, and that school officials never received any reports that he had committed acts of violence.

Instead, records indicate that Boise State was concerned with Ukwuachu's mental condition, since the university's medical director had diagnosed him with a depressive disorder. Three days after that determination, and after Ukwuachu told coaches he wanted to transfer to be closer to home, he was dismissed from the Broncos football team.

Meanwhile, the judge for Ukwuachu's trial handed down a sentence of 180 days in jail with 10 years of felony probation and 400 hours of community service.

As for Briles, he was getting the needed support from his superiors, giving him peace of mind that his job was secure, although he still had to read and hear his name dragged through the proverbial mud.

Despite the fact that football coaches typically want the most time possible to prepare for an opponent, especially one like SMU that had a new head coach in Chad Morris, all Briles wanted to do was get back on the field.

Enough prep time or not, September 4 couldn't get here soon enough.

Sunday

Finding time to check out what's on TV, especially in the fall, just doesn't happen for football coaches—at any level. For many TV is simply one in a long list of in-season distractions—the kind of thing that takes up your time and doesn't give you anything in return.

During the football season, the only time you might catch Cowboys head coach, Jason Garrett, watching any television would likely be when an NFL game is on. Probably some matchup between the New York Giants and Washington Redskins, knowing he'll see both of those teams on the schedule twice.

But in the off-season, Garrett likes to wind down in the evening with his wife, Brill, the two enjoying everything from shows such as *Homeland* to movies, sporting events, and, of course, the news. The Princeton grad likes to keep up on world events.

It was one night in May when what he was watching not only caught Garrett's attention, but also ended up becoming a theme for his football team in the 2015 season. He was mesmerized by the words of U.S. Attorney General Loretta Lynch in an interview he saw on the evening news. The coach listened closely to Lynch tell her story, which included growing up with a minister father and a librarian mother. Her message was about learning the importance of honor and integrity.

"It really was about as eloquent an eighteen seconds as I'd ever heard," Garrett said. "She ended up being the valedictorian of her high school class. She went to Harvard Law School, was a district attorney, and eventually the Attorney General of the United States. It's a great arc. And for her to share that idea that we're not going to let other people outside us define us, we're going to define ourselves by what we do and what we say and don't say, and how we present ourselves each and every day, that's a message that we shared with our team. It's something I think is really important in life for individual people and certainly good for football players, coaches, and a football team."

Right then and there, Garrett came up with the year's message:

We Do.

To him, it was short but simple, much like last year's battle cry, "Fight," which eventually became "Finish the Fight" when the Cowboys made their run to the playoffs. He wanted his team to realize that this season's success or failures would be in the players' own hands: that they controlled their own destiny.

So like he did in 2014, Garrett called up the equipment staff and had them print out hundreds of navy Dri-FIT shirts, designed by Nike but printed at the Dallas Cowboys' merchandise facility, also known around the organization as DCM. In July, when the players arrived at their hotel rooms for training camp in sunny Oxnard, California, about an hour north of Los Angeles, they found their "We Do" T-shirts laid out on their beds.

While "We Do" was the real message, there were others that Garrett had printed up. Throughout camp, navy shirts were seen floating around that also read "Team 56," which was the coach's unique way of reminding his players not to dwell on last year's accomplishments and focus only on this season's group—the fifty-sixth football team in Cowboys history.

Another shirt simply read, "Hah!" Garrett's creation was meant to represent the sound made when a player or coach does something in a positive way.

"You get off the ball and make a big block—Hah!" said Garrett. "Or you come out of your break, catch the ball, and make someone miss—Hah!"

The phrases were short, but they were catching on. Whether or not they were making a difference mentally inside these players' heads was up for debate, but they were at least conversational pieces for the media, who were inquisitive enough to ask around about the meanings.

And for Garrett, if people were talking about it, the message was getting across.

And Garrett expected the message to get across for all of his team— from the coaching staff up through the team's top talent.

And while new players had been added all across the team, the top talent still included the familiar faces of the franchise: Dez Bryant, Jason Witten, and of course, quarterback Tony Romo. All three of them had taken vastly different journeys to reach this status. Bryant was the ultra-talented lightning rod of a player who could be just as explosive off the field, including a few brushes with the law during his first five years in Dallas, but had developed into a dynamic star on the field who seemed to finally have football as his top priority.

Witten was the most constant thing about the Cowboys other than their mediocre record since he arrived in 2003. The tough-as-nails tight end had missed only one game in his previous twelve years, and not one since a broken jaw in his rookie season forced him to miss the only game of his illustrious career.

And then there was Romo, who might have rivaled Witten when it came to toughness, as he had fought through two back surgeries the past two seasons but managed to have a career season in 2014, amidst unreal and often unrealistic expectations that come with being the starting quarterback of the Dallas Cowboys. Romo earned a few NFL MVP votes in 2014 as he was the league's most efficient passer and got his team to within a controversial play from perhaps reaching the NFC Championship Game.

Romo, Witten, and Bryant all arrived at Oxnard, not only uttering similar messages from Garrett, but donning his shirts as well. One player who wasn't sporting any of the shirts during the first six days of camp, though, was veteran defensive end Jeremy Mincey. He had been a pleasant surprise in 2014, not only posting a solid year rushing the passer, but also providing leadership in the locker room, despite it being his first season with the team.

But when he refused to report to training camp, it was a surprising setback for the Cowboys, who didn't see it coming. Mincey, entering the final season of his contract, was hoping for at least another year to be added to the deal. In 2014, he missed a $500,000 playing-time incentive by just eleven snaps. He also knew that while the Cowboys signed fellow defensive end Greg Hardy in the off-season, Hardy's four-game suspension would leave them even more vulnerable if Mincey weren't in the mix.

Moments like these were yet another example of why the NFL is indeed a business. A high school or even college player doesn't have the leverage to send a message by missing a week of practice, or even one day, without extreme consequences.

However, Cowboys' Executive Vice President Stephen Jones, the son of owner Jerry Jones, was pretty firm when asked about Mincey's negotiating ploy. Stephen was also the director of player personnel and was expected to take over for his father one day.

"We won't discuss anything with Jeremy if he's not here," he said.

After nearly a week, Mincey showed up, met with the Joneses, and was on the field soon thereafter. The Cowboys waived the $30,000 in fines that Mincey had accumulated for missing time, but did not cave on the request to add another year to his contract.

"This is the business side of it," Mincey said. "I wanted to take care of my family. But there's no hard feelings. I'm ready to work."

That was in front of the cameras. However, whispers around camp were starting to surface that Mincey's real issue wasn't so much about another year, but the team's decision to fork over so much money to Hardy, who had a chance to earn more than $12 million for just one season. Here was Mincey, who had become one of the vocal leaders of the defense last year, now taking a backseat on the field, financially, and perhaps even as the established veteran in the locker room.

Despite any concerns, Mincey's infectious smile never wavered and the usually happy-go-lucky lineman carried about his business.

Meanwhile, not everyone was smiling around camp, especially following an afternoon practice that saw a couple of Oklahoma State alumni trading punches in the middle of the field. Dez Bryant and cornerback Tyler Patmon got into a heated scuffle during a play, which before long escalated into a full-on fight with Bryant landing a haymaker punch to the back of Patmon's head.

Eventually those two would make up, but things wouldn't end so pleasantly a few days later when the then-St. Louis Rams came to town for a combined practice with the Cowboys. With hundreds of California-based fans hoping the Rams would make the move back to Los Angeles, the stands were flooded with blue and gold jerseys and flags, as the locals were able to get an up-close look at the intense workout.

And once again, Patmon and Dez—who wasn't even practicing because he was rehabbing a hamstring injury, but still limping his way some two hundred yards to get in the mix—were right in the middle of what became an ugly scene that stretched across two fields.

Last year's motto was "Fight," but it was certainly carrying over into 2015.

Garrett's messages could come in many ways. Not only were there dozens of motivational signs around the locker room at the team's training facility in Valley Ranch, but the walls of the team meeting room were covered with quick, striking signs that read "Attack" or "Relentless" and "The Ball, The Ball, The Ball" to stress the importance of turnovers.

On road games, players, coaches, and staff members would often get Cowboys-decorated key cards for their hotel rooms. Messages such as "The Team, The Team, The Team" were printed on the back.

As the Cowboys left Oxnard for their second preseason game, having already dropped their exhibition opener at San Diego, 17–7, Garrett used the location to send yet another inspirational message. This would be the club's first trip to San Francisco's new Levi's Stadium, which would just so happen to also be the site of Super Bowl 50 the following February.

While it was customary for the Cowboys to head straight from the airport to the hotel on the night before the game, this time Garrett wanted the team to hold a walk-through practice at the stadium instead. Now, one of the reasons could've been the newly sodded turf that had been a cause for concern for both teams. At least that was an easy excuse for Garrett to take his players to the field the night before.

But the visit could have also been just another calculated message from Garrett, the coach wanting his players to get a firsthand look at their desired destination. When asked by a reporter about the reasoning behind the scheduling change before the team's departure to San Francisco, Garrett smiled.

"We just thought it was a good idea to go up there," he said. "If you're a player, coach, or staff member in this league, and you don't have a goal of winning the Super Bowl, you're doing the wrong thing."

Once in San Francisco, Garrett indeed hammered the point home to his players about returning in February, telling them all, "We've got to focus on the task at hand, and that's winning this game, but the overall goal of this team is to get back here again."

Unfortunately, the Cowboys looked like anything but a Super Bowl contender against the 49ers, a game that saw few starters play more than a handful of snaps, if any. The Cowboys lost, 23–6, but that was nothing compared to the even bigger loss they were about to suffer back in Oxnard during the final week of camp.

"It's my ACL!" cornerback Orlando Scandrick yelled on the practice field during a team drill. "It's my ACL. I know it. It's gone. Shiiit!"

Scandrick had been run into by rookie receiver Lucky Whitehead, who caught a pass over the middle, but couldn't stop his momentum before ramming into the cornerback, whose leg was planted in the grass. Scandrick immediately hollered, writhing in pain as he tried to roll over, unable to bring his right leg with him.

Considered one of the smartest players on the team and a student of the game, Scandrick also happened to be the Cowboys' best cover cornerback. That's why a sickening feeling was shared among the team, coaches, and, of course, the fans around the fence line as they watched Scandrick being carted off the field with his head buried in a towel. He knew what the MRI was going to say. He knew his season was over before it even started.

"Man, we've got to get out of here," cornerback Brandon Carr joked, referring to the near five-week stay of training camp. "It's time to go home. We can't have another injury like this."

And while he wasn't aware of it at the time of his comment, his head coach was thinking the same thing. On the Monday of that week, he informed his operations staff of his desire to leave one day early and head back to Dallas on Thursday instead of the initial plan of Friday.

In fact, Garrett tried his best to hide the news from all of the players and coaches. However, by Thursday morning, with the weight room already being cleared out and loaded onto an eighteen-wheeler for the trip back, word started to spread like wildfire.

Garrett called the team up for a huddle at the end of the morning walk-through, hoping to spark a celebration from a group that was dying to get back to its families, friends, and own beds.

"Here's what we're going to do," Garrett said. "We're going to put six linemen, three offense and three defense, down here to catch a punt. If any of these six guys can catch the punt in the air . . . we're going to get on those buses over there . . . and we're going to the Point Mugu Air Force Base . . . so we can go home today!"

"Woo-hoo!" shouted out one—and only one—player, who sounded sarcastic in his tone.

The players had found out, somewhat ruining Garrett's attempt at delivering the special news. Still, they all wanted to make sure they'd get to go home. And sure enough, rookie defensive end Randy Gregory made a diving catch on the first punt, creating a rather loud ovation from his teammates, who joyfully jogged off the field, knowing they had just a couple of hours to pack for the flight back to Dallas—even though some might have already been packed.

On Saturday night, the Cowboys then took on the Minnesota Vikings in their third preseason game, also known as the dress rehearsal for the regular season. The starters always play about a half, and this affair was no exception. Quarterback Tony Romo had two touchdown passes, including one to Whitehead that was proof enough that the savvy veteran was ready for the season. Romo stood in the pocket for nearly five seconds, twisting and turning his body to avoid the rush before stepping up to find his darting target over the middle.

"Thatta baby, nine!" Garrett said, as he often referred to his players by their jersey number. "That's how it's done."

It might have just been another preseason touchdown, but to Garrett, it was a sign that his quarterback still had the moves that had made him one of the more electrifying players he'd ever been around.

Garrett's eyes always widened and oftentimes turned glossy when asked to speak about Romo, a quarterback that he could certainly relate to. Unlike many of the NFL's top passers who were first-round picks, including number one selections such as Peyton Manning, Eli Manning, Cam Newton, and Andrew Luck, Romo's path was a bumpy one.

After a successful career at the Division I-AA level, Romo left Eastern Illinois as one of the school's most prolific passers, but NFL teams weren't exactly knocking down his door. The only reason he was invited to the scouting combine in Indianapolis—a showcase for the top rookies to work out in front of NFL teams to improve their stock for the annual college draft—was to be an extra thrower for the defensive players in drills. Romo wasn't one of the top quarterbacks in a class that included Carson Palmer, but he showed just enough talent to get a call from both the Cowboys and Broncos after the completion of the 2003 NFL Draft. At that point, Romo was an undrafted free agent and could choose his team. While he had a couple of former Eastern Illinois alums fighting for his services in Sean Payton, the Cowboys' quarterback coach at the time, and Broncos head coach Mike Shanahan, Romo picked Dallas, thinking he had a better shot of making the roster that included Quincy Carter, Chad Hutchinson, and Clint Stoerner at the time.

Romo's first head coach, the legendary Bill Parcells, didn't like everything about his rookie quarterback's game at first glance. But he knew there was potential. And that's why he kept him on the roster without playing him for three full seasons before finally giving him his shot in the middle of the 2006 season. Romo took over a 3–3 team and helped lead them into the playoffs, where cruel fate would end his storybook run. Romo, also serving as the holder on field goals, dropped the snap that likely would've given Dallas a playoff win in Seattle, but instead sent the Cowboys home early, and sent Bill Parcells into coaching retirement for good.

The following season was where Romo would get a new quarterbacks coach in Garrett, who not only had playing experience, but also traveled a scenic route to the league. He was also undrafted after a stellar career at Princeton. Garrett spent a season in San Antonio in the World Football League before making the Cowboys' roster in 1992, serving as the third backup to Troy Aikman. Garrett eventually played eight years in Dallas, winning three Super Bowl rings as a backup quarterback who started just nine games.

But as coach and player, Garrett and Romo went to new heights in 2007, as the Cowboys went 13–3 before stumbling in the playoffs. And that would serve as the recurring theme for both of them: regular-season success, only to see their seasons end in disappointment.

Garrett's first three seasons as the full-time head coach of the Cowboys ended with gut-wrenching losses in the final game with the NFC East title and trips to the playoffs on the line. Each time, Romo and Garrett faltered, as the Cowboys limped to an 8–8 record. But in 2014, Romo was able to manage a back injury that required surgery just eight months earlier, then guide the Cowboys to a 12–4 mark and the team's second playoff victory in twenty seasons.

So as the Cowboys embarked on this new season, one full of high expectations, Garrett had a little extra power in his helmet slap with Romo, knowing that the veteran leader of this team was ready for the season.

And with that, Romo was finished for the night and for the rest of the preseason, as the Cowboys traditionally rested all starters and some key backups in the fourth exhibition game.

Dallas lost this one to the Vikings, 28–14, but was more victorious in other areas, most notably on the injury front. Not only did they escape their final meaningful preseason game—perhaps an oxymoron—without any serious damage, they also started to see some of their pressing training camp questions answered.

The question of Terrance Williams' speed was put to rest as he zipped past Minnesota defenders for a 60-yard touchdown. The question of Gregory continuing to play at a high level was answered with his third sack in three preseason games.

And perhaps the biggest non-quarterback question of the off-season, just who would step up in the race for the starting running back position, got a little clarity when veteran Darren McFadden showed he still had some speed and quickness, rushing for thirty-seven yards on four carries. If anything, it gave the Cowboys some hope that both McFadden and Joseph Randle were capable of filling the void left behind after De-Marco Murray signed a free-agent deal with Philadelphia.

The Cowboys didn't necessarily bring McFadden on board to be a starter. That would've been foolish, considering he had played only sixteen games in a season just once in his seven previous years in Oakland. Then again, the Cowboys didn't trust Randle either after his off-the-field issues of the past year, which included a shoplifting charge and then a domestic violence dispute earlier in the summer back in his hometown of Wichita, Kansas.

As of now, Randle was still the favorite to win the starting job, but at least McFadden's performance gave the Cowboys some hope that he could handle the load if Randle were to falter once more. There were coaches, scouts, and even some players who just figured Randle's lack of accountability would surface again sooner or later.

But in the end, the question mark at the running back position wasn't enough to dampen what had been a highly successful camp. In a preseason with messages coming out from every side, it seemed all the signals were getting clearer by the day.

Chapter 2

CLOUDS ROLLING IN

Friday

The weekly schedule of the Plano Senior High school football team is nothing if not predictable. For the players, the weekends are spent recovering, trying to turn their attention to schoolwork, hanging with their friends, and just generally trying to pretend they are like anyone else in Plano.

While the players do come in on Saturdays to review the game film from the night before, their day is nothing like that of the coaches, who put in another ten- to twelve-hour day, with one eye on the previous game and the other getting ready for next week. Long gone are the days of having to meet up with opposing coaches to exchange game tapes. Now, the digital game films can be traded on the Internet, taking anywhere from two to three minutes for one coach to get his hands on all of the games for his upcoming opponent.

While one might assume that would make for shorter days for these coaches than in the past, the easily-accessible game tapes instead allow coaches to watch even more games than before, keeping them at the field house as long as ever. At Plano, the Sunday schedule always starts around 1 p.m., letting the coaches get to church with their families in the morning; but the afternoon consists of another six to seven hours, mostly getting the game plan ready to install for the team.

During the school week, practices are designed to experiment with new plays while also working on the weaknesses from the previous game. Monday through Wednesday are full practice days, with Thursday as a shorter practice. Each day focuses on different things, but they all have one thing in common: Friday. For everyone, the week builds and breathes around Friday. Unless, of course, the week's game is on a Thursday.

Such was the case with the Wildcats' second game of the season against MacArthur High School of Irving, Texas. With a Thursday night game, the biggest change was that Tuesday practice got cut short. For Thursday games, the game plans were usually a bit more simplified, which sometimes could become a good thing. And to top it off, kickoffs on school nights were typically at 7 p.m., which got the team out of the field house a little earlier than normal.

On this Thursday night, the Wildcats arrived in the Dallas suburb of Irving with hopes of a 2–0 start to the season, while also knowing that this would be the last real tune-up before district play began. So far, everything this team had wanted to see had come to fruition, albeit just one game into the year. Matt Keys handled his first start with moderate success, Brandon Stephens scored three touchdowns and showed signs of dominance, and the defense appeared to have some playmakers. Even a couple of unproven contributors such as Nic Melson and Darion Foster were pleasant surprises.

But just six days later, the Wildcats were again under the hot Texas sun, this time donning their traditional white jerseys with maroon pants and, of course, their white helmets, which now featured a few stickers on selected helmets after last week's win.

Plano had beaten MacArthur in each of the last five years, dating back to a loss to the Cardinals in the 2009 season opener. Since then, the Wildcats had largely dominated the series.

But the coaching staff had more of an uneasy feeling about MacArthur this time around. They had a game-changing wide receiver in Joshua Hodges, a big-time recruit who at the time was looking at schools such as Texas A&M. Throw in a running back that had played varsity since his sophomore year in Artiss Henderson, and the Cardinals had quite a one-two punch at the skill positions.

But in the week before the game, assistant Plano coach Chris Fisher couldn't stop thinking about MacArthur's quarterback. It was not that Kane Hardin was an all-state player, but every time Fisher watched him on tape he saw someone else—someone that was like a brother to him.

"He's Tanner," Fisher said when describing Hardin. "They're not the biggest guys in the world, but are just tough as nails and will do whatever it takes to make the play."

Tanner would be one Tanner Craven, who meant much more to Fisher than just being his cousin. They basically grew up together in the Amarillo area. Craven had a few college stops, including the University of New Mexico, before finishing at Midwestern State University in Wichita Falls, Texas, where Fisher spent two seasons on the football squad himself and eventually got his degree. Tanner also spent nine years on the Plano staff, serving mostly as the quarterback coach before leaving in 2014 to run the offense at R.L. Turner High School in Carrollton, Texas. Thankfully, Tanner and Chris hadn't had to face each other as coaches, but they saw each other and talked football all the time, each pursuing his own role in the small world of big-time high school ball in Texas. The bond between Chris and Tanner was stronger than oak, and the respect they shared was even greater. So when Chris compared a player to Tanner, it was a big deal.

The combination of a gritty quarterback in Hardin with the playmakers in the backfield and on the outside was enough to get the coach's attention. The Wildcat players, on the other hand, well, they were a little more confident.

Bopping around with their headphones, a loose group exited the bus. They weren't exactly overconfident because McCullough would never allow that, but just six days removed from a big win over John Tyler, they could smell a 2–0 start.

For the majority of the first quarter, though, any stench they could sense was probably theirs. It was a foul start for the Wildcats, who struggled in all three phases. The offense could barely muster a first down, while the defense had trouble with Hodges, who had two 36-yard catches on one drive, the latter resulting in the game's first touchdown. And to make matters worse, even though MacArthur botched the extra point, Plano would then mishandle the kickoff return, eventually falling on it in the end zone for a safety.

Just like that it was 8–0 in favor of the Cardinals, and that confidence and swagger on the faces of the Wildcats had faded.

But Plano has some playmakers as well, especially Brandon Stephens. Even before kickoff, the all-state running back had already scheduled a press conference for the following day at the school to announce his college decision, having narrowed his choices down to Texas A&M, Texas, Alabama, and Stanford, among a few others. It was a decision that both Plano fans and college scouts had been anticipating eagerly for a long time.

Stephens' father, Tim, said the first inkling he ever received that his son could be special occurred about nine years earlier.

"When I signed him up for football in third grade, I couldn't see the talent," Tim admitted of his son. "Other people saw it. But to me, he was just my son. But this third-grade coach told me that he'd been coaching kids a long time and never saw anything like Brandon. I brushed it off. But when he got to the fifth grade, that's when I started believing."

Now, seven years later, Tim and his wife, Charlotte, never could've imagined the type of attention placed on their son, simply for his athletic ability. The phone calls from college recruiters began around his sophomore season but increased to about "four to five every night" during his junior season, Brandon recalled. During his 2014 season, several college coaches, from both inside and outside the state, would line up on the sidelines, proudly wearing a colorful team polo, pullover, or cap to show what institution they were representing.

Stephens was a laid-back kid with a serious side that he got from his father. So publicly, he never let the attention get to him. Instead, he'd put up solid numbers, becoming one of the standout elements of the team's 2014 season. It was a strong sign to all those who came to see him play: through the pressure of his biggest year, he only seemed to get better. In Texas, the lights are already bright—any player that can succeed on this stage will be walking into the pressure of college ball with an advantage already.

Stephens had ridden the wave of last season into a bidding war of coaches looking to bring his talent to their top-tier college programs. During the run-up to the season, speculation was rampant about where he was going to end up. Now, after years of courtship, it seemed he'd finally settled on a university. That announcement, however, would have to wait until the next day. If he didn't carry his team to victory on this night, he knew it would definitely sour his moment.

And so he did just that. Stephens had runs of nineteen and twenty-eight yards to set up Plano for its first touchdown, a strike from Keys, who was absolutely blasted on the play before heaving a pass to Kaleb Macaway, the receiver making a leaping grab in the end zone. Down 8–7, Plano then used big plays from Stephens again, who ran through the Cardinals' defense for twenty-seven yards to set up a 1-yard touchdown plunge by Keys, which put the Wildcats on top.

But as good as things were looking offensively, the defensive coaches were scrambling on the sideline. Senior cornerback Obale Enoweyere went down with a broken leg, ending his prep high school career on the spot. Considered a raw athlete that still needed to understand the ins and outs of the game as a freshman, Enoweyere had worked his way up through Plano's program, from a talented sophomore with skills, to a serviceable junior on the varsity who got extended playing time, to now a senior starter the team was counting on.

Fisher, his position coach who had told his peers just earlier in the day how much progress Enoweyere has made from last season, typically didn't go on the field for injuries, but he made an exception this time.

"When I got there, tears were rolling down his face," Fisher said. "Immediately, I had tears rolling down my cheeks, too. I just knew how hard he worked to be a guy we could count on. He had a chance to have a special season and in the second game of his senior year, he breaks his leg. He'll never play football again, and it just breaks your heart."

Fisher wiped away both Enoweyere's tears and his own, kissed the fallen cornerback on the forehead, and said, "We've got you."

With the teams exchanging touchdowns to put Plano up 21–15 going into halftime, the shootout continued into the third quarter as Henderson gave his team the lead on a 35-yard reception when he weaved through half of the Wildcats defense, which had now lost yet another starter in safety T.J. Lee. A fearless, hard-hitting senior who was one of those "glue" players, his high-ankle sprain wouldn't just keep him out for the rest of this game, but eventually half of the season.

But again, the focus had to remain on the present, and the Wildcats kept finding answers, even from the unlikeliest of sources. Just moments after another false start penalty on his offensive line had him visibly frustrated, Keys calmed himself just enough to make a huge play. Fighting off a would-be sack by a rushing Cardinals defender, the big-bodied Keys stayed on his feet and heaved the ball to wide-open receiver Daniel Rodriguez, who had somehow slipped past the entire secondary, for a 62-yard touchdown, giving Plano the edge again, 28–22.

The sideline erupted, including the coaches this time around. This back-and-forth game might have been just a Week 2 non-district affair that was more of a tune-up for the rest of the season, but the intensity level was sky-high. McCullough nearly tackled Keys as he came off the field, giving his quarterback a forearm to the chest, in approval of course.

Gasping for air, and needing a serious break, Keys had no time to rest. This was a shootout, remember? After Henderson busted up the middle for a 41-yard MacArthur touchdown, Plano answered with a 70-yard kickoff return, setting up a field goal to take the lead, 31–29.

All night, the offense had found one answer after another, but deep into the game, now the defense finally had to take a stand. Senior defensive tackle Darion Foster watched the next series from the sidelines, still reeling from a mistake he'd made on MacArthur's previous possession that had led to Henderson's last touchdown. He'd been caught out of position on the inside, leaving a gaping hole for Henderson to exploit all the way to the goal line. As he watched MacArthur move the ball once more, he knew he had to make up for it.

Going in on MacArthur's next set of downs, Foster stayed in his lane this time and stuffed the Cardinals' running back for a short gain on first down. On second down, he chased the quarterback to the sideline and swarmed him for a 2-yard loss. And on third down, he held his own at the line of scrimmage while the pass went incomplete. Three plays and off the field with about seven minutes left in the game. Little did Foster or his defensive teammates know that they wouldn't return to the field.

In just his second start for Plano, Keys looked like a pro, squeezing every second from the play clock as the Wildcats managed to grind out yard after yard and first down after first down. Stephens was slicing and dicing with runs left and right, but the pivotal play occurred on a fourth-and-five at the Cardinals' 17-yard line with 1:45 on the clock. McCullough had faith in his kicker, Blake Mazza, who had booted a 36-yard field goal earlier in the quarter to give his team the lead. But in a game this back and forth, the head coach wasn't interested in upping the advantage to five points and then having to kick off. After calling a timeout to think about the situation, he sent his offense back on the field to finish the job.

As the offensive line walked to the line of scrimmage, the chatter from the hometown MacArthur crowd grew louder, while the Plano fans, clustered together in the stands behind the Wildcats bench along with a constellation of banners in support, held their breath. This was a win they expected for their team, and while this game certainly didn't lack entertainment, the possibility of a loss hung in the humid air. This was a game they were supposed to win—and now the team had to do just that.

With the defense focusing on Stephens, Keys was able to juke up the field on an option play, keeping the ball for fourteen yards to the 3-yard line. Mission accomplished. Stephens, standing twenty yards behind, went down and slapped the turf with two hands in excitement, knowing his work was done as well.

All that was left was a couple of kneel-downs from Keys, who not only improved to 2–0 as a starter, but also won a little respect from his teammates and coaches.

"All I know is that Matt Keys is as tough as they get," said Fisher, who entered the game praising the toughness of MacArthur's quarterback, but hopped on the victorious bus raving about his own.

After the game, McCullough couldn't say enough about his signal caller. "Matt just found a way to win. That's really all you can ask your quarterback to do. He made plays in the passing game, and when we needed him to run, he did that. He showed a lot of heart tonight."

The players were absolutely exhausted. The emotions of the game, coupled with the ninety-degree heat and then a very joyous locker room that included more chants and a few dances, took everything out of the Wildcats. And to think it was a school night.

The players had class on Friday morning, but one of them had an announcement to make.

With a few teammates, some faculty and staff, some media members that included a couple of Dallas TV stations and Plano's local beat writer, Matt Welch, the do-it-all reporter for the *Plano Star-Courier*, a handful of coaches, and several members of his family, Stephens sat at a makeshift table set up in Plano's indoor practice facility.

After a few deep breaths, proving just how much this decision had been weighing on him, Stephens finally announced to the anxious onlookers his collegiate choice.

"I'm going to Stanford."

Applause came from the crowd and handshakes all around.

"This was the right opportunity," Stephens said to reporters after the announcement. "If I get it over with, I can just focus on school and football, of course, and not have that extra stress on my shoulders."

While moving to the West Coast would undoubtedly be quite the journey for anyone, especially a soon-to-be nineteen-year-old, Stephens made it clear that he had work to do with the Wildcats before he became a member of the Stanford Cardinals.

With Stephens' announcement made, it put to rest one of the questions being asked by everyone outside the team, but it did little to change what was happening in it. While everyone was happy for Stephens, they were focused, not on the story of next year, but on the story of this one. And right now, all anyone could seem to think about was the unexpected brilliance of Matt Keys. Through two games he'd already shown himself to be a consistent playmaker, someone whose presence could help alleviate the pressure on Stephens and open up new possibilities for the offense.

It was almost enough to make you forget there had ever been doubts about him. Almost.

Saturday

Heat waves in Texas have a way of spreading to cover the entire state. But the heat is never the same everywhere. Houston's heat isn't like Austin's heat, and it certainly isn't like Dallas' heat, especially in August when rain is often a hard thing to come by. This is the case in the best of times, but during a heat wave, it takes on new significance. For the last couple of weeks, much of Texas had been consumed by temperatures hovering in the triple-digit range; and as Art Briles stepped off the bus in Dallas, he felt it immediately.

But considering what had been going on behind the scenes surrounding their campus, Briles and the Baylor coaching staff didn't need to walk outside of any bus to feel the proverbial heat. The Sam Ukwuachu conviction in August led to weeks of questioning, from both the media and Baylor's administrators, on not only the number of incidents that had been occurring on campus but the process in which they had been handled. Sadly, this wasn't the first time in recent years Baylor had dealt with this type of situation. Former defensive end Tevin Elliot was sentenced to twenty years in prison in 2014 for two counts of sexual assault from a 2012 incident. While Elliott was removed from the football program immediately after he was charged and was kicked out of school, he did finish his playing career at Central Arkansas in Conway. Still, the rape trial not only led to a conviction but also brought out testimonies from other victims who claimed they had been assaulted but never reported the incidents to the police. Some of the alleged incidents with Elliott occurred at a junior college before he transferred to Baylor in 2009.

The Elliott case was seemingly closed in 2014 but resurfaced again after Ukwuachu's conviction. While it might have been premature to call this behavior a pattern at Baylor, the incidents certainly weren't isolated. And that had Baylor officials somewhat scrambling to get a better understanding of these situations—and figure out if there were more that hadn't been reported.

After one of the school's law professors finished an internal inquiry on how the school dealt with these prior allegations, Baylor's president, Ken Starr, decided to take a proactive approach in the matter and hired outside investigators to look into incidents involving sexual violence, both on campus and especially within the athletic department and the football team.

On September 2, two days before Baylor's first game of the season, the school hired attorneys from Pepper Hamilton LLP, a Philadelphia-based firm that has over a dozen locations, mostly in the northeast area of the country. Attorneys Gina Smith and Leslie Gomez arrived on Baylor's campus in the days leading up to the first game, quickly becoming a fixture in the hallways of the football offices, as they interacted with coaches and staff members. Before too long, the investigation dug deep into records of cell phones of the coaching staff and email history over the previous eight years.

While no one likely enjoys dealing with an investigation into their own records, there wasn't great concern from Briles and the coaching staff. Sure, there were some incidents involving players but nothing that they felt was handled improperly. The Baylor coaches and football staff were asked to cooperate in full with the investigators, who, from the start, began to make some findings.

Though the investigation remained confidential to the public, there were some prior incidents that led to Baylor's having to suspend a pair of defensive starters. Shawn Oakman's senior season hit a road bump as he was forced to miss the opener at SMU for what Baylor specified as "team violations." Safety Orion Stewart was suspended as well, although both of them made the trip on Friday with their teammates to Dallas for the season opener. Briles was informed of the issues regarding both players on Thursday before the game, but was told that nothing more was needed than a one-game suspension. From a football standpoint, he certainly wasn't happy to miss a pair of defensive starters who had practiced with the team for all of the off-season, only to make a last-second change the night before.

Still, just like the team had done a few weeks before by seemingly overcoming the dark cloud that hovered over the program during the Ukwuachu ruling, Baylor and its team pushed on, straight through to Dallas for a nationally-televised showdown with SMU.

Standing by the bus, Briles recalled a recent visit to this very campus. While visiting his oldest daughter, Jancy, who lived in Dallas' uptown district just a few blocks from SMU, the two went for an afternoon run. The goal wasn't exactly to wind up at an in-state rival's school, but thanks to the unbearable heat, the best route back to her house actually took them right through the heart of SMU's beautiful location. Wearing a gray Dri-FIT shirt—long-sleeved, of course—with a Baylor logo on his chest and black shorts with another BU logo on the leg, the head coach of the Mustangs' first opponent was turning some heads and even catching a few glares from the onlookers who seemed to recognize him.

Was he sending a message? Was Briles taunting them by taking a run right through their campus? That was hardly the intention, but the coach quickly visualized the thought of one of his rival coaches taking a jaunt through Baylor's campus and McLane Stadium, and realized he would've likely been put off had the tables been turned.

"We better get on out of here," he said with a chuckle, and the two put their heads down and pretended to focus solely on their journey as they trekked on back to the house.

But now, on this Friday afternoon in early September, Briles and his team were the main attraction, not only on the Dallas campus, but also in the college football world. This game, their season opener, would be taking place on a Friday instead of a Saturday, and while Friday night games have a way of throwing the schedule off a bit, Briles was never worried about this one. Not only was it the first game of the season, meaning a routine hadn't even been set yet, but he knew they'd be the only college game on TV nationally.

"The world is watching," he said to his team as they prepared to dress for the game. And unlike most weeks where Briles picked a handful of seniors to go into the equipment room and literally select the entire uniform for the upcoming game, the head coach gave them a rather strong suggestion for this matchup.

SMU had publicly promoted the season opener to its fans as a "White Out," encouraging the students, alumni, and other onlookers to dress in white in support of Chad Morris and his first game as the Mustangs' head coach. But since SMU decided to wear its traditional blue jerseys, that gave the Bears an opportunity to match, and perhaps mock, the home team's publicity stunt.

"Let's show them a white-out," Briles said to his players as they started to trickle out onto the field, wearing white helmets, jerseys, and pants. If anything, it gave the Bears an advantage, considering the first quarter of the game with this 6 p.m. kickoff would be played under the sun.

But like everything else swirling around the Bears program, what the team wore on the field wasn't really a concern. Uniforms, suspensions, investigations, accusations—all of these matters were being put to the side. This Baylor team was finally going to be able to simply play a real game of football.

"It's already hot," said one of the Bears' strength coaches. "Might as well start hot. Let's go. Let's go show them who we are."

Briles typically liked to get the football first, and this game was no exception. Winning the toss allowed him to see what the entire staff had been waiting for all off-season, dating back to spring football when Seth Russell won the starting quarterback job.

When Russell showed up on Baylor's campus in the fall of 2013, he didn't have many supporters who imagined he would one day be the team's starting quarterback. In fact, during Russell's final high school game of his career—a playoff game for Garland High School at the Cowboys' AT&T Stadium in Arlington—he was benched in the third quarter and replaced by an underclassman who rallied his team into overtime. Russell was inserted back into the game but threw a costly interception that proved to be his final attempt of his high school career.

Still, Russell landed at Baylor, and immediately surprised his coaches, teammates, and any other onlookers with his uncanny athleticism. While his 6–3, 200-pound frame wasn't overly impressive looking, his ability to run the forty-yard dash in around 4.5 seconds didn't hurt. He quickly gained some popularity with his teammates during pickup basketball games when the scrawny, baby-faced "white kid from Garland" would throw down a thunderous reverse-slam dunk with relative ease.

For a redshirt season, and then two more as a backup to All-Big 12 standout Bryce Petty, Russell certainly was well-liked by his teammates. And his coaches trusted him enough to give him the starting job.

But none of them actually knew just how Russell would respond when the (ESPN) lights came on.

On the first play of the season, Russell calmly took a shotgun snap, set his feet, and lofted a perfectly thrown ball into the hands of Corey Coleman, who got behind the defense for a 42-yard gain right in front of Baylor's bench.

"Here we go," passing game coordinator Jeff Lebby said on the headsets. "That's a hell of a connection for the 2015 season."

And off the Bears went, as they hurried up to the line of scrimmage, calling three straight running plays, including a 25-yard rush by Shock Linwood on his first carry of the year. Goal-line specialist Devin Chafin entered the game and scored on his first touch, plowing into the end zone to cap off a 75-yard drive that took four plays and all of fifty seconds.

"Welcome to the show," Briles said to Russell as he walked off the field, garnering head-slaps from his teammates as he quickly went to the bench for a breather. What he didn't realize was how quickly he would be back on the field.

Briles was right. This was indeed a show, despite the Bears being favored by 35.5 points by the Las Vegas oddsmakers. SMU was here to play and after a long kickoff return to midfield, the Mustangs' new quarterback, Matt Davis, one-upped Russell with his first pass, firing a touchdown strike to tie the score.

Russell knew where to go as the second drive began—back to Coleman, who caught a slant over the middle and raced sixty yards to set up another touchdown, this time a run by Russell, who read the defense on an option play to find the end zone.

But SMU was just as inspired, and the White-Out crowd had started to fill up the home side of the stadium rather nicely. The Mustangs were hanging around, tying the game at 14, but their defense couldn't stop the Bears, who scored on their third possession and had the ball back near midfield just before the end of the first quarter.

Sophomore receiver KD Cannon was one of Baylor's highest-touted recruits just one year earlier. Unlike many of the Baylor receivers who redshirted as true freshmen, only to play four more seasons, Cannon quickly exploded onto the scene in 2014 with 1,038 receiving yards to earn consensus Freshman All-American honors.

But Cannon, who ran his mouth seemingly as much as he ran routes, had been jawing with the SMU secondary from the start. After Russell carried the ball for a first down, cornerback Ajee Montes had finally had enough and decked Cannon after the play, which resulted in a personal foul penalty.

But Cannon was heated. The fifteen yards for the offense just wasn't enough.

"You and me, let's go," he barked at Montes, waving him up to the line of scrimmage for the next play. "I've got you, right here."

Almost the equivalent of calling a home run shot in baseball, Cannon barely made any moves off the line, but easily sprinted past the cornerback as well as his safety help. Both players were five yards behind Cannon, who hauled in Russell's perfect pass at the goal line for a touchdown.

"What?!" Cannon exploded, nearly getting a penalty for spiking the ball, but instead just receiving a warning from the official. "We're going to eat all night!"

Four possessions, four touchdowns for the Russell-led Bears with the quarterback already owning two touchdown passes and another score on the ground—and that was just in the first quarter of the first game of the season. Apparently shootouts were in the Texas air along with the heat.

Although on pace to surpass one hundred points on the night, Baylor cooled off dramatically, failing to add to its point total in the second quarter as the Mustangs hung right with the number four–ranked Bears, trailing 28–21 at the half. And it could've been much closer had SMU managed its time better before the break. Instead, the team let the clock run out with the offense on the Baylor 10-yard line, failing to even get a field goal.

In one locker room, the Mustangs had to be ecstatic, trailing Baylor by just a touchdown. They still had the momentum, the home crowd, and a young team with growing confidence.

"We were pretty confident, too," Briles recalled of his team's thinking in the other locker room. "We knew we just needed to settle down. I think we had a better understanding of what (SMU's offense) was going to do."

They were so confident that the Mustangs never scored another point. Anchored by nose tackle Andrew Billings, who controlled the line of scrimmage from start to finish, Baylor applied more pressure in the second half and never allowed SMU to get on track again.

Meanwhile, Russell kept the train rolling for the Bears, firing two third-quarter touchdowns to Jay Lee, who had plenty of family and friends in the stands from his hometown of Allen, a northern suburb of Dallas. Lee only had three catches in the game, but all went for touchdowns as Baylor pulled away dramatically in the third and fourth quarters.

While Russell was slicing up the Mustangs on the stat sheet, it was a play that didn't count that seemed to get his coaches the most excited. Midway through the fourth quarter, he kept the ball on a run option, darted through an opening in the line, and then took off for a 60-yard touchdown that was actually called back because of a holding penalty. But the move showed that Russell had turned the corner. It was clear things had now changed with this offense.

Kendal Briles, the son of Baylor's head coach who was beginning his first full season as the offensive coordinator, shouted on the headsets to his fellow coaches.

"We've got a different animal now, boys," Kendal said. "This is a new toy for us. He's different."

The younger Briles was referring to Russell's speed, an element the offense hadn't been accustomed to since Robert Griffin III, who hoisted the Heisman Trophy in his final year with the Bears in 2011.

Baylor decided to pull Russell from the game after that negated touchdown, inserting freshman phenom, Jarrett Stidham, the highest-recruited quarterback Briles and the Bears had ever landed. He could run, he could throw, he was big, and he was smart. And, he was just eighteen years old. Still, the thought of redshirting him was never really considered because the coaches knew if anything were to happen to Russell, Stidham would be the next-best option, despite his lack of experience.

On the first play of his collegiate career, Stidham reared back and flung the ball deep to a wide-open Chris Platt, who had to adjust on the fly but hauled in the pass for a 42-yard touchdown. Platt, a speedster in his own right, was greeted first by Stidham, the youngster turning on the jets in excitement and sprinting to greet the recipient of his first college pass.

The colorful and always playful Cannon gave his own assessment of the play to the freshman quarterback.

"Man, that throw was terrible," he said with a smile, but not exactly joking. "That was behind him. He made you look good."

Stidham was too excited to care. He was one-for-one with a touchdown pass to open his career. Meanwhile, Russell was thinking about one of his passes as well.

"Hey, Seth, how many touchdowns did you get tonight?" asked one of the backup kickers on the sideline.

Russell responded with an honest shrug. "I don't really know. But I do know I had an interception. I know that. I threw a pick, so that's really all I know."

The answer was five, and whether or not Russell was aware of that, he knew his coaches would pay more attention to the one SMU caught, rather than the ones that helped his teammates reach the end zone.

Baylor had a chance to score late, something that would've pleased the gamblers who thought the Bears would easily cover the spread, but instead, Briles opted not to kick a late field goal, giving Baylor the 56–21 win.

After addressing his team in a joyous locker room and speaking to the media in a makeshift interview area, Briles found some familiar faces from Stephenville, Texas—where he coached the high school team for twelve years from 1988 to 1999 and won four state championships—waiting outside. Some of his former players, who still lived in the small Texas town, were on hand to watch their local product, Stidham, in his first game.

For all of the great quarterbacks who have rolled through Stephenville—several of which were coached by Briles, including his own son Kendal—there were many who thought Stidham was the best. And recruiting services would tend to agree, ranking Stidham in the Top 10 nationally among dual-threat quarterbacks who could run and pass. Originally committed to Texas Tech, Stidham changed his decision during his senior season and reopened the recruitment. That opened the door again for Briles, who made sure he didn't miss out on the hometown hero for a second time.

Even though Briles had been the head coach of Baylor for years, in many ways he was still the quintessential Texas high school coach. His years in Stephenville were formative ones, and you could still hear in his voice the traces of the Texas high school coach he once was. One of the things his former Yellow Jacket players recalled the most was Briles' ability to relate to the students as people, not just their coach. Briles wouldn't just oversee the weight-lifting period, but he would partner up with some of the bigger lineman and participate in the lifting program right along with them. To lighten the mood, Briles would often crank up the radio in the weight room and try to name the band of the song before anyone else in the room. One player once recalled Briles' yelling in the middle of a bench-press lift, "Six . . . seven . . . eight . . . Led Zeppelin . . . nine . . . ten."

At Baylor, Briles hadn't changed his ways, trying even harder at times to relate to the players' needs. Like them, he was also a college football player back in the 1970s at Houston and understood the challenges of balancing school, football, a social life, and doing all of it while fighting off homesickness as well.

Some college coaches will elevate themselves above their players, becoming larger than life figures and ruling from on high; maybe it was because his time at Stephenville stayed with him, but that was never Briles' style.

As the freshman quarterback approached his head coach, Briles teased him in a fun-loving way—his way of letting Stidham know he played well but not to get too proud of himself since he had just one college game under his belt.

They shared a laugh, as did the others. For Briles and his family, it felt good to laugh a little. The last few weeks certainly hadn't been filled with an abundance of comedy.

As it turned out, the next couple of weeks weren't going to be that much fun, either.

Sunday

Expectations are a tough thing in Texas. It doesn't matter what level of play: accountability is often demanded for even minor failure to live up to expectations.

Perhaps no one knows this better than the members of the Dallas Cowboys. When you play for the Cowboys, wins are expected, even when things seem at their most unrealistic. This is in part because everyone in the state is watching. Texas has thousands of high school football programs and dozens of college teams. But there is only one Dallas Cowboys.

There is an infamous quote from the introductory press conference after Jerry Jones bought the Dallas Cowboys franchise in 1989 that still gets replayed seemingly every year when it's close to football season.

"There is no substitute for winning," said Jones, then forty-six years old. "We must win. We will win. Win is the name of the game."

And while Jones has indeed won three Super Bowls, it had now been twenty years since he last hoisted the Lombardi Trophy after his team claimed Super Bowl XXX with a 27–17 victory over the Steelers at the end of the 1995 season.

Hanging on the wall in his Valley Ranch office was a cartoon with two buzzards sitting on a branch, the popular caption reading, "Patience my ass! I want to kill something." Given that, imagine what had been festering inside of Jones as the 2015 season approached. The soon-to-be seventy-three-year-old was still searching for his elusive fourth Super Bowl, which would be the sixth title in the Cowboys' illustrious history.

Less than a week after undergoing hip replacement surgery, Jones gingerly walked to the stage for the annual Cowboys Kickoff Luncheon, held on September 2 at AT&T Stadium. This suit-and-tie pep rally of sorts was for fans and sponsors to meet the team, but the event also raised funds for the Courage House at Happy Hill Farm, a private day and boarding school that helps at-risk children.

Never one to shy away from bold predictions, in 2001, the team's first year after Hall of Famer Troy Aikman's retirement, Jones recognized that winning with a rookie quarterback such as Quincy Carter might be a challenge, so he "softened" his stance in front of those attending the luncheon and predicted a more conservative number of regular season victories—ten. The Cowboys won just five games. The following year, Jones suggested to the crowd that a Super Bowl run was possible, but his team again struggled and finished 5–11 for the third straight season.

Nevertheless, Jones continued his preseason optimism until he changed his stance somewhat in 2014. He took the stage and spoke of the "uphill battle" the Cowboys would face that season, but reminded the audience that teams sometimes played their best "when backed into a corner." The club responded with a 12–4 campaign followed by a playoff win over the Detroit Lions before a controversial loss in the next round against the Green Bay Packers.

Once again, the eternal optimist was back in 2015.

"We understand the opportunity we've got. Last year, we needed to circle the wagons, and we did that," Jones said as he looked around the stage at his players, who were seated on either side of the podium. "Men, I'll tell you this. This is an opportunity for you. We've got players up here who could've gone somewhere else and been on other teams. There're some great players up here. Let's get it together. We're ready to go."

But it wasn't just Jones feeling the Super Bowl vibes. Several others who took the stage echoed his statements. Former Cowboys great Emmitt Smith, a Hall of Famer and the NFL's all-time leading rusher, was honored with the Tom Landry Legends award. At one point in his speech, he turned toward the current players and coaches and said, "I want you to achieve the things we were able to achieve."

Smith's running mate and fellow Hall of Famer Michael Irvin wasn't as cryptic. The event's honorary chair took the microphone and tried to connect numerical coincidences to a possible Cowboys trip to Super Bowl 50. He told the audience that the Cowboys had been around fifty-five years, and then pointed out that the Cowboys had won five Super Bowls.

"I'm into omens," he said. "Fifty-five minus five . . . that equals fifty."

Irvin also pointed out that it had been twenty years since the Cowboys won the thirtieth Super Bowl.

"Thirty plus twenty equals fifty," Irvin continued. "I don't care how you get there. You just make sure that at the end of this year, the golden team in the NFL is winning the golden Super Bowl in the NFL."

Naturally, Irvin and Smith were a little more flamboyant on stage, but other former players in the audience, including quarterback Roger Staubach, also couldn't avoid the "Super" elephant in the room.

"I think this has a chance to be a really special team," the Hall of Fame quarterback said.

Respectfully, head coach Jason Garrett sat and listened to all of it. Super Bowl talk can make a laid-back, careful-with-his-words type of person like Garrett cringe, which he likely did several times when Irvin was up there preaching Super Bowl or bust.

When it was finally Garrett's turn, he found a middle ground. He recalled a story about the late Buck Buchanan, a longtime equipment manager of the Cowboys who had passed away in June. Buchanan's son, Bucky, had been on the team's equipment staff for more than twenty years.

Just days before the luncheon, Garrett had gotten misty-eyed prior to the team's preseason game against the Minnesota Vikings during a moment of silence honoring Buck.

Garrett shared a story of his first season with the Cowboys in 1992, when he was just a young quarterback with seemingly long odds to make the roster. He sheepishly entered the equipment room and apologetically asked Buck if he could possibly get a smaller T-shirt than the baggy one he was issued. Garrett said he was shocked at Buchanan's answer: "Here at the Cowboys, we pursue excellence. We'll get you a shirt that fits."

Garrett also shared his story of watching U.S. Attorney General Loretta Lynch on television and the inspiration for the "We Do" shirts, along with the constant theme of the previous year's message, "Fight."

"A lot of people at these kind of luncheons want to make guarantees," he said. "We ain't making any of those. But, I will guarantee this: This team will define itself by what it does. This team is going to pursue excellence. This team is going to be a team that fights."

As the luncheon concluded, the players exited the stage and headed toward the charter buses that would take them back to Valley Ranch or their own personal cars. However, the media members in attendance scurried to find a few answers to questions that had popped up during the nearly two-hour event. While more than seventy players were on the stage, the focus shifted on the players not in attendance.

Where was Greg Hardy? What about Joseph Randle? And no Randy Gregory or Corey White?

Heading to his car, Executive Vice President and Director of Player Personnel Stephen Jones assured the media that all had excused absences and that their status with the team was safe, despite the Cowboys having to trim the roster to fifty-three players in three days.

The Cowboys' official statement was "personal reasons," but for all of them, especially Randle, Gregory, and Hardy, any kind of absence was a red flag, considering their off-field troubles. Hardy, however, was gone to attend the birth of his child.

The most serious of the no-shows was Randle, who had to return to his hometown of Wichita, Kansas, for another court appearance. This was not related to the previous February incident in which his ex-girlfriend accused him of pointing a gun at her and shattering a car window. It was another minor legal matter that he needed to take care of before the season began.

Despite all of his off-the-field issues, Randle had plenty of support from the Cowboys, who not only let DeMarco Murray leave but also didn't draft another running back.

Randle didn't get much competition in training camp from Darren McFadden, so for now, this starting job was still Randle's to lose. But with each non-football matter that popped up, his grip on the starting job seemed to get a bit looser by the day.

Missing the kickoff luncheon isn't ideal, but this close to the season, the Cowboys would prefer these kinds of events be skipped rather than a practice or, of course, a game.

Speaking of games, the Cowboys wrapped up the preseason on September 3 with what had become one of the more futile sporting events in the NFL—the fourth exhibition game. With most of the starters around the league never even putting on shoulder pads, the last preseason tilt was typically a sixty-minute affair of second- and third-stringers with only a few hopefuls still having a shot to make the team.

Facing the Houston Texans for statewide bragging rights in a game known as the "Governor's Cup," the Cowboys rested thirty-three players, including all of their starters and top reserves. Hardy was again excused and missed the game, while Gregory and Randle returned but joined the rest of the key players in not suiting up.

As for White, a cornerback sitting squarely on the bubble of making the roster, he not only played, but even scored a touchdown on an interception return in the third quarter to temporarily tie the game, 7–7. Third-string quarterback Dustin Vaughan, who desperately needed a solid showing to stick around for another season, then led a fourth-quarter drive that put the Cowboys in the end zone for a third time, securing a 21–14 victory and avoiding a second straight winless preseason.

Vaughan, an undrafted rookie free agent in 2014 out of Division II West Texas A&M near Amarillo, spent his first season on the Cowboys' 53-man roster, but never took a snap. A six-five frame with a strong arm is a good start for any quarterback, but his footwork, struggles reading defenses, and limited athletic ability had been exposed in the first three preseason games of 2015, and even at times against Houston.

But in the end, Vaughan led the Cowboys to the win, only stirring the pot even more about his chances of making the team.

Undrafted quarterbacks obviously hold a special place in Jerry Jones' heart. He often wonders what would've happened had he not given Tony Romo the years to develop. Back in 2004, Romo's second season, he was nearly released and likely would've been had the team not shockingly cut incumbent starter Quincy Carter in training camp. And, of course, Romo went on to become one of the NFL's most prolific passers.

For two years, Vaughan had drawn comparisons to Romo, mainly because of their small school background and undrafted status. Now, Vaughan had rallied the troops in the second half, which seemingly was enough to convince the coaching staff to keep him. If anything, he had his offensive linemen on board.

"You just made the team," one of the rookie linemen yelled at Vaughan as they walked off the field after the score. "They ain't getting rid of you, boy!"

Except they did. Two days later, Vaughan was released, as was rookie Jameill Showers, another quarterback who had flashed some potential during camp but just wasn't worthy yet of a roster spot.

Perhaps Vaughan got caught up in the Cowboys' raised expectations for this season. A year ago, they could take a flyer on a rookie quarterback from a small school and keep him on the roster all season. But in a year where there were legitimate Super Bowl aspirations, Vaughan just wasn't good enough to keep around. His foot speed never developed like the Cowboys had hoped, coupled with just an average throwing arm. So the Cowboys cut ties with Vaughan, a player that never figured into the 2015 plans anyway, especially with Romo and then Weeden on the depth chart.

On cut-down Saturday, Garrett personally visited with all twenty-two players who had been waived, a day he dreaded every year.

"It's the worst part of our job," he said after the final moves were made on September 5. "There're a lot of guys whose dreams and aspirations of being a pro football player are going to be cut short or at least detoured for now. That's not easy. But we have to do what's in the best interests of the Dallas Cowboys."

The preseason was done. The 53-man roster was set. Now it was time for the Cowboys to start their long regular-season journey.

And somehow live up to the expectations.

Chapter 3

FULL OF SUSPENSE

Friday

High school football runs much deeper than the players who suit up on Friday nights. This is likely true in all parts of the country, but none more so than Texas, where football is undoubtedly the king.

Sure, the players, coaches, band members, drill team, and cheerleaders live for the spotlight of Friday night. But in high school, you don't have to wear any kind of uniform to be a part of the action.

At Plano, there is no better way to keep up with the social circles that come with the teenage life than to simply go to the football games—home or away. The movie theaters, the mall, or even fast-food parking lots might be popular hangouts on other nights of the week. On Friday nights in Texas, the grandstands of the football field are where all groups, organizations, and even cliques come together as one.

Just before kickoff, hundreds of Plano students who made the twenty-minute drive over to Hawk Stadium locked hands as the national anthem was played by Hebron High School's marching band. Each of them waved a mini American flag as a tribute to 9–11, even though none of the high school students could've been older than five years of age when tragedy struck both New York City and Washington, D.C., on the fateful day of September 11, 2001.

But patriotism and honor had no age requirements. These students stood tall, kept quiet, and raised their flags high in the sky. Two students even had red-white-and-blue face paint, along with maroon "We Are Plano" T-shirts, of course.

And even before kickoff, this group of honorable students showed that they were into the game just as much, already engaging in across-the-field banter with the Hebron students on the opposite sideline.

Unfortunately, it didn't take long for the biggest fears of Plano's fans to become a reality. Forced into his first start because of the previous week's injury to Obale Enoweyere, sophomore Seagol Mbua gave up an early score on Hebron's first possession, a 32-yard touchdown over the middle on third-and-11.

Head coach Jaydon McCullough glared over at his defensive coaches, coordinator Clint Stewart and assistant Chris Fisher, with an "I told you so" look that reiterated his concerns entering the game. Whether or not he believed it, Fisher shrugged it off. "We'll be all right. He's fine. Let's go O. Let's get it back."

And they did, just like that. Matt Keys heaved a 52-yard strike to Garrett Frederick on Plano's first play from scrimmage, and eventually tied the game with his own 1-yard run, providing just the response the Wildcats needed.

"They can't stop us, guys. Let's keep it up. This is our game!" Keys shouted on his way off the field, as he was greeted by just about every player in uniform. The score was tied 7–7, but perhaps even more importantly, that answer by the Wildcats seemed to indicate a major shift in momentum.

The defense started to calm down as Plano made some adjustments on the fly in the secondary, mixing up the coverages and providing more safety help to the corners, especially the young Mbua.

Hebron had a shot to take a second-quarter lead with a field-goal attempt, but Aaron Ragas, flying off the right side of the formation, got a hand on the kick, deflecting the ball about ten yards back and into the hands of safety Nic Melson. He was not the biggest player on the field—by a long shot—but Melson was one of the Wildcats' fastest and shiftiest players. He simply took off with the ball, darting down the right side in front of his Plano teammates, who were already bouncing on the sideline after the block. Melson got to the Hebron 40-yard line before he completely juked a defender, leaving him flat-footed in his tracks while he flew on by.

The only person seemingly running as fast as the junior was . . . another Melson. His father, Marty Melson, tried his best to keep up from the 30-yard line to the 20. Once his son reached the end zone, the proud papa then showed a little hops on his vertical with an emotional jump.

The stellar runback gave the Wildcats a 14–7 lead, and stunningly, gave Melson his second touchdown in just three games.

Some of Marty's colleagues, who stood next to him during each game charting plays, were beside themselves. "Coach, did you teach him those moves?" shouted one seventh-grade coach.

Even the rather quiet, laid-back Melson couldn't resist a big smile after that one.

But that was just the beginning of the second-quarter's big plays. Brandon Stephens, in his first game since announcing his decision to attend Stanford on a full football scholarship, ripped off a 45-yard score that resembled a Division I athlete facing players who will likely never suit up for organized football again after this season. Stephens was considered a smooth runner with moves on top of moves. On this touchdown, he danced his way through the line and around a linebacker before cutting up the field and running untouched to the end zone.

Leading 21–7, Plano's defense made a play that seemingly would bust the game wide open. A fumbled reverse was recovered by Ragas at the Hebron 33-yard line. But three penalties later, followed by a failed fake punt, and Hebron had the ball right back, actually gaining four yards in the process to the 37. In just six plays, the Hawks then drove right down to score on a 30-yard touchdown over the middle, where the tight end couldn't have been more wide open.

Still, Plano had plenty of confidence on offense, and with three minutes left before the half, that was more than enough time to get back on the scoreboard. Keys worked the short passes, while Stephens had two big runs down to the 2-yard line. From there, Keys tried a quarterback sneak on first down and was met in the hole by a blitzing linebacker who stood him up with a helmet to the throat.

"I got rocked on that play," Keys admitted afterward. "I still feel that hit."

But at the time, his adrenaline was pumping enough for him to score on a similar third-down run with just twenty seconds left on the clock, giving Plano a commanding 28–14 halftime lead.

"Twenty-four minutes!" McCullough yelled at his team as they were coming off the field, presumably telling his team that they had two twelve-minute quarters standing in the way of their first district win. Perhaps that was exactly how many minutes his team had to sit in the locker room while both bands played at halftime, but considering McCullough's no-nonsense intensity, he was likely referring to the amount of football left to be played.

Whatever happened during that half hour in the locker room, though, wasn't something McCullough and the Wildcats wanted to bottle up for the future. Plano went into the break with 28 points, the most they scored in a first half all season. But no one, not even some of the more pessimistic coaches on the staff, would've dreamed they wouldn't tally another point—for two weeks.

Just before the second-half kickoff, Fisher had a nervous look about him. Knowing the offense would get the ball first, he kept saying, "We've got to go down and score. We just have to score right here. If we don't score, it's going to be a long game."

It was a long game—a game that would need an extra session.

The offense that went into the locker room wasn't the same one that came out for the last two quarters. A three-and-out followed by a short punt led to an easy touchdown for the Hawks, who cut the lead in half in less than three minutes.

Although the score remained the same going into the fourth quarter,

Hebron drove to the Plano 9-yard line, and on a third-and-goal, tried a reverse pass with the receiver throwing it back to the quarterback. But the Wildcats had it sniffed out and Ragas, who had been around the ball all night, was in a prime position for an interception at the goal line. Instead, he decided to just knock the ball down with one hand and not attempt the catch.

McCullough went nuts on the sideline, even yelling at his position coach, Fisher, in disgust. "We made that play right there. We've still got the lead!" Fisher responded, assuming Hebron would make its chip-shot field goal. Instead, the kick sailed wide right and Plano held on to its 28–21 advantage.

Moments later, Hebron was close to the end zone again, thanks to a crazy play that almost gave Plano another turnover. After a 36-yard screen pass to the Wildcats' 2, the Hawks fumbled near the sideline and a mad scramble knocked the ball out of bounds. However, the Plano defenders claimed the ball hit the orange pylon first, which would've resulted in a touchback and Plano's possession.

"Hebron ball!" the side judge official shouted in response to the defender's claims.

"That's a touchback, ref . . . the ball hit . . ."

"Heee-bron BALL!"

On the next play, the Hawks reached the end zone and the score was tied.

The game would go to overtime, where Hebron's momentum continued. On a fourth-and-3 at the Wildcats' 8-yard line, the Plano coaches didn't expect the Hawks to actually run a play, despite coming to the line of scrimmage.

"Don't jump offside!" Stewart yelled about six times. "Don't jump! Don't jump!"

Plano jumped. Now it was first down for the Hawks, who would score two plays later for a 35–28 lead. The Wildcats took over possession and got down to the Hebron 5 for their own fourth-and-goal. But despite Stephens' consistent play all night, the Wildcats elected to use Keys on a run-pass option rollout. The problem wasn't the play-call, but the direction of the play. While they were discussing the play in the huddle during the timeout, Keys was positive he was told to roll left, despite having trips to the right side. It didn't make sense: "I thought maybe they're doing this on purpose to focus on the short side."

But Hebron wasn't fooled, and Keys was stuffed for no gain. By the time he got himself off the ground, the entire Hebron team, coaching staff, and everyone else on their sidelines had rushed onto the field in celebration.

Walking off the field, the coaches were upset with their quarterback, since they had wanted him to roll to the right. He even had to get other teammates in the huddle to vouch for him that the play was called to the left. Either way, the Wildcats, who were up fourteen at the half, ended up losing the game by seven, falling to 0–1 in district play.

But it was much worse than that. This one was the game they had to have. The players wouldn't say it out loud, but deep down, going 0–1 in district pretty much meant going 0–2. The Wildcats knew that they had to travel to Allen High School the next week, the three-time defending state champions who hadn't lost a game since the 2012 season.

That made the walk back to the locker room even more depressing for the dejected players and staff.

In the locker room, McCullough wasn't very sympathetic. In fact, he painted a not-so-pretty picture to a bunch of already disappointed players.

"Losing this game is tough. We had to have this game because we know who we play next," McCullough said, referring to the upcoming game with three-time defending state-champ Allen. "We can't point fingers at each other. We have to stick together. But it's not going to be easy now."

As the players and coaches exited the locker room, heading for the buses, Fisher wondered out loud, "How did we lose that game?" But he knew the answer. Everyone in the stands knew the answer. Getting shut out in any half, especially the second half, was a recipe for failure.

Fisher overheard two of his players making small talk en route to the buses.

"Well, looks like we're just going to have to go beat Allen," said senior linebacker Tucker Pollacia to a teammate.

"Hey Tuck, I like that," said Fisher. "You're right. I like that attitude, son."

Meanwhile, an eager newspaper reporter, assigned to interview the Plano head coach for the first time, was asking just about every staff member the whereabouts of McCullough.

"Are you Coach McCullough? I need to do an interview with him?"

"Nope, sorry. He's still inside."

Finally, the reporter found his target, stopping McCullough just outside the field house for an interview.

"Hey coach, how are you doing?" he asked with too much pep in his voice for the moment.

"Well, son, I've been better. But what you do need?"

And so McCullough patiently answered his questions, even though he really didn't want to talk to anyone. It was just one game, but it was certainly a big game—no matter what team was looming on the schedule next.

Saturday

No state in the country produces more Division I college football players than Texas. In an eight-year span from 2007 to 2014, the Lone Star State averaged 377 signees per year. Coming in second was Florida with an average of 333, followed by California at 247.

Texas had plenty of talented players to choose from, so despite Baylor's transformation into a national power in college football, the Bears hadn't stretched their recruiting circles too far past the Texas state lines.

Not only were there plenty of good players to go around, but the Baylor coaching staff knew the state as well as any other staff. Of the fifteen full-time coaches, including head coach Art Briles, ten of them had played high school football in Texas. Of those ten, eight of them stayed in Texas to play college football as well. All told, they knew every corner of this state. With its success, Baylor hadn't changed its geographic focus, but the school was now eyeing better players—players that never considered Baylor before, but were now picking the Bears over the likes of Texas, Texas A&M, and even some of the SEC schools like Alabama and LSU that came in and tried to poach some Lone Star talent.

But with newfound success, scrutiny oftentimes follows. Not only was Baylor in the middle of its own independent investigation for how it handled disciplinary matters; now the NCAA was questioning the football program about totally different matters.

The NCAA's rulebook for institutions and their players is nearly 500 pages long. Inside, you can find rules regarding everything from giving players too much food on their plate to putting team-logoed stickers on an envelope. Like the latter, most of the procedures pertain to recruiting and even include updated standards that cover the latest social media policies for Twitter, Instagram, and Snapchat.

As impossible as it might sound, it's the job of every school and its coaches to have a full understanding of the rules, regardless of how petty they might be.

The previous spring, two of Baylor's coaches, one of whom was Kendal Briles, the son of the head coach and the team's current offensive coordinator, attended a high school track meet that had some potential recruits participating, including two who had already committed to Baylor.

Football coaches use track meets as another opportunity to talk with recruits, these competitions serving as a loophole during the NCAA's quiet periods when visitations are not allowed. The NCAA has specific rules that coaches aren't even allowed to watch the races of potential recruits, but what makes these guidelines a bit tricky is that other participants are still eligible to be contacted.

Kendal and wide receivers coach Tate Wallis attended a track meet in the Dallas area to watch a high school junior. Another coach from a different Big 12 team reportedly spotted the pair and turned them into the NCAA for improper conduct, including not properly turning around in the stands while the recruit ran a particular event.

By early September, the NCAA was fully investigating the accusation. To be proactive, and oftentimes to soften the blow of the punishment, schools will impose a penalty beforehand, just to put a hopeful end to the probing. So as his team practiced in preparation for its Week 2 game against Lamar, a lower-level Division I school from Beaumont, Texas, Art Briles was forced to do the unthinkable.

Both Kendal and Tate would be suspended for the entire game, could not attend any team functions that day, including pregame meetings, or even be at the stadium.

Jeff Lebby was way more than Baylor's running backs coach and passing game coordinator. Married to Art's youngest daughter, Staley, Lebby just happened to be the head coach's son-in-law. But his connection to the family was also rooted in a lifelong friendship with Kendal, whom he considered to be one of his best friends.

On Thursday afternoon, two days before the home opener, Kendal poked his head into Lebby's office.

"You've got it."

"What?" Lebby responded, although he knew exactly what this meant. He just needed to hear it again for his own clarification and perhaps to stop his heart from beating so fast.

"You've got it, coach," Kendal said, telling Lebby that he would have to handle the play-calling duties for the upcoming game.

About ten seconds later, Art made his way into Lebby's office.

"Are you ready?"

"You're damn right, I am," he responded, even if he wasn't 100 percent sure just yet. "Shit yeah, let's go."

For Lebby, the moment was bittersweet because every coach relishes the opportunity to further his career. Getting the chance to call a game—for Baylor and this high-powered offense, no less—was something that all young coaches dreamed of. At just thirty-one, he had already done more and seen more than many in his profession. At the same time, he hated what his friend and colleagues were going through, and hated that yet again the Bears were in the news for the wrong reasons.

While outsiders might think a team like Baylor could beat Lamar with the ball boys calling plays, coaches don't operate that way. All week they had watched tape of Lamar's 66–3 win over Bacone College. They also knew that any opponent could come in and beat you—if you weren't ready.

Jeff wasn't going to allow that to happen, so over the next two days he worked with offensive graduate assistant Brad Willard, who was now going to assume the role of signaling the plays in from the sideline. In a quiet coaches room on Friday, Lebby would call out the plays, and Willard would signal them. That night, Willard even went home and had his wife call out the plays while he practiced the signals.

Jeff didn't sleep much on Friday night, but when he finally got up on Saturday morning, he saw a text message from Kendal, who he knew was upset and hurting over not being able to coach the game.

"I'm good. Go light 'em up! Have fun!"

With Kendal's blessing, Jeff started to get excited about his moment again, although the drive to the field house was rather strange. Jeff and Kendal live about eight minutes away from each other, and it had always been a game-day tradition for Jeff to pick up his friend along the way. But once he arrived at McLane Stadium, Jeff tried to maintain the same routine as always, which included a pregame chat on the bench with longtime offensive line coach, Randy Clements.

Meanwhile, back at his home, Kendal was subject to the same Fox Southwest broadcast as everyone else, watching the game from his living room, twisting and turning with every Baylor possession.

On Baylor's first possession, the Bears didn't have any dynamic big plays, but were effective in both running and passing the ball and soon enough found the end zone for a touchdown. When Shock Linwood crossed the goal line, it was a huge relief for Lebby, who wasn't counting on the offense to score on every drive, but "damn sure wanted to score on the first one."

Even if Lebby might have been calling a good game, the Baylor players weren't exactly playing one. In fact, the first half was as sloppy as Art Briles could recall. The defense, even with the return of Shawn Oakman and Orion Stewart, was letting Lamar move the ball up and down the field.

On offense, quarterback Seth Russell was finding receivers such as Corey Coleman and KD Cannon, but had also found a Lamar defender as well. Leading 21–14 in the second quarter, Baylor had a third-and-1 from its own 11-yard line when Lebby called for a short pass. But the receiver ran the wrong route, and Russell was intercepted for a second time, which led to a game-tying touchdown minutes later.

"Jeff?" Briles called for Lebby, whom he typically called "Lebb" or "Lebbo" when he was in better moods.

"Yes, coach."

"Run the damn ball."

"Yes, sir."

The entire first half was just a mess. Here was the number-four team in the country facing a squad that competed at the Football Championship Subdivision level (what was once known as Division I-AA), and yet the game was tied, 21–21, midway through the second quarter.

The Bears were truly missing Kendal and Tate, just for their roles on the sideline if nothing else. Wide receivers at all levels are often considered "divas" who want the ball and want their egos stroked. Sometimes they just need a calming voice. Without those two coaches, however, the receivers were somewhat on their own.

In fact, a mini-quarrel between Coleman and Russell was taken to Briles in the middle of a defensive series.

"You guys handle it," Briles said in a way that let them all know that they needed to come together really quick or this embarrassing first half was going to get even worse.

Eventually, talent and depth prevailed and the Bears started to pull away in the second half. Russell finished with 342 passing yards and four touchdowns, three of which went to Coleman, but also had three interceptions, prompting his coach to be rather blunt in his postgame interview.

"Well, as good as he was good, he was bad as he was bad," Briles said. "He needs to balance between being fearless and being smart."

Speaking of balance, the Bears also dominated the ground game as three different backs rushed for one hundred yards en route to a 66–31 win.

No matter the competition, calling plays for an offense that put up 66 points isn't a bad first outing for any coach, especially under these odd circumstances. Lebby received high praise afterward through calls and texts from his colleagues, peers, and friends, including one right after the game from Kendal.

Still, it was a little weird for Lebby to have so much attention thrown his way. But he was about to get more than he could have ever wanted.

Sunday

In Texas, football players on all levels share at least one main goal every year: make it to AT&T Stadium in Arlington, Texas.

For high school players, it means they have reached the playoffs and sometimes deep into the brackets, as this luxurious $1.2 billion stadium has housed a half-dozen state championship games. For the college kids, three Division I schools in Texas, including Baylor, and five other Division II teams have played under the same bright lights at one time or another. And now that the Cotton Bowl has regained its status as one of college football's most prestigious bowl games, and has since moved from Fair Park in Dallas to AT&T Stadium, getting there is now a goal for many college teams outside of Texas.

And then there's the NFL. Every year the Cowboys bring in twenty to twenty-five rookies, and at least half of them admit the Cowboys were either their favorite team growing up, or certainly the favorite team of their families. Making the team and playing games inside the stadium is the ultimate goal: proving to everyone they have indeed reached the pinnacle of pro sports, playing for the Dallas Cowboys, also known as America's Team.

As the Cowboys prepared for the 2015 season, with preseason out of the way, it was time to shift the focus to the games that counted. Aside from a few minor roster alterations, the team was getting itself ready for the season opener against the New York Giants the following Sunday night.

The Cowboys might have been ready. The stadium, however, was not.

In fact, five days before the Cowboys and Giants would meet in front of an expected crowd of more than 90,000 fans with millions more watching at home on NBC, AT&T Stadium was hosting a more globally significant event—if that were even possible.

If Tony Romo, Eli Manning, Dez Bryant, and Odell Beckham Jr. are the best of the best in the NFL, soccer stars such as Lionel Messi are seen as even more iconic throughout the world. Messi and Argentina's national team played an international "friendly" against Mexico on September 8 in a game that drew more than 82,000 fans.

Whether it's football, or fútbol, events at AT&T Stadium usually bring out the best in superstars, and Messi was no exception as he scored a game-tying goal in the final minutes to preserve a 2–2 tie.

But as soon as the final whistle blew and the fans started to head for the exits, members of the stadium's change crew were already in the process of transforming the venue from one colossal event into another. Perhaps the biggest challenge involved altering the field, as real grass was rolled out for the soccer game, only to be removed and replaced by the NFL turf, which had been stored in a warehouse-type location within the bowels of the stadium.

In fact, by the time the Cowboys and Giants took the field on Sunday, September 13, it would be the third different playing surface used at the stadium. On September 5 the Cowboys' home had also hosted the AdvoCare Classic, the annual early-season college football matchup that featured two of the nation's best teams, Alabama having defeated Wisconsin, 35–17. Because of the different hash marks and field logos between the college and NFL turfs, the stadium kept two synthetic playing surfaces, along with the occasionally needed grass. In a span of eight days, AT&T Stadium would use all three.

Back at Valley Ranch, the Cowboys were welcoming some new faces to both the 53-man roster and the practice squad. The latter is a 10-player developmental group who practices with the team and has lockers at the facility, but isn't eligible to play in games unless they are officially signed to the active roster. Their $6,600 weekly salary is about a quarter of the league minimum for rookie players on the actual team. Still, practice-squad players can earn up to $112,000 per season and have an opportunity to get called up to the roster at any moment.

Not among those on the practice squad, though, was Dustin Vaughan, the second-year quarterback who just couldn't wow his coaches enough in the preseason and training camp. However, the Cowboys did place two quarterbacks on the unit, including Kellen Moore, a veteran who had been with the Detroit Lions for the past three years. While in Detroit, he was coached by Scott Linehan, a former Lions assistant but now the current Cowboys offensive coordinator. He undoubtedly wanted to reunite with the prospect.

Moore, who became the first quarterback in FBS history to earn fifty collegiate wins as a starter at Boise State, walked into the locker room at Valley Ranch on the Tuesday before the Cowboys' first game. When he did, many of the media members on hand wondered, some out loud, just who this was.

"Man, they get new equipment guys in here every week," one of the beat writers said with a serious tone.

"No man, that's the new quarterback they signed," said another reporter from a different newspaper. "That's Kellen Moore."

With a generously listed height of an even six feet, Moore and his baby face, rosy cheeks, and less-than-stellar physique more than blended in inside the locker room, especially with the equipment interns and media present.

Then again, his presence didn't seem to matter much either way. The

Cowboys had Tony Romo playing at the highest of levels coming off the 2014 season and even Brandon Weeden looked to be an adequate backup if called upon. Behind fellow practice squad–mate Jameill Showers, Moore arrived as the fourth quarterback on the team. The chances of him ever getting on the roster, much less getting in a game, seemed to be the longest of long shots.

Conversely, the Cowboys added a fourth running back with every intention of playing him. In fact, former Texas A&M standout Christine Michael was acquired in a trade with the Seattle Seahawks and given a chance to possibly win the starting job ahead of Joseph Randle and Darren McFadden.

Quietly, some of the offensive coaches were hoping to add a veteran such as Michael weeks earlier when McFadden was sidelined with a hamstring injury, and Randle never ran away with the starting job despite getting all of the first-team reps during training camp and the preseason.

For this first game, though, Michael's lack of knowledge with the Cowboys' playbook hindered his chances to suit up against the Giants, giving Randle and/or McFadden at least one game to shine. As it would turn out, a different running back would end up stealing the spotlight altogether.

Of course, when it comes to opening night in the NFL, there's certainly plenty of spotlight to go around. Al Michaels and Cris Collinsworth are the "A" team of broadcasters for the league's marquee game of the week, which is shown on NBC's *Sunday Night Football*.

However, across the field in the radio booth, there was a major change behind the mic as the team had to find a temporary fill-in for longtime "Voice of the Cowboys" Brad Sham, who was entering his thirty-seventh season as the club's play-by-play announcer. Due to the beginning of Rosh Hashanah, the start of the Jewish New Year, Sham was unable to work that evening. Each year he looked for any potential conflict when the NFL schedule was released each April, but remarkably, this was the first time the holiday had actually forced him out of the booth.

So what did the Cowboys do instead? They approached one of Sham's predecessors in longtime CBS analyst Verne Lundquist, who actually served as the team's play-by-play announcer for twelve years before moving on after the 1983 season. It wasn't Sham's idea to call Lundquist, but he wished it was, calling it "an honor" to have his former partner fill in for this game.

Lundquist worked the Vanderbilt–Georgia matchup for CBS on Saturday, September 12, before flying directly to Dallas to prepare for his first Cowboys game in thirty-two years.

By the time the showdown kicked off, the electricity in the stadium could've powered both the radio and TV broadcasts combined. Cowboys fans had waited eight long months since the controversial Dez Bryant non-catch call in the team's loss to the Green Bay Packers in the divisional round of the 2014 playoffs.

Now, it was time to right the wrong, and the Giants happened to be the team in their way. Still, the visitors weren't about to step aside for their NFC East rivals.

Ironically enough, the infamous Dez-catch resurfaced early in the second quarter when the Giants' Larry Donnell had a similar play over the middle. The tight end caught a pass for a first down, but when he was brought to the ground by rookie cornerback Byron Jones, the ball popped loose and rolled out of bounds. Jason Garrett, standing five feet from the football, immediately waved his arms in an "incomplete pass" motion. But when the two side officials discussed the play, Garrett nearly dropped to his knees when he heard them rule the pass was complete with a fumble that kept the ball with New York.

"You've got to be kidding me," Garrett said to his coaches on the headsets. "This is the same damn play as Dez."

Out of spite, Garrett had no choice but to drop his red challenge flag and when the lead official came over to hear the head coach's reasoning, referee Bill Vinovich got more than he bargained for.

"I mean, we've been talking about this rule for eight months now," said Garrett, referring to the NFL's competition committee's attempt to clarify the ruling of a completed catch during the off-season. "Well, if this is a catch, then I don't know what's a catch and you guys don't either."

Garrett even told Vinovich to relay that message to Dean Blandino, the NFL's director of officials, when he went under the hood on the sideline to review the play. Whether or not Vinovich passed along Garrett's thoughts to anyone, Dallas did win the challenge, as the ruling was reversed to an incomplete pass.

But the Cowboys still weren't doing much on offense, settling for two field goals in the first half. Randle fumbled on his second carry of the game but managed to recover the ball at the bottom of the pile, avoiding an embarrassing way to start the season, considering the Cowboys had named him the starting tailback the Friday before the game.

The Giants' defense had a lot to do with the Cowboys' problems. New York scored one touchdown in the second quarter when cornerback Dominique Rodgers-Cromartie picked off a pass and returned it fifty-seven yards to the end zone. They then set up another in the fourth quarter with an interception by fellow cornerback Trumaine McBride that was returned to the Cowboys' 1-yard line.

The problems on offense, though, were even worse—way worse—than what the numbers on the stat sheet suggested. After a catch early in the fourth quarter, Bryant gingerly walked to the sideline and told the trainers that his foot didn't seem right. He was experiencing a "funny feeling."

What he was feeling was a broken right foot. The training staff took him to the locker room, where X-rays revealed the fracture, ending his night, his first month, and essentially the next one as well.

Still, the Cowboys had to power on without their most explosive player. Midway through the fourth quarter, with the team trailing 23–13, Romo engineered a quick drive, spreading the ball around to receivers such as Cole Beasley and Terrance Williams, and then to trusted tight end Jason Witten, who scored a touchdown to narrow the gap to 23–20 with just more than five minutes to play.

However, the Giants looked again like it would be their night. On third-and-goal at the Cowboys 1-yard line with 1:45 left, Manning had his team in position to either put the game away with a possible touchdown or at least run the ball and tick another forty seconds off the clock. Instead, the Giants quarterback threw an incomplete pass and settled for a field goal, giving possession back to Romo and the Cowboys with 1:29 to play and seventy-two yards needed for a touchdown.

No timeouts, no Bryant, no problem—at least on this night.

Romo absolutely carved up the Giants, using running back Lance Dunbar out of the backfield with two of his career-high eight receptions. Romo masterfully rushed the offense down the field and had the ball on the Giants' 11-yard line with just thirteen seconds remaining. As the offense got to the line of scrimmage and viewed the New York secondary, Witten yelled over at Romo and put two fists up by his forehead, a signal that showed his quarterback that the middle of the field would be open. A few seconds later, still barking out signals, Romo then did the exact same motion with his fists to let Witten know that he saw the same thing.

With the snap, however, usually reliable center Travis Frederick dribbled the ball back to his quarterback on two hops. But Romo, a former all-state high school point guard in Wisconsin, calmly got a handle on the ball, picked it up, moved into position to throw and found Witten—over the middle, of course—for the game-winning touchdown.

Cowboys fans absolutely roared with excitement. Romo couldn't pump his right arm any harder than he did just after the score, and then he ran to the bench, where he was mobbed by his teammates and coaches, including an equally amped-up Garrett, who can head-slap his players with the best of them.

Just when it appeared all hope was lost, Romo had pulled out his magic wand and saved the Cowboys from an 0–1 start against a division rival.

With the 27–26 victory, the Cowboys players were greeted back in the locker room by a barely dressed and hobbling Bryant. Wearing only biker shorts, the star receiver couldn't hold back his excitement.

"Hey, hey, that's what I'm fuckin' talking about," said Bryant while giving fist- and chest-bumps to anyone in the vicinity. "That's how we fight! That's how we fight. What? What?"

At that point, Bryant already knew his foot would keep him out for at least four weeks, if not longer, but he didn't care. His team had found a way to win a game without him. And he was going to find a way to get back earlier than expected.

One of the last players in the locker room was Romo, who had done a live interview with NBC immediately after the game. On the way to his locker, the quarterback was congratulated by owner Jerry Jones while standing next to HBO's Bernard Goldberg, a respected reporter from *Real Sports with Bryant Gumbel,* who was doing a long story on Jones.

"Did you enjoy that one?" Romo said to Goldberg.

"Wow," the veteran reporter responded.

"I know you can't, because you're impartial, but don't be afraid to say you enjoyed it," Romo said again.

"Ha, I'm impartial, but I grew up in New York," Goldberg quipped.

Romo laughed, but stopped mid-chuckle. "No one's perfect," he said as he patted the reporter on the chest and casually walked back to his locker.

When the shouting, hollering, and commotion finally stopped, an already hoarse Garrett got his players' attention, praising them for their grit and ability to fight.

"You guys are relentless . . . badass . . . motherfuckers," Garrett said, creating a rousing response from the team. "And there will be T-shirts in your lockers on Tuesday."

The players roared again, although they wondered just how the head coach was going to pull that off. Sure enough, thanks to even more hustling by the team's equipment staff, players arrived back at the facility to see navy T-shirts hanging in their lockers with "Relentless" printed on the front.

On the back there was also a short, subtle message that carried more than one meaning. It stood for Garrett's affectionate nickname, but also the manner in which the Cowboys had come back to steal a victory against their division rival.

"BAM!"

Chapter 4

BROKEN DREAMS

Friday

High school football coaches watch fifteen to twenty-five hours of football in a given week.

About three of those hours are during a live game, and maybe seven to ten are on a practice field. The rest come from a screen, whether it's a computer screen, film projector, or TV.

On this particular Sunday night, assistant defensive coordinator Chris Fisher was watching football on the biggest of big screens. He was also watching it live. That kind of double-dip only happens in places such as AT&T Stadium in Arlington, Texas, home of the Dallas Cowboys.

Fisher and his cousin Aston had scored some free tickets to the Cowboys–Giants season opener—and not just any seats, but a pair in the Club Level around the 45-yard line. They got a perfect view of the field but were also eye-level with the massive yet beautifully sharp video board that stretched from one 20-yard line to the other 20-yard line, extending sixty yards.

Make no mistake, Fisher was a huge Cowboys fan, having grown up in Amarillo as part of a family that never missed a game on Sundays. In fact, for those noon kickoffs, he recalled his grandfather Forrest getting a tad antsy at church if the preacher went a little long, and always managing to be the first one up and into the aisle after the final "Amen."

But for Fisher, his mentality of "once a coach, always a coach" surfaced even when he was trying to be a fan.

"I'm constantly looking at the defense. How they line up in formation, coverages they run. It just never stops," Fisher said. "You want to look at pass rushers and see who is bringing pressure. You're looking at all of that. You're a fan, yeah, but your mind just starts racing. I'm trying to figure out what's going to happen pre-snap, looking if they're showing pressure, looking at the alignment of the safety. How wide are the outside linebackers? You look for all of those things. You find yourself not following the ball.

"And then something awesome happens, you high-five your cousin, and you're a fan again. But you're not far from it. It's what we do."

While the Cowboys were able to pull out a last-second victory, the nail-biting finish kept the majority of the 93,579 fans in the stands, which meant the traffic outside the stadium put the two back in their Plano homes well past midnight for the start of the week.

And not just any week—this was Allen week.

Sure, Plano has crosstown rivals in Plano East and Plano West, but the argument can be made that Allen is the Wildcats' biggest rival. From a location standpoint, the neighboring communities are so close that there are some families who have a Plano address but are inside the Allen school district.

Although there is a healthy debate about whether the city is big enough for more than one high school, Allen remains just a one-team town. And that team, for the last few years, had been the best in all of Texas, having won three straight titles heading into the 2015 season. Leading up to this year's Plano showdown, the Eagles had won 46 straight games.

When it came to district play, Allen hadn't lost since 2005. The team's closest scare occurred against the Wildcats in 2012 on its way to the first state championship in the three-peat. But it took a dropped two-point conversion pass by Plano for Allen to escape with the 35–34 win at its brand-new Eagle Stadium, the plush $60 million venue that comfortably seats over 18,000 spectators and rivals any high school stadium in the country, as well as several Division I home fields.

But as dynamic as the stadium looked on the outside, the foundation was a different story. The Eagles had to shut down operations at the venue in 2014 due to cracking in the concrete, forcing the matchup between Plano and Allen that year to be played at the Wildcats' regular home turf, John Clark Field. The stadium was closed for fifteen months, reopening in May of 2015.

Now the Wildcats were returning to Allen, three years after their last visit. And it was that reality that didn't quite sink in with the Plano coaches until the team got off the bus and started walking into the place.

"This is a high school stadium?" the players quipped, but with modest seriousness.

As the defensive coaches sat on the sidelines, overseeing their squad take the field, it dawned on them that while this might just be "another big stadium" to them, many of these players hadn't seen the field—or anything like it.

"We started looking around at our kids and realized that only two of them had ever played here before," Fisher said. "You get caught up in things and don't realize that it's natural for them to look around and be a little intimidated."

But make no mistake, the kids might have been a little star-struck with the stadium, but oddly enough, they didn't seem so afraid of an Eagles team that hadn't been whipped in three years. And this despite Plano's last two meetings against the team having gone Allen's way by a combined score of 84–16.

Minutes before kickoff, Jaydon McCullough acknowledged the mountain his team was facing, but seemed ready to climb it.

"Men, it doesn't really matter what anyone else thinks about us," he barked to his huddled players. "It doesn't matter what anyone outside of this locker room thinks. We believe in you. Believe in yourself and believe in each other. Let's go out and show them who we are."

Similar to a college or NFL venue, the players walked down a large hallway under the stadium before entering the field. "Shock the World" statements were being tossed around left and right as the Wildcats were starting to believe they had a chance to win.

The problem was, the guys on the other side simply knew they would.

Allen needed just four plays to score as Eagles quarterback Seth Green scrambled fifty-five yards for a touchdown. After a three-and-out by the Wildcats, Allen reached the end zone again on a 44-yard pass, giving them a 13–0 lead just four minutes into the game.

Coaches usually drop the usual "We're all right" or "We'll get it back" lines when the defense gives up a score. But maybe this time, Plano's assistants weren't so sure that would be the case.

"Let's go! Get off the field," the coaches yelled at some of the players walking—not jogging—to the sidelines. "Hustle off. Get some water."

Plano's biggest fears had come to life, and the line of cars trying to get into the game was still piled up on East Exchange Parkway, outside of the stadium.

"Get the ball to Brandon!" McCullough said on the headsets, trying to get his star running back involved.

Brandon Stephens answered with a 34-yard reception that might have been a touchdown had quarterback Matt Keys had a little more time to set his feet on a wheel route out of the backfield. The pop-fly pass was hauled in by a waiting Stephens, who jaunted to the 21. Plano then got to the 12-yard line, but on second down, and Stephens somehow on the sidelines, the Wildcats handed the ball to Tarence Raymond, who fumbled it away, giving Allen possession again.

"We can't waste those chances, guys!" offensive coordinator Joey Stone barked at both the skill players and the offensive linemen who missed some key blocks. "Concentrate!"

Stone shook his head in disbelief. He called plays last year in the 42–3 loss to the Eagles and knew just how difficult it was to score touchdowns against the Eagles. They had just wasted a golden opportunity.

What he didn't know then was that it would be the Wildcats' *only* real chance to score.

Even though Plano's defense started rising to the challenge, forcing a missed field goal and two turnovers as play continued into the second quarter, the offense could barely block Allen's four defensive linemen, much less generate a drive.

Late in the second quarter, still trailing 13–0, the Wildcats got the ball to the Allen 47-yard line and faced a third-and-6. Then three blitzing Eagles hit Keys as he released the ball, attempting to throw deep down the left sideline. Allen's Anthony Taylor picked off the pass with ease and scampered seventy yards to the end zone untouched.

Just like that, Plano was now down 20–0. The floodgates were open. The chatter, the bounce in their step, and the waves of confidence that had started to return to the visitor's sideline ended with a thud.

The turnover was so shocking for the Wildcats that Keys, who had taken just about every snap to that point in the season, couldn't shake the play out of his mind right away. In fact, he looked out onto the field and noticed something missing from the next offensive huddle—himself.

"Oh shoot," Keys said, seemingly forgetting that he was the quarterback and needed to be in the game. He ran out there to execute the plays, but the damage was now done.

To make matters worse for McCullough, a little injury to insult was added just before halftime. A play spilled over to the sideline and an Allen player ran into him, smacking the coach squarely in the chest.

"That's the hardest I've ever been hit on the sidelines," McCullough said after the game. "I felt it the entire game. Probably a pretty good bruise there."

Bruised egos would fill Plano's sideline in the second half, which began with another pick-six for a touchdown on the first play of the third quarter. A fumble here, an interception there, a fumbled kickoff, the turnovers just kept piling up, reaching eight by the end of the game.

Allen kept scoring, and kept trying. After a fourth-quarter touchdown pushed the lead to 58–0, the Eagles just had to have the ball back, calling for an onside kick, which they recovered, prompting even their coaches to get off the ground with celebratory jumps and fist-pumps.

On the other sideline, the Plano coaches were a little surprised by the act, but not shocked. Unfortunately for them, they had been on the wrong side of these blowouts against the Eagles not just on the varsity level, but also with the junior varsity and occasionally the freshman teams.

With Plano's defense on the field nearly the entire second half, it could've been easy to drop the rope. Darion Foster didn't operate that way. Undersized for a defensive tackle and playing his first season on the varsity, he had come too far to stop.

He ran sideline to sideline for nearly the entire fourth quarter, even getting blindsided and knocked on his butt a few times, but he kept getting back up. Darion was in on four tackles in the final frame, even catching the attention of his uncle, whose eyes were usually fixed on the secondary.

Eventually, the game would come to a merciful end with the Wildcats losing, 65–0, easily the worst defeat of McCullough's tenure at Plano High.

Mad about the lopsided score and losing for the tenth straight time to Allen, Fisher put his uncle hat on in the final seconds as he watched with pride. "I know this, my nephew is a grown-ass man—a grown-ass man. He's never going to stop."

Fisher grabbed Darion by the neck for a quick hug after the game, but nothing too extreme, maintaining their player-coach relationship.

It was one of the more uninspiring renditions of Plano's school song afterward, the band serenading players who had their hands up to honor the school, but really just wanted to get into the locker room and put the 65-point loss behind them.

Inside, McCullough told them to do just that.

"Men, we can't have this one back. It was a really tough loss, but it's one loss. One game. If we let this loss turn into another loss down the road, I'm going to be really disappointed. That's not who we are."

Usually, after the head coach talks, it's on to the team prayer, but Keys rose from his kneeling position to address the team.

"We have six more games guaranteed. For a lot of us, we're not going to play football after that," Keys said to his peers. "We're going to have to win five or six to be where we want to be. To do that, it's going to take everyone buying in. We can still be the team we thought we were. You have to believe that you and everyone surrounding you are talented as we are. You guys are my family for the six weeks. We have to do everything and anything we can for each other."

Both players and coaches were nodding their heads in approval. The bitter taste of 65–0 was hanging over their heads but Keys' words of encouragement seemingly had a positive effect.

The last person out of the locker room was McCullough, which is usually standard for all games, but in this case was also a result of just moving slow. His chest aching because of the sideline hit and his heart hurting even more because of the final score, McCullough was rather shocked when he stepped outside of the stadium and went up the stairs toward the buses.

About twenty adults—some parents, some school administrators, and perhaps family and friends—were there waiting for the head coach to come through the line just as all of the players and assistants had done in the last ten minutes.

"We're all right, coach," one father said with some enthusiasm. "We'll be back next week. Get 'em ready next week."

McCullough shook his head in amazement. His team had just lost to a bordering rival by sixty-five points, and he was getting encouraging words from a group that even he would expect to express more frustration. The head coach was able to kiss his wife and then grab the first seat on the first bus, which was the signal for the convoy to take off.

As he sat there during the quiet ride, the optimism in McCullough started to return. The 65–0 shellacking by Allen was less than thirty minutes old, but there was only one thought he couldn't ignore:

This Flower Mound team will be tough, but we just have to win.

Saturday

Of the ten full-time assistant coaches on Baylor's staff, nine of them are married with children.

Without a doubt, coaches love what they do, but their jobs are a grind. Whether or not they've got the bye week circled on the calendar, it's a safe bet that their wives do.

Of course, it's not vacation time for all of them. Head coach Art Briles rarely got a chance to indulge in one of his favorite passions—high school football. He'd been involved with Texas high school football at just about every level, including the Class 1A ranks when he was the star quarterback for Rule High School near Abilene, Texas.

Now, he used his time off to recruit. Or in this case, keep an eye on some of his committed players. Down in the Houston area, Briles went to see prized running back Kameron Martin, who not only had been fully committed to Baylor for nearly a year, but also had a massive new BU tattoo on his left arm to prove his allegiance. Getting a chance to see Martin for a few plays gave the coach time to head over to Silsbee, Texas, and check up on a bigger recruit—literally—in tackle Patrick Hudson, one of the top offensive linemen in the country.

But it was another coach on Baylor's staff who would find himself in the news. And for the second straight week, it was another member of the Briles family.

Son-in-law Jeff Lebby and his wife, Staley, were able to make a friend's wedding in Norman, Oklahoma, on Friday night. Lebby knew coaches rarely get to attend such events during the football season, but thanks to Baylor's bye week, he and Staley jumped at the chance to return to Oklahoma, a place where he spent five years as both a player and then a graduate assistant before eventually landing a job at Baylor in 2008.

In the weeks leading up to the trip, Lebby never even bothered to inquire about OU's game that weekend. He knew his team was off, so the last place he wanted to be was at another stadium. But when he realized the Sooners were hosting Tulsa, a team that had just hired longtime Baylor assistant Philip Montgomery, who basically filled his entire staff with coaches who had some kind of tie to the Bears and/or Briles, Lebby called "Monty" to see about possibly meeting him at the hotel on the day of the game.

"When he told me the game was at 11, I said, 'Shoot, Coach, we're going to be in town.' He said, 'I'll get you two sideline passes.' And I didn't even think anything else about it," Lebby recalled. "That Friday night, I talked to OU's director of football operations and told him I was going to be there, and he said, 'Great, we'll see you tomorrow.' But I seriously had no idea this was against any rule."

Jeff and Staley picked up their passes and made their way down to the field. They had been standing on Tulsa's sideline for a few series of the first quarter when he got a tap on his shoulder.

"Are you Jeff Lebby?" said a well-dressed man he didn't recognize.

"You've got 'em," the Baylor coach sarcastically fired back.

"I'm the director of compliance here at OU. You can't be down here. It falls under the bylaws of scouting. You probably need to get on the phone with your compliance guy."

By the time he could get his phone out to call anyone over at Baylor, Lebby could see "Coach Briles" dialing in on the screen.

"He wasn't happy at all," Lebby said. "And he shouldn't have been. It was a bonehead mistake. I just didn't realize it was an issue."

And to be honest, Briles wasn't sure it was against any NCAA violation as well.

"I was very upset," he recalled. "I just knew it wasn't kosher. I did not know it was an NCAA violation because it shouldn't be. The last place you can tell anything is on a football field. If you're going to scout somebody or take advantage, you're not going to gain anything on the field."

Even though Jeff and Staley left immediately, the firestorm didn't die down. Despite receiving an explanation and apology from Montgomery following the game, OU coach Bob Stoops fanned the flames when asked about it by a reporter during his Monday press briefing.

"That's not allowed," Stoops said. "I don't know what he was doing here. . . . It's something that needs to be reported and needs to be dealt with through the Big 12 office and our people, so I'm sure they will."

Like Briles did with his son, Kendal, and receiver coach, Tate Wallis, for their recruiting violation, he suspended Lebby. This suspension was for the first half of Baylor's game against Oklahoma on November 14.

"It was an overblown incident that we punished ourselves for and moved on," Briles said. "If it was a big deal, they're looking for small things to make big deals out of."

Lebby, a graduate of OU, was disappointed, but not too surprised by the reaction of Stoops, a man who had come to his living room to recruit the former four-star lineman from Andrews, Texas.

"Bob knew he had a chance to take a shot and took it," Lebby said. "They had been playing second fiddle to us. He got to take a shot and he did. I expect nothing less, that's for sure. But I was wrong, and shouldn't have been there."

The irony of this story is that Stoops and the OU coaches were no strangers themselves to gaining any kind of edge—even at Baylor's expense. In 2008, Briles had just taken over as the head coach at Baylor, which was then no match for teams like OU and Texas, as the Bears went only 4–8 in each of his first two seasons. But before Baylor's game with the Sooners in Waco that year, word got back to the coaches that Oklahoma assistants had asked for and received faxes from the University of Houston pertaining to some of Baylor's favorite plays, signals, formations, and so on, that Briles had actually left for the new head coach of the Cougars, Kevin Sumlin. He, of course, had come from the Oklahoma staff under Stoops.

Briles thought of mentioning that to the media before the game, but instead, kept it under his hat. In fact, he considered it a compliment that national power Oklahoma was already a little worried about his offense and what to expect. And he knew there would come a day when Baylor would reach their level.

In 2014, the Bears handed Oklahoma its worst home loss in the Stoops era, crushing the Sooners, 48–14, for the third win in their previous four meetings with OU.

For that alone, the two teams' November 14 showdown was already circled on every calendar from Waco to Norman. But the action, and then reaction, of this latest event just pushed the rivalry to another level.

Sunday

One way to beat the Monday morning traffic in Dallas is to get a head start on the rest of the drivers. Anything before 7 a.m. typically avoids the bumper-to-bumper routine. For the true early risers who are on the road at 5 a.m., they are privy to one of the more popular sports talk shows in the country, *The Musers,* on KTCK—1310 "The Ticket." Together since 1995, the trio of Craig Miller, George Dunham, and funnyman Gordon Keith have hosted the highest-rated show in their time slot for over twenty years.

On this Monday morning, some six hours after the Cowboys' improbable comeback over the Giants, there was little room to poke and prod this team. Finding negatives about the Cowboys' 27–26 win just wasn't justifiable this morning.

The Cowboys were supposed to have this magical response to the 2015 season and after one game, there was certainly magic in the air.

"When this team goes to the Super Bowl this year, we're going to look back at games like this one last night," said one of the hosts.

"Who knows, just maybe this will be their year," said another.

Sure, it was only one game into the season, but if "The Ticket" was buying in, there couldn't be a lot of others who weren't.

But while the NFL is on a completely different stratosphere from college and certainly high school, the routine is the same. There is little time to waste either patting yourself on the back or dwelling on a loss. The next game is always staring the team in the face.

But never was this more of a reality than in the Cowboys' second game of the year.

When the NFL released its regular-season schedule back in April, one of the first games that popped off the page was the Week 2 trip to Philadelphia, where last year's NFL rushing champ, DeMarco Murray, had soared in free agency.

The league's schedule makers obviously didn't want to wait too long for Murray to face his former team, for he had become the first player in NFL history to win the AP Offensive Player of the Year award before switching teams in the ensuing off-season.

Had Joseph Randle, who backed up Murray the last two seasons in Dallas, not provided any juicy headlines over the summer, the reunion between the Cowboys and their former running back still would've been worth watching. Randle just made it a must-see event.

During an interview in May, Randle was asked about the possibility of winning the starting job in 2015 and replacing Murray, who had just set the Cowboys' all-time single-season record with 1,845 yards, surpassing Emmitt Smith's MVP season in 1995, when he rushed for 1,773.

"He had a good year last year," Randle said of Murray. "I got to sit back and watch a lot, and I felt like there was a lot of meat left on the bone."

Days later, and after a meeting with head coach Jason Garrett on being more careful with his words, Randle tried to clarify the statement, citing no disrespect toward Murray but only mentioning that his goal was to not only reach the lofty standards, but try to surpass them.

By then, the quote had already made its way to Philadelphia, where Murray jokingly responded with a jab, saying, "Hopefully he'll be able to taste some of that meat this year."

Game on.

A month later, Randle was doing an interview with the Cowboys' in-house Internet and TV departments, and he prefaced the sit-down by saying he didn't want to get himself in any more trouble with his comments. After a five-minute interview in which his answers were basic and harmless clichés, Randle didn't seem satisfied.

As he got up to take his clipped-on microphone off his shirt, he matter-of-factly explained how he was already behind in his own personal goals since joining the NFL two years earlier.

"I should already have two 2,000-yard seasons by now," Randle said. "I think if I had been starting, I already would've rushed for 2,000 yards twice."

Instead, Randle had just 507 yards in 29 games played as a backup. But he was showing at least some maturity because when it was asked if he wanted to get back on camera and make that statement, he nearly did, before it was decided he was better served to hold back on those proclamations just yet. Come September 14 in Philadelphia, Randle knew he could let his on-field performance do the talking for him.

As the players got to Valley Ranch on Tuesday, they noticed a new member of their team standing just outside the locker room. Veteran Jeremy Mincey was quick to point out, "This guy looks pretty stiff."

That's because it was a mannequin, one from a department store to display men's clothing. He was actually given to the Cowboys and head coach Jason Garrett by a suit salesman in an attempt to do business with players who needed to purchase a suit, perhaps for the annual kickoff luncheon a few weeks back.

But with the mannequin remaining at the facility, Garrett used him to send another message to his team.

With no face and wearing a nameless white 55 jersey, this mannequin was the "nameless, faceless opponent" Garrett had been referring to for several years, standing right here before the team in real life (sort of).

This was Garrett's way to remind his team once again to focus on themselves, and not worry about the opponent, and of course, one particular player on that team, regardless of where they were a year ago.

"It's been around a long time," Garrett said of the phrase. "Nameless, faceless opponent. It's not really about anybody else but us. So putting that out there has nothing to do with this week, but it has something to do with every week."

While he was supposed to be nameless, the players gave him plenty of nicknames, such as "Woody" and "Rolando," for the number it wore. And even Barry Church said the players just started calling him "Randy" because they thought it was fitting.

Either way, he got to make all of the road trips, as the equipment staff would take him apart, put him in a long duffel bag, and send him on each road trip, where he would eventually be placed in the team meeting rooms.

The Cowboys actually did bring a living and breathing new player during the week in an attempt to provide some help at wide receiver. Dez Bryant had undergone foot surgery on Tuesday, September 15, and was hoping to return in just four weeks, although the Cowboys' medical staff thought six weeks was more realistic.

The Cowboys traded for veteran Brice Butler, who had been with the Raiders the past two years. Right away, Butler impressed some of the members of the Cowboys' operations team with his knowledge of team history, something that often escapes the younger generation of players, especially one such as Butler who grew up in California.

Butler had worn 12 on his jersey for three years with the Raiders, but he knew better than to even ask the equipment guys for that number.

"I know Roger Staubach wore that, so that's out," Butler said on the phone to a Cowboys' personnel staffer who was trying to line up his flight information to get him to Dallas before Wednesday's first practice.

Butler began his career at Southern Cal before heading to San Diego State. But he chose 19, knowing that Keyshawn Johnson had once donned that jersey for two seasons in Dallas. More important than the number he wore, Butler made it to every practice that week, showing the coaches enough to make him active for the game. To put that in perspective, the Cowboys were now on their second week with running back Christine Michael, but he still wasn't suiting up for games.

As the Cowboys arrived in Philadelphia the Saturday before the game, Garrett reminded the players of a team outing they took back in Oxnard, California, just three weeks earlier. When his players, coaches, and staff members crammed into the movie theater one evening at camp, they were all rather stunned to see *Rocky III* come up on the screen.

Yes, everyone has heard the song "Eye of the Tiger," but many of the players hadn't seen this 1982 film starring Sylvester Stallone. And shockingly enough, many of these players hadn't heard of Mr. T, who played the role of "Clubber Lang" and had two matches with Rocky in the film.

But Garrett had a reason to show this particular movie, which actually turned into a challenging project for staff members, who searched for a movie theater with the capability of showing this thirty-five-year-old movie on the HD screen. Garrett didn't reveal his reason for showing *Rocky III* until the night before the Philly game.

"Guys, it's going to get loud out there, and they're going to play that Rocky music and get the fans all fired up," Garrett said. "But what they don't realize is that's our song now. That's the movie we saw. That can be our song. Don't let them get fired up over our song. Let's create the environment for ourselves."

When the game began, the Cowboys' defense didn't let the Eagles do much of anything, especially run the ball. Not only did Philly have Murray, but they also had signed Ryan Mathews in free agency, both to go along with speedy, all-purpose back Darren Sproles.

Together, those three ran for seven yards—for the game. The Eagles ran it seventeen times and got seven whopping yards. Murray's much-anticipated matchup against his former club was a complete non-factor as he rushed for two yards on thirteen attempts. Linebacker Sean Lee, who had missed the entire 2014 season with a knee injury, was all over the field, chasing down Murray from sideline to sideline. Lee got an interception in the end zone as well and was eventually named NFC Defensive Player of the Week.

But the Cowboys' offense wasn't taking advantage on their end. While Randle wasn't being shut down like Murray, he only finished with fifty-one yards on eighteen carries for the game. In fact, it was a blocked punt for a touchdown on special teams that gave the team its only touchdown through three quarters.

Still, the Cowboys were holding on, leading 13–0 at the start of the fourth quarter and looking for some insurance on the scoreboard. What happened next was an on-field disaster that would change the course of the entire season.

Flushed out of the pocket and rolling to his left, Tony Romo tried to avoid the pressure coming from Eagles linebacker Jordan Hicks. Romo fumbled the ball, while Hicks drove Romo to the ground, landing on his left shoulder.

The Eagles recovered the ball, but that wasn't the loss the Cowboys were sick about. Lying on the field holding his shoulder, Romo knew this was the same injury he experienced in 2010, when he missed ten games with a broken collarbone.

"I felt it right away," Romo said after the game. "I've had that feeling before. Your body goes into a little bit of shock."

The Cowboys' owner did as well. Up in his owner's suite, surrounded by his family, Jerry Jones could only bury his head into his hands, refusing to hide the sickening feeling. After the game, when asked how he felt to see his star quarterback writhing in pain and not getting up to his feet, Jones didn't mince words.

"Just about as low as a crippled cricket's ass," Jones said, prompting a few laughs from the media members, although he wasn't joining them in laughter. "And I was feeling sorry for myself. I thought the world was picking on me. I just thought about Tony, how disappointing it was because of the expectations."

The Cowboys still managed to win this game, as backup Brandon Weeden came in to complete seven straight passes, including a 42-yard strike to Terrance Williams, who burned the Eagles defense for a touchdown, giving the Cowboys a 20–10 win and a 2–0 start to the season.

Without Dez Bryant was one thing. Without Romo was another.

Without them both was something the Cowboys didn't even want to think about. But it was stone-cold reality, one that even the head coach couldn't avoid, but not before praising a defense that limited the high-powered, fast-paced Eagles to just 226 yards of offense, nearly all of it by air.

"Defense, one of the greatest efforts I've seen in my life," Garrett said in the middle of the locker room. "I've been around ball a long time, and I haven't seen a defense shut down an offense like that in a long, long time. And special teams, you ignited us when the game was nut-cutting time. That's big time.

"I'm going to be real with you guys. We're going to have some adversity. We had guys step up today but we have to keep stepping up. We're going to do this thing together. Let's get on in here, guys."

And with that, the team huddled up and raised their hands together as one. One week after losing their emotional sparkplug in Dez Bryant, the Cowboys had now lost their general.

With his sport coat draped around his shoulder, Jones had been fielding questions for about forty-five minutes in the middle of the locker room. As he was finally set to walk away, one more reporter came in, asking the owner/general manager if the Cowboys were built to win just as easily without Romo.

"Of course not," Jones said. "We're a different team. But we're a team that can win football games in the NFL without Romo."

Or so he thought.

Chapter 5
GOING, GOING ... GONE

Friday

When the Plano coaches arrived at the school on Saturday morning, some of them might have been surprised by the glare coming from the sky.

Yes, that was indeed the sun. And as bad as the 65–0 loss to rival Allen felt the night before, the sun did come up as it always does and was shining brighter than ever on the quiet campus, which had just a dozen or so cars in the parking lot.

Win or lose, Saturdays are always long days for the Plano coaches, who get in around 11 a.m. and review the Friday night game film, grade out each player at his position, start evaluating the next opponent, and also meet as a staff throughout the day as they formulate a game plan.

Typically, the coaches stick around for eight to nine hours, but after the Allen game, they knew this day would be even longer. The Wildcats were now 0–2 in district play, and none of them could recall a beating like the one they had just received.

"We had to make sure we didn't lose more than that one game," Jaydon McCullough said, referring to the psyche of his team. "It was a bad loss, but it was one loss. As a coach, you have to get your kids believing they can win. We knew we couldn't dwell on one game."

While different ideas were being tossed around by the coaches on how to approach the upcoming week, one of which was to only show the first half of the tape to the team and not remind them of the second-half turnovers, the best motivational tool with which they could come up suddenly landed square in their laps.

And they didn't have to do a thing.

While looking through the scouting report of the upcoming opponent, Flower Mound High School, the coaches were made aware of a three-word tweet that came from Jaguars quarterback Noble Newton, who had just led his team to an upset win over Boyd High School in McKinney, Texas, the previous night. And he most certainly knew of the Wildcats' 65–0 loss to Allen.

So he took to Twitter to share his thoughts on the next matchup, which was still six days away.

"Plano ain't ready."

That's it. Just three little words, but they were powerful. The coaches were able to screenshot the tweet, print it out, and insert it into the scouting report for the upcoming game, making sure every Plano Wildcat saw it. Many of them had already been made aware of Newton's tweet at some point during the weekend, but seeing it again on Monday in the scouting report served as a quick reminder.

If there was one player not too fired up about what Flower Mound's quarterback was saying on social media, it had to be Plano's own quarterback, whose thumbs had gotten him in trouble just a few days earlier.

Going against McCullough's advice early in the season when he told Matt Keys to "be very, very careful about what you say on Twitter," Keys had tweeted before the Allen game that despite the school's three-year run as state champs, he "wasn't afraid" of their upcoming opponent.

He should've been. Not only did the Eagles dominate the game, hitting him so hard that he even threw up into his facemask while on the field, but Keys also had to see members of Allen's team flood his Twitter timeline with messages regarding his "not afraid" tweet.

"A couple of players found it," Keys said. "They tore me up. I should've listened to Coach McCullough about Twitter. He was right."

So while Keys was trying his best to ignore the Twitter messages on his end, his teammates were using Newton's tweets as pure motivation.

On the day of the game, Plano's buses rolled out of the parking lots of the Senior High around 3:30 p.m., giving them ample time to make the 25-mile trek across town, despite heavier traffic on Fridays. But while everyone expected to break quite a sweat later that night, nearly all of the players and coaches were perspiring long before kickoff. Thanks to old air-conditioning units in the school buses, the afternoon ride was a steamy one. Getting slowed down by traffic only made it worse as the players started to voice their displeasure.

"The kids usually don't say a lot on the buses," McCullough said. "They're always pretty focused, but they were ready to get off that bus and get on the field."

Whether it was ridding themselves of the sour taste from the Allen loss, or being 0–2 in district play, or perhaps looking to show Flower Mound and its quarterback how ready they were, Plano came firing out of the tunnel.

After two losses, star running back Brandon Stephens was embracing the role of a leader, knowing that all eyes were looking at him to right the ship. Just before the opening kickoff, Stephens went up to every offensive lineman, hugging each of the starters while adding an encouraging word. He then turned around to see defensive backs coach Chris Fisher approaching him for a quick, but blunt message.

"Put on a show tonight," Fisher said. "Put on a show. We need it."

"Yes, sir, coach. Yes, sir."

Knowing that his future teammates at Stanford were also playing that night at Oregon State in a rare Friday game, Stephens obliged Fisher's request and delivered his best performance of the year, although it took a while for him to heat up. Plano recovered a fumble on the second play of the game, but only managed a field goal on its opening possession.

Later in the second quarter, Plano trailed 7–6 with the Jaguars driving past midfield. From the sideline, Fisher saw the Flower Mound coaches call an audible and couldn't get his defensive backs to adjust, leaving the middle of the field wide open. Just before the snap, Fisher ripped his headset off in disgust and said to bystanders within earshot, "Well, here comes a touchdown for them."

Sure enough, Newton found his tight end running free down the seam for a 45-yard score that was never contested.

Plano trailed 14–6 before the half, when Keys then got hot, hitting Garrett Frederick for a 41-yard pass down the sideline to the 23, and then teaming up with Frederick again on the next play for a touchdown, trimming the Jags' lead to 14–13 at the break. The score prevented Plano from going eight quarters and an overtime without finding the end zone.

In the second half, with the help of Stephens, Plano lit up the scoreboard for 23 points. The senior running back weaved through Flower Mound's defense for a 67-yard touchdown early in the third quarter with Keys throwing his second touchdown of the game on Plano's next drive. In the fourth frame, Stephens added another 10-yard score, which put him over the 200-yard rushing mark.

The Wildcats didn't exactly put the game away, but with Plano leading 36–24 in the final four minutes, the team's defense came up with critical stops on the goal line to burn precious seconds off the clock. When the Jaguars finally scored, only 1:36 remained on the clock. Plano then recovered the onside kick, preserving the victory.

Seven days after getting beat by sixty-five points, the Wildcats responded with a win that, according to the Plano coaches, saved the season.

"Guys, we still control our own destiny," McCullough told the team afterward. "We still have everything in front of us, and we know what we have to do. I'm so proud of the effort tonight. It was a fight from the start. We were challenged, but we fought back, and that's all we ever ask from you. We know we can play better and we will, but let's enjoy this win tonight."

And the players certainly did, not wasting any time busting into their victory chant, which began just three years earlier when defensive standout David Griffith, who was now playing at the University of Louisiana-Monroe, began a postgame chant that has since continued.

The captains, who on this occasion included Stephens, jumped up and down in the middle of the group the entire time, igniting a raucous back-and-forth exchange.

"Plano! . . . (Plano!) . . . Plano! . . . (Plano!)"

"Yeah, we rock! . . . (Yeah, we rock!) . . . Yeah, we rock! . . . (Yeah, we rock!)"

This went on for about a minute, with even some of the coaches getting involved in the mosh pit–style celebration.

Beating Flower Mound didn't stay on the players' minds for too long, though. Sure, they needed the win, but moving on this week would be easy.

"We had to get this game," Keys said afterward, "but now we can really focus on West. That's all we care about right now."

Somewhat true, but Stephens had his mind on another game that was going on simultaneously.

"What's the score?" Stephens asked a few friends and family around him, figuring they were keeping track of his future team as it faced Oregon State. It didn't take long for someone to relay an update: "Stanford up by seven."

"That's good. That's good. Let's keep it up. I'm looking for two wins tonight," Stephens said as he slung his equipment bag over his shoulder and headed toward the buses.

Stanford would win the game, 42–24, making Stephens' night complete. And now, like his teammates, he could shift his attention to Plano West, a school for which he had developed quite a disdain. Well, for at least all but one of its students.

Saturday

For most college teams, the regular season would still seem rather new and fresh after just two games. With ten more to go on the schedule, and hopefully eleven, late-September is very early in the grind.

So why did Art Briles feel so tired?

Well, it certainly wasn't age catching up to him. Briles was probably in better shape than 99 percent of the fifty-nine-year-olds out there, whether they coached football or not. He preached physical fitness not only to his players, but to his assistants as well. You won't see many overweight coaches on his staff, and if they are, it's not for a lack of trying.

That actually stemmed from Briles' coaching days at Stephenville High School, when he amazed his players with not only his willingness to hit the bench press with them, but also his brute strength to boot. He's always had the philosophy of "don't ask players to do something you're not willing to do yourself."

Even at Baylor in 2011, star receiver and future first-round draft pick, Kendall Wright, made a bet with Briles that if the Bears upset Texas Christian University in the season opener, Briles would take his shirt off and show how "rocked up" he was. Sure enough, Baylor outlasted the Horned Frogs, 50–48, in a wild shootout that seemed to spark a rivalry that has now gone to new extremes. But after the game, Briles busted through the locker room doors, ripped off his shirt, and the players absolutely erupted into a mosh pit scene for the ages.

But three weeks into the season felt like three months for Briles in 2015. Without a doubt, the off-season distractions had taken their toll.

Even though things had died down from the August sexual assault charges against former player Sam Ukwuachu and the claims that Briles knew of his alleged violent history at Boise State, the backlash was damaging.

There were nights when Briles didn't eat much and certainly had difficulty sleeping. Now, getting ready for an opponent like Rice would cause him to stay up regardless, thinking about any type of advantage he could gain for his team. But throw in the ongoing Pepper Hamilton investigation, which led to him having to suspend two defensive starters before the SMU game; and the Lamar outing that violated NCAA rules, which resulted in the suspension of two coaches, including his son. He also had to suspend and eventually dismiss tight end Tre'Von Armstead from the squad on September 18 for violating team rules, also stemming from the Pepper Hamilton investigation, in which it was revealed that Armstead and teammate Myke Chatman had been named in an alleged sexual assault that was never reported to authorities in 2013.

Needless to say, the stress was piling up for Briles.

And he didn't forget about the recent slip-up with passing game coordinator Jeff Lebby, also Briles' son-in-law, which caused Lebby to get suspended for a half when the Bears played Oklahoma on November 14.

Make no mistake, Briles knew exactly what the problem was, and maybe that was one reason why the Bears had struggled in the first half against both SMU and Lamar before pulling away for 35-point wins.

"I lost my edge," he said, something he even shared with the media in the week leading up to the Rice game. "I had an edge about me for a long time as a person and a coach. I don't want to lose that or let somebody take it away from me."

And sure enough, people were trying. Not just the media, but even coaches he was going to face later in the season.

There's certainly no love lost between TCU and Baylor, which has become one of college football's most intense rivalries. The 2013 meeting in Fort Worth included Briles and Horned Frogs' head coach Gary Patterson exchanging words near midfield in the middle of the game and then again afterward when, while shaking hands, Briles told Patterson to "leave it on the field and shake it off." Patterson then used his postgame press conference as a platform to call out Briles, Bears safety Ahmad Dixon, and just about everything else, saying he wouldn't "take a backseat to anyone," despite his team's going on to finish with a 4–8 record and miss a bowl game.

That was just the beginning, though. The 2014 contest was absolutely epic as Baylor rallied from twenty-one points down in the fourth quarter to win, 61–58, a score that resurfaced many times throughout the year as the polls continued to put TCU ahead of Baylor despite their identical records.

And before the 2015 season began, Baylor's team photo showed offensive linemen Jarell Broxton and Spencer Drango standing side by side, putting numbers 61 and 58 together. Coincidence or jab? Baylor officials said it was not planned and explained that seniors stand together by position, and that Broxton and Drango were two of just four senior linemen.

Still, the picture went viral, adding yet another dimension to this rivalry between private schools that are less than ninety miles apart.

Leading up to Baylor's game against Rice, Briles saw about seven phone calls and texts from friends, colleagues, and even family members, wanting to know if he had "heard what Patterson said."

At the time, he hadn't, but it wasn't long before word trickled "south."

Patterson was dealing with his own off-the-field issues after two players were arrested for robbery. In the middle of a press conference to announce the news, he got a little testy with reporters who were digging for more information on the case, in particular about TCU defensive end Mike Tuaua.

"I'm not going to let you all say this guy (Tuaua) is a bad person. If he made a mistake, he made a mistake," said Patterson. "It's not even close to what happened south of here."

South, as in Waco—as in the Baylor incident, which was most likely a situation Patterson didn't know much about. A few days later, Patterson denied any reference toward the Bears, but said it was reactionary to outside comparisons between the two cases.

As expected, Briles was asked to make a comment by Waco reporters, but he didn't take the bait. "Casually, yeah," Briles answered when questioned about whether he had heard Patterson's comments. "But what did David say? Did [Rice head coach] David Bailiff say something? No? Okay, well, I'm worried about Rice. We're playing football. That's where we take our shots, on the football field."

Whether or not that was added fuel for the Bears, or it was just the fact that they were at full strength on the coaching staff and injured players had returned to the field, Baylor came out and dominated Rice on a beautiful Saturday afternoon at McLane Stadium. The traditionalists in the stands were happy to see the Bears trot out of the tunnel wearing gold helmets, green jerseys, and gold pants—the staple combination for Baylor in the 1970s and 1980s. The younger folks may like the different uniform looks, but this game had a throwback flavor, especially against a former Southwest Conference member in Rice, who was facing the Bears for the eightieth time, dating back to 1914.

Flamboyant defensive end Shawn Oakman, sporting a green Mohawk, pumped up his defense with a playful jab at Rice's much-publicized offense.

"They came here to watch us," Oakman said, pointing to the fans piling in. "We're the show. Let's put on a show."

And while the defense did just that, the offense matched it and then some. For the third straight game, the Bears scored a touchdown on their opening possession as KD Cannon showed off his speed by catching up to Seth Russell's pass in the back of the end zone. Russell then hit Jay Lee and Corey Coleman with two more touchdown passes before the end of the first quarter.

"They've all got one now," Russell joked to offensive coordinator, Kendal Briles, referring to Baylor's top three receivers; like all players at that position, they never got the ball enough, always claimed to be open, and loved scoring touchdowns.

In the second quarter, Coleman hauled in another score, making a highlight-reel grab over a defender in the end zone. When it eventually came time for All-America and Biletnikoff Award honors for Coleman, this highlight of him jumping into the screen for the touchdown would be remembered as one of his best. It even got his usually calm head coach to rip off his headset and throw his ball cap in the air with excitement. Coleman later scored again before halftime, showcasing his own speed down the left sideline.

"Best in America," Art Briles yelled at Coleman as he made his way back toward a jubilant and packed sideline. Briles used to call Kendall Wright "BIC" for Best In the Country, but this revised nickname for Coleman seemed applicable as well.

Baylor cruised to a 70–17 win over the Owls, with Russell completing only twelve passes, although six went for touchdowns. For the third straight game freshman backup, Jarrett Stidham, played the majority of the fourth quarter and threw another touchdown pass, the second of his career.

"We played with energy today," Briles said in his postgame press conference. "We hadn't played with a lot of energy in the first two games. We challenged our players this week. We challenged the coaches. I was happy with this good, solid win, but I was really happy with the energy we had."

Briles showed some energy of his own when talking with the media, asking Bob Simpson, the owner of the Texas Rangers and a Baylor supporter who was standing nearby, if the Rangers had won a crucial late-season game against the Astros. He also wrapped up the briefing by talking about his big men up front.

"We've got four seniors on the (offensive) line. They have some experience, so they should play good, or well, if you're an English teacher," he said while getting up from the table. "Which, I am."

And with that, it appeared Briles had his edge back.

Briles left the press conference room and was eager to meet up with his wife and daughters and grab some much-needed dinner. While there might have been a healthy traffic jam outside the stadium, Briles knew there was clear sailing in his path back home.

With their house right off the Brazos River just outside of Waco, Jan drove their pontoon boat to McLane Stadium, participating in the new tradition of "sail-gating" outside of the stadium. So afterward Briles met up with his family, hopped on the boat, waved to a few fans still relaxing in their party cruisers, and they headed back to the house.

With his feet up near the front of the boat, Briles grabbed his phone and went to work on responding to the hundreds of calls and text messages he received from friends and family after a game.

About a month removed from what was a tumultuous month of August, Baylor was now 3–0 after a crushing win over an in-state school. For the moment, at least, it was literally smooth sailing for Briles and his football team.

Sunday

From the Pop Warner stage to junior high, high school, college football, and on to the pros, there is one constant that typically holds true: lose your starting quarterback for any length of time, and the situation can get dire.

In high school, there are typically a couple of backups on the roster; however, teams often move talented players from running back or receiver into the quarterback slot, allowing a more skilled player the opportunity to handle the ball every snap.

In college, the backup quarterbacks are scholarship players with talent, but perhaps lack game-day experience. Yet, they are still recruited for a reason, and when their number is called, they are expected to deliver.

But either way, injuries in high school and college football are somewhat the same in that adding help from the outside is out of the question.

The NFL is obviously a different story, especially early in the season.

With Tony Romo out for eight weeks with a collarbone injury, the Cowboys had to turn their attention to Brandon Weeden, a first-round pick of the Browns in 2012, who was waived by Cleveland after two unproductive years.

As a backup to Romo, Weeden was seemingly a good fit, providing a strong arm and if anything else, a strong pedigree as the twenty-second overall pick just three seasons earlier.

In the NFL, backup quarterbacks are hot commodities, strictly for the "just in case" scenarios like this. Now, the Cowboys were headed for a backup plan for the backup.

Even though both Jerry Jones and Jason Garrett expressed extreme confidence in Weeden, the Cowboys covered their own bases by trading for an experienced veteran in Matt Cassel, who had actually started the first game of the season for the Bills just two weeks earlier.

Cassel had bounced around the league for ten years, starting in New England as Tom Brady's backup for four years before becoming a starter in Kansas City, where he made a Pro Bowl in 2010. But his 34–38 all-time record as a starter was both the reason he kept getting jobs and also the reason why he was often available. Teams want quarterbacks who have won games. But when they lose a little more than they win, they become expendable.

Cassel was expendable to Buffalo, who dealt him to Dallas for a better draft pick two years down the road. By sending over a veteran quarterback, the Bills now got the Cowboys' fifth-round pick in 2017 in exchange for a seventh-rounder that year.

It seemed trivial to swap late-round picks in two years for a quarterback because it was. The Bills had no interest in keeping Cassel in the fold but didn't want to give him away for nothing. By trading for Cassel, the Cowboys had to absorb his contract, which counted about $1.75 million against the team's salary cap, which was a little north of $143 million in 2015.

Oddly enough, Cassel's addition put a strain on the camp, forcing the Cowboys to shuffle around some money on the cap, a common procedure that occurs far more than it ever gets announced. However, one move the Cowboys made this week was to restructure tight end Jason Witten's contract. In a move that was more semantics than anything else, Witten saw his $5.1 million base salary reduced to $3.6 million, but turned it into a $1.5 million roster bonus, which he received immediately. It helped the Cowboys gain some cap room for the current year in case they needed to sign other players or trade for more veterans such as Cassel. And the Cowboys didn't mind pushing more money into next year's cap, especially for Witten, who hadn't shown much sign of slowing down—at least on game days.

Witten had played through broken ribs, sprained ankles and knees, and most famously, a lacerated spleen injury that occurred early in training camp in 2012. That injury figured to keep Witten out at least six weeks, if not longer.

But Witten had no interest in that medical opinion, or even the second and third opinions that he received from various doctors. Finally, Witten found a New York doctor that eventually cleared him to play in the Week 1 opener against the Giants, of course. The tight end clearly wasn't his usual self in that game or even the next two, where his lack of mobility to catch passes over his head was evident, even forcing some media members to question if the end of his brilliant career was starting to surface.

Instead, Witten continued to improve that season and wound up setting an NFL record for catches in a single season by a tight end, hauling in 110, including a franchise-record seventeen in the rematch with the Giants later in the season.

So doubting Witten and his availability to play seemed rather worthless, as he entered 2015 with ten Pro Bowls in his first twelve seasons. That's why few people in the organization, from coaches to teammates and even the team trainers, were concerned to see Witten actually on crutches the Monday following the Philadelphia game, nursing two sprained ankles.

Some of the more veteran media members in the market, the ones that knew better, purposefully asked Witten his chances of missing Sunday's game with the Falcons.

"Come on, man," Witten said with a piercing grin because he knew the cameras were on, and he didn't want to come across as surly or disrespectful. "We'll see how the week goes, but I think I'll be all right."

When the interview was over, Witten put on a ball cap, changed shoes to go work out, and muttered a few things to some other reporters who had stuck around by his locker to chat.

"Tony is out. Dez is out. You think I'm going to miss my first game in twelve years because of an ankle injury?"

"What about two ankle injuries?

"I think you know where I'll be on Sunday."

And to Witten, it was in no way a jab at Romo or Bryant, two players he didn't have to question when it came to toughness. Sure, there had been times in the past when Witten had seen some teammates take themselves out of games or decide not to play with injuries that he wouldn't even report to the training staff about.

So as expected, Witten got himself healed and ready to play, and when he walked to the center of the field Sunday afternoon at AT&T Stadium for the noon kickoff as one of the team captains, Witten indeed extended his consecutive games streak to 190 games, closing in on the franchise record held by Bob Lilly at 198.

Witten's ankles seemed rather fine when he was hopping around in the pregame team huddle, head-butting anyone in his path as he yelled, "Every play. Every snap. From the first play to the last, let's get after 'em today."

And from the very beginning, the Cowboys indeed got after the Falcons, whose 2–0 record not only matched the Cowboys, but they had also defeated the Eagles and Giants in the first two games.

All eyes were fixed on Weeden, who was one of two active quarterbacks in the game along with Kellen Moore, who was promoted from the practice squad. Cassel, who arrived just a few days earlier, was deactivated for this game and stood on the sidelines in street clothes.

The Cowboys came out with the perfect way to help a backup quarterback—run the football with authority. Joseph Randle racked up sixty-five yards on his first two carries, including a 37-yard touchdown that sent the AT&T Stadium crowd into a frenzy.

Randle bounced off defenders at the line of scrimmage and on the goal line, but never went down. His hardest hit might have come from coach Jason Garrett, whose flying head-slap more than showed the coach's approval and excitement in what was Randle's best run of the season so far. Along with Garrett, Romo, with his left arm in a sling, was rather animated with his celebratory fist pumps as the offense came off the field.

But despite Randle scoring the next Cowboys' touchdown, he wasn't the only running back to shine in the first half, as Darren McFadden got into the scoring act, with his first touchdown run of the season, giving Dallas a 21–7 lead.

On the sidelines, Cowboys running backs coach Gary Brown, a former NFL standout with the Oilers and Giants for eight years in the

1990s, had nothing but praise for both of his backs, who had battled for the starting position through camp and the off-season.

"You guys are like Batman and Robin today," Brown said. "And I don't really know who's Batman and who's Robin, but . . . whatever."

Randle looked more like the Caped Crusader when he scored his third touchdown of the half, leaping over the pile just before halftime to give the Cowboys a 28–14 lead. When he got to the bench, however, the only criticism he got from Brown and other coaches was to be extra careful when stretching the ball over the goal line during those running-back leaps that Walter Payton made famous back in the 1980s.

But a questionable timeout the Cowboys called with forty-six seconds left, coupled with their touchdown on the next play, gave the Falcons enough time to drive for a field goal just before the half. The score not only trimmed the lead to 11, but also gave Atlanta some momentum in the second half that Dallas had no answer for. The Cowboys also had no way of stopping Falcons receiver Julio Jones, who torched them with twelve catches for 164 yards and two scores. While Jones' big day was expected, Atlanta running back Devonta Freeman came out of nowhere to rush for a career-high 141 yards and three scores.

On the flip side, the Falcons had made all of the necessary adjustments against the Cowboys' running game. Randle had rushed for eighty-five yards on his first three carries, seemingly a lock to earn his first 100-yard game of his career. But his final eleven carries of the game netted just two yards.

So the onus went back to Weeden, who was completing passes left and right (22 of 26), but mostly short dump-off passes to the receivers and backs, including shifty tailback Lance Dunbar, who caught ten passes for one hundred yards.

As the Cowboys watched Atlanta take the lead, they still couldn't get themselves off the mat. After scoring twenty-eight points in the first half, they were shut out completely in the second as the Falcons gave them a stunning 39–28 defeat.

All week long, the players and coaches had preached the words "next man up" as a battle cry to overcome injuries to players such as Romo, Bryant, and even Jeremy Mincey, who was out with a concussion.

So when one of the first questions at Garrett's postgame press conference touched on his team's missing key starters, the head coach stopped the reporter in his tracks.

"There's no excuses who was there and who wasn't there," he said. "We had guys out there, and we didn't get the job done. They did a better job than we did, and they won the ballgame."

In the locker room Weeden said the right things by taking the blame for the loss, which dropped him to 5–17 in his career.

But the higher-ups, both Garrett and Jerry Jones, praised him for his accuracy and moving the offense in the first half.

"I liked what I saw out there," Jones said in his typical postgame media powwow, which occurs after every game either inside the locker room or just outside the doors. "The stage wasn't too big for him. I thought he made some good decisions. I know there are some throws he'd like to have back, but I think we've got something we can work with here."

About two minutes later in this media session, the always candid team owner pointed out that Cassel was brought in for a reason.

"I'm excited to see what he can do. He'll get a shot," said Jones, who was making it clear that Weeden wouldn't lose his job, but there might be a quick hook if things didn't turn around quickly.

Chapter 6

THREADING THE NEEDLE

Friday

For ninety years, the city of Plano had one football team. The Wildcats were the only game in town, and on seven occasions, they'd been the best team in the state.

In 1981, the Wildcats were handed their first intra-city opponent when Plano East Senior High opened. The two shared some memorable games, and it was easily the fiercest rivalry for each school.

But that changed in 1999 when a third high school opened. Plano West Senior High, located just 4.9 miles away from the original Plano Senior High, was a little too close for comfort for the Wildcats' faithful. Plano East is one thing, sitting on the other side of town where players, coaches, and fans don't regularly cross paths. Having campuses located less than five miles apart, though, is a different story. Even today, the two schools share an intense rivalry that goes a little deeper than just their annual forty-eight minutes on the football field.

For starters, many of the kids from these two high schools went to elementary school together. Several of them attend church together and some have formed relationships outside of school.

Over the summer, quarterback Matt Keys had gone on a few dates with a girl that was attending West. It wasn't anything serious, but of the many reasons he wanted to win this game, performing well in front of her was admittedly on the list.

It was a little more intense for Brandon Stephens, whose girlfriend was a star basketball player at Plano West. The week of the game, he asked her where she might sit on Friday night. Torn between her allegiances to her West friends and her boyfriend, the decision was made to watch a half from each side of the stadium. "I was fine with that," said Stephens, whose plan all week was to beat the rival Wolves and then ask his girlfriend to Plano's homecoming dance, which was coming up in two weeks.

First thing's first, Plano had to take care of business. This was personal, especially for the players, who had referred to the days leading up to the Plano West game as "WukFest." While it sounded like a wonky name for some festival, it was actually a derogatory play-on-words with switched letters that showed just how many of the Plano players felt toward their nearby rivals.

A couple of years earlier, a Plano senior referenced "WukFest" in a pep rally before the game and was disciplined immediately. This year, both Keys and Stephens were told by the emcee of the pep rally that any mentioning of that phrase would result in a trip to ISS, Plano's in-school suspension.

But the rivalry between the schools goes deeper than just spirited teenagers. Plano West head coach, Scott Smith, not only graduated from Plano Senior High and was on the Wildcats' coaching staff during the early 2000s, but was a finalist for the head-coaching job that eventually went to Jaydon McCullough in 2008. Smith was hired for the West job in March 2015, and formed a coaching staff that had several Plano ties.

"I have so much respect for Scott Smith," Wildcats defensive backs coach, Chris Fisher, said. "When I got to Plano, he was a guy that took me under his wing and taught me the Plano defense. So when we play those guys, it's just always an intense game, physically and emotionally. We see these coaches all the time. We see them at track meets and coaching clinics. You see them around town. And you just want to win so bad."

Big games might change the intensity level for Plano. The preparation might be even more amped up. What doesn't change, and never changes for the Wildcats, is the look—at least not during the regular season.

In today's world of fancy uniforms with bright colors and shiny helmets and snappy designs becoming the norm at seemingly all levels of football, Plano chooses tradition and basics over glamour.

When they are the home team, the Wildcats sport their solid maroon jerseys that simply feature a tiny font with the word "Plano" above the numbers on the front. Maroon pants and the traditional white helmets make up this classic uniform that has been altered very little since the 1950s.

The only change you'll ever see with the Wildcats' uniform occurs in the playoffs. If the team is successful enough to reach the postseason, the players will get their last names stitched on the back—something that many high school teams do for all games. But at Plano, it's a tradition that current athletic director and former Plano head coach, Gerald Brence, began back in 1994.

In fact, when he asked his staff to vote on whether it was a good idea, every assistant coach was in favor of it, except one.

"I didn't see the need to put names on the back," said McCullough, who was then in his first year as a Plano assistant. "I mean, we didn't have names when I was playing. But, I didn't win that vote, and the kids like it. It gives them something else to be excited about if they get to the playoffs."

McCullough loves to tell the story of their 1994 team picture, when Brence finally got up the nerve to tell Plano coaching legends John Clark and Tom Kimbrough his idea to add the names on the jerseys for the playoffs.

After what seemed like a four-minute pause, Clark finally responded to Brence.

"You better win."

Luckily for Brence and the newest tradition, Plano did win, claiming its seventh state championship that season.

Those types of statements were what likely changed McCullough's mind back in 2008 when he decided to change the jersey as well, adding a stripe down the panel.

He informed Brence, who had moved up to athletic director that year, of his proposed change and at first wasn't told no. In fact, Brence never did put his foot down and reject the idea.

"But he came in my office several times and said, 'Are you sure you want to do this?' " McCullough recalled. "Finally, I realized that I didn't want to change it. I called up Nike and said, 'Okay, solid maroon again.' You just don't change the tradition. It's a big deal to the fans who played here. It's important for them to look down and say, 'Hey, I played in that same uniform.' "

In his own family, McCullough routinely has conversations with his brother, Joey, the head coach of crosstown rival, Plano East, which has just thirty-four years of history and has never won a state championship.

"He gets these gold chrome helmets," McCullough said. "The players love them and they look great. And I even got a call from the booster club the next day wanting shiny helmets, too. I had to tell them we can't do it. We just can't. And they understood."

As for the players, most of them don't fully appreciate the tradition until they get further along in the program. The younger kids watch ESPN like everyone else and see college teams such as Oregon and Baylor changing up uniforms every week with a variety of combinations. They even play against high school teams with alternate uniforms.

"The upperclassmen start to buy in and love the tradition," McCullough said. "They start to understand the history behind a lot of things we do, so it's really not a big deal to them. I think they embrace it."

On this night, the kids were permitted to make a slight alteration to their uniforms with the addition of pink accessories to honor Breast Cancer Awareness Month, as the game was played two days into October. The coaches allow just one game in October for the players to add pink in the form of towels, wristbands, ankle tape, or even shoes.

A few years back, McCullough thought the players were "overdoing it" with the pink attire, thinking they were more interested in a unique fashion statement than the actual reasons behind the color.

"We had a team meeting and talked about how this is a great cause and we need to take it serious, instead of mocking it with a selfish 'look at me' attitude," he said. "So I asked them to raise their hands if they had been affected by cancer in their family or friends at any point. And, of course, just about all of them raised their hands. So we just got together and decided we would pick a game and wear the same stuff and really honor the cause and not mock it."

By the time kickoff finally arrived, uniform colors, district lines, and even girlfriends' seating locations all took a backseat to the actual game. And Plano West showed right off the bat that they weren't going to wait around for something good to happen. The Wolves called for an onside kick to start things off, but the Wildcats were able to recover, setting up near midfield for their first possession.

But Plano couldn't even get a first down, the first sign of what kind of game this would be. Both defenses were on point all night, slugging it out with hard hits and forced turnovers.

The Wolves posted the first touchdown on a 39-yard pass in the first quarter, but Plano finally responded with a game-tying score before halftime when Stephens took a direct snap in the Wildcat formation on third-and-3 and found a gaping hole in the middle of the defense for a 41-yard touchdown.

The score remained tied, 7–7, all the way into the fourth quarter, when Plano West mounted a drive that ended with a forceful touchdown run, which gave the Wolves the lead with less than six minutes to play.

Pinned back at their own 23-yard line, the Wildcats would have to drive the length of the field just to even the score. Walking toward the huddle before their first play of the series, Keys told Stephens, "It's you and me right here. Right here, we're going to work together and go tie this game."

Sure enough, Keys and Stephens ran the ball—literally—right through

West's defense. A 14-yard run by Keys was followed by an 11-yard run and then a 26-yarder by Stephens to get Plano in position. On a crucial fourth-and-3 with less than two minutes to play, Stephens then busted through the line and nearly scored before getting tackled at the 5-yard line, directly in front of Plano's pink-wearing student section, which had been yelling back and forth with the West students in what has become the custom.

Close finishes between the two schools have become the custom as well, with West scoring in the final seconds to beat Plano, 37–35, in 2012. The Wildcats did defeat the Wolves by 17 in 2013, but had to narrowly upset West, 17–14, in 2014. This game was shaping up to be another great finish with perhaps even overtime—if the Wildcats could get five more yards.

Unfortunately, instead of moving forward, the Wildcats went backward, thanks to a 2-yard loss on first down, a false start penalty, and then a rush for no gain, which set up a third-and-goal from the 12-yard line with just 30 seconds remaining. Deciding not to pass, Plano stuck to the run, but Keys was stopped after only one yard. A do-or-die fourth down from the 11-yard line loomed.

Plano called a timeout to set up the biggest play of the game, and perhaps the season. In the huddle with offensive coordinator, Joey Stone, Keys was a little surprised with how it unfolded.

"We basically just made up a play for Brandon right there," Keys said. "They asked Brandon what he wanted, and he called for a pass in the seam. So we set up a play for the receivers to just run outs to free up the middle. We hadn't even run the play before, so I didn't really know where he was going to be. I just had to throw it out there."

Stephens lined up in the backfield and then darted toward the goal line, where he was bumped by a defender, causing him to stop for a moment before he lunged for the pass in the back of the end zone. The ball barely hit his fingers, ricocheting to the turf for an incomplete pass.

The star running back, lying flat on his stomach, popped his head up hoping to see a pass interference flag, but to no avail. He then buried his head back in the ground, trying to drown out the rowdy West fans and players who were already celebrating.

As he collected himself around the 10-yard line, Keys actually spotted the girl he had dated, along with other friends and acquaintances he knew from West.

"It sucks to stand there and see these people you know, and they're so happy to see you lose," he said. "But, that's how it goes."

And it wasn't just the students and players. The wives of the Plano West coaching staff didn't even wait for the postgame handshake to finish before rushing to their husbands for an emotional hug.

Meanwhile, the devastated Wildcats made the long walk up the ramp at John Clark Field toward the locker room, most with teary eyes and broken hearts. Like he did after every game, Keys met with reporters, refusing to hide his raw emotions.

"This is the worst night of my life," he said. "I put this game on me. I didn't get the job done, and I have to live with that. We were so close to scoring and we came up short. It doesn't get any worse than this."

On the bus ride back to the school, all Stephens could think about was the final play.

"I just kept replaying it over and over," he said. "I've actually thought about it several times since then. But that night, I kept thinking, what if I would've run faster or got off the line of scrimmage cleaner. It was just an awful feeling."

Keys, however, had more than just an emotional heartache. His right throwing hand was throbbing in pain, swelling up to the point that he was unsure just how serious it was.

In a world of hurt, Keys later sat on his couch at home reliving the game and trying to forget it at the same time, while also thinking about the severity of his injury.

"I just sat there looking at my hand," Keys said. "Right then and there, I thought, 'I hope it's broken. I hope I'm done.' I just sat there and cried and wanted it all to be over."

Saturday

When it comes to recruiting, Art Briles isn't picky about where to land the best players. He obviously has a soft spot for the small-town kids, considering he was once one himself growing up in Rule, Texas, which has a population now of just more than six hundred residents. But he also knows some of the best are right in the middle of the biggest cities, which is why he spends many hours in San Antonio, Houston, and, of course, the Dallas-Fort Worth Metroplex.

There are a couple of reasons why Briles loves playing Texas Tech every year in the Texas Farm Bureau Insurance Shootout at AT&T Stadium. For starters, he knows the neutral-site game against the Red Raiders benefits his school, with Waco being much closer to Arlington, Texas, than Lubbock. Secondly, getting to tell recruits that they will play at least one game in the luxurious stadium, which is not only the home of the Dallas Cowboys, but has also hosted a Super Bowl, a Final Four, and an NBA All-Star Game, is quite a recruiting tool. That selling point works as well on a kid from way down in Beaumont, Texas, as it does for the ones living right in the middle of Dallas who have probably already been to the stadium a dozen times.

"Kids want to play at home," Briles said. "They want mama and daddy to be there. So getting to play in Dallas, in one of the greatest places in the world, is a big deal."

In this rivalry game, the teams alternate each year as the home team. For this one, it was Baylor's turn to be the home squad, which was huge for the walk-ons and redshirt players, considering that they got to hop on the buses and travel up to Dallas for the game. The NCAA limits the number of players who can travel for road games, but with Baylor being the home team, the entire roster of more than one hundred got to make the trek north. And for the twenty-six kids from the Dallas-Fort Worth area, it was a chance to play in front of an adoring crowd.

"It's always a thrill to go up to AT&T Stadium," said Baylor safety Chance Waz, who is from Pflugerville, Texas, near Austin. "The bulk of our team is from Dallas. It's fun for them to go to their hometown and have their families supporting us. NFL teams play there, so it's a fun time."

Fun for the players, but not always as fun for the coaches, considering how intense and wild the rivalry has become.

Texas Tech hadn't beaten Baylor since 2010, with the Bears averaging 57.25 points in their last four wins. The Red Raiders had averaged over forty-one points themselves in those losses, and rallied back the previous season to tie Baylor before falling short, 48–46. There's a reason this game is called a "shootout."

A caravan of ten buses carrying players, coaches, cheerleaders, band members, and other support staff rolled out of Waco around 8 a.m., arriving at the stadium by mid-morning.

As the buses pulled into the parking lot, Briles couldn't help but have flashbacks to just eight months earlier when his team surrendered a 20-point fourth quarter lead in the Cotton Bowl to Michigan State, losing 42–41 at this very stadium. Briles called it "one of the toughest losses" he's ever endured, knowing that a win would've given his team a 12–1 record and probably a number-three ranking in the final polls, instead of a seventh-place finish.

"This stadium owes us one," he said to the coaches within earshot of him, sitting like always on the first row of Bus 1. "We didn't get to fulfill our destiny. I don't know if we can clean the slate, but we can at least clear it. It'll never be cleaned until we win a Cotton Bowl."

For now, winning this game would at least help.

Already, Baylor and Tech fans were in the stadium's parking lots, barking back and forth with "Sic 'em" and "Wreck 'em" chants, respectively.

AT&T Stadium has at least eight different locker room areas, aside from the Cowboys' home locker room. Even when the Cowboys aren't there, the room remains intact for stadium tours, as fans always cherish the opportunity to take pictures in front of the lockers of players such as Tony Romo or Dez Bryant.

The Bears had used the same locker room for each of their games at AT&T, right outside the end-zone tunnel in the southwest corner of the stadium. But the yelps and howls that sounded like grade-schoolers could likely be heard all over the stadium when the Baylor players arrived.

They had already seen these new "gunmetal" gray uniforms before, but now as the uniforms hung in front of their lockers, it brought out a different level of excitement. The players had wanted to break out these uniforms for the first game against SMU, and then for the first home game against Lamar.

"Nah, we held these back for this game," Briles said. "It was the first conference game, it was indoors; we knew everything would look good and pristine under the lights."

Whether they admit it or not, college coaches do care about what their schools' uniforms look like. Oftentimes, it's a battle between tradition and style, with the boosters and older alums rarely wanting to see changes, while the younger generation always asks for something new, hip, and "out there."

For most schools, tradition wins out. At Baylor, Briles goes the other way, a decision he made about two years after arriving in Waco.

"I decided to do that when I decided to get more attractive to good football players," Briles said. "That's the bottom line. Some universities can operate with decades of tradition and some can't. We are in a position where we needed to stand out and be different. People tend to like to look good. You don't put on something to wear and say, 'This doesn't look good.' It's the same with uniforms."

In the last few years, with the help of Nike, Baylor has become one of the more fashionable teams in college football, donning chrome gold helmets in its last two bowl games. Their equipment manager, Jeff Barlow, did an interview before the season with ESPN, stating they have 120 uniform combinations, meaning they could switch out either the helmet, jersey, or pants to give themselves a different look in every game for ten straight years.

Initially, there was some flak from older fans who remembered seeing nothing but green and gold, which just so happens to also be the last words of the school's fight song.

"We had some of that at first, but once you start winning more games, it died down," Briles said. "But really, it's about the kids. Looking at the big picture, our brand has to be attractive to fifteen- to twenty-five-year-olds, initially. That's who is judging us first—kids. We have to be attractive to the young people."

Needless to say, these all-gray uniforms were quite attractive to the Baylor players.

"This is the best uniform I've had since we've been here," senior defensive end Kevin Palmer said. "It's just tight. You want to look clean out there, and I think we did. When you look good, you play good."

On this day, Baylor did both.

Right before kickoff, Kendal Briles, standing in the center of a huddle that included the quarterbacks and running backs, set the bar high for his offense.

"Let's get out there, take care of the football, and score every time we have the ball."

In the first half, Baylor nearly did just that, scoring on its first four possessions and seven of its first eight, totaling forty-nine points before halftime. The tone was set on the third play from scrimmage when Shock Linwood did something that finally got his position coach, Jeff Lebby, off his back. On third down from the Bears' 21-yard line, Linwood busted a huge run right up the middle, outracing the entire defense for a 79-yard touchdown, the game's first score.

"We hadn't had a run over sixty yards in two years," Lebby said. "I stay on the backs about breaking off a big run, and we give them hell when they don't. So for him to break one like that, and really just get us off on the right foot, was a huge play."

With one half of the stadium already in a frenzy, the red-and-black side got going just a few plays later as Tech answered with a 55-yard touchdown pass to Zach Austin. The receiver had gotten behind safety Orion Stewart, who also jumped too early trying to knock the ball down.

"What was thaaaat?!" defensive coordinator, Phil Bennett, screamed at Stewart in disbelief. "You know better than to do that. Watch the ball!"

Stewart, already beating his chest as if to say "my bad," went straight to his defensive teammates and said, "I'll get it back."

But he didn't have to, as the Bears offense was absolutely rolling. Knowing games like this are going to be high scoring, every possession is critical just to hold serve. But as Baylor had a third-and-long at the Tech 18-yard line, Art Briles had one thing on his mind before quarterback Seth Russell took the snap.

"Can I get some water real quick," he said to anyone within earshot behind him. After a young trainer hurried over with a water bottle, Briles calmly grabbed a quick swig, and then went back to the edge of the sidelines, seemingly knowing that Russell would indeed hit wide receiver Corey Coleman over the middle for a touchdown—as if it was a foregone conclusion.

And perhaps it was for Briles and the coaching staff. Running up and down the field on the Red Raiders was something they were getting used to, although it didn't mean they were comfortable. They all remembered having a 45–20 lead late in the third quarter of the 2014 game. Starting quarterback Bryce Petty got knocked out with a concussion, leaving Russell to finish the job. The offense stumbled and Tech made a huge flurry, nearly coming all the way back before Baylor's defense prevented a two-point conversion and then recovered an onside kick to escape with the win.

"Remember what happened last year," the strength coaches, led by the ultra-intense Kaz Kazadi, repeatedly shouted up and down the sidelines. "We're not letting them come back on us. Don't let up on them. Don't let up."

However, it was the Baylor coaching staff that eventually let up, calling off the dogs midway through the third quarter with the Bears comfortably in front by twenty-eight points. Baylor still ran its offense, though, and still scored a fourth-quarter touchdown. They even waited until the last possession to insert freshman Jarrett Stidham, who always received a warm welcome from the observant Baylor fans when he took the field, knowing he was likely going to be the future star quarterback of this team.

But on this day, the other side of the stadium was paying attention as well. A round of boos came from the Red Raiders fans who hadn't forgotten that Stidham initially committed to Tech, but changed his mind and eventually signed with the Bears.

For the fourth straight game, Stidham saw action in the second half, but this would be the first time he didn't throw or run for a touchdown. The high-paced action slowed down immediately. And Tech knew it.

Just before the final gun, coaches from both teams who were upstairs in the booth got on the elevators at the same time to head down to the field. One of them leaned over to the group of Baylor offensive coaches, trying not to let his fellow Red Raiders colleagues hear him.

"Thanks. I think we both know you could've scored eighty on us if you wanted to."

Probably so, but Briles didn't want to. The head coach on the other side of the field, Kliff Kingsbury, used to spend hours upon hours in his office when Briles was the running backs coach at Texas Tech from 2000 to 2002, and Kingsbury was the Red Raiders' star quarterback. Briles thought highly of Kingsbury and wanted him to succeed as much as one coach from the same conference can hope for.

The 63–35 win was lopsided enough for his taste.

At the podium in his postgame press conference, Briles was absolutely out of breath. And his comments sounded more like a guy coming off one of the rides at Six Flags, which is only two miles down the road from the stadium.

"It's just an insane game and has been for the last four or five years," he said. "You can't breathe for a half-second. If you had any hair, it's blowing backward, and you're just screaming the whole time. But we've got some firepower, too. We can get on people when we really want to. This is probably the best team win we've had, certainly this year."

Outside of the press conference room, which is the same one the Cowboys use after their home games, Briles jumped in a golf cart to head back to the Bears' locker room. Before he took off, a couple of Baylor boosters stopped him to shake hands and congratulate him on the win.

"Thank you, thanks for coming," he said with a big smile. "This was big. This ride will feel better than the last time."

The last ride left Briles wondering just how his team would respond to such a gut-wrenching loss to end the season. This ride let him know that his team had bounced back better than he ever could've imagined.

Sunday

Other than the state championship, it rarely happens in high school. In college, maybe it occurs with a few selected bowl games.

But in the pros, at least three times a week, teams will find themselves playing the only football game on in the country.

Each Sunday and Monday, and now every Thursday, the only game is the NFL's featured matchup, putting eyeballs across the nation solely on that game. For some, the week is nearing the end and fantasy football owners need a big conclusion with whatever players they've got in these final games. And others, they're just football junkies that will watch whatever is on the tube.

There's a reason the Cowboys have the moniker "America's Team." Sure, they've got a sizeable fan base in their own state, even in Houston, where the Texans reside as the state's other NFL team. But outside the Lone Star State and even the country, there are many die-hard fans who bleed the Blue & Silver.

These days, cable packages such as DirecTV's Sunday Ticket offer fans opportunities to watch outside-of-market games from their living room. And just about every legitimate sports bar will offer up all the games as well.

But for this Sunday night, watching the Cowboys was made easy—as the team beloved by so many traveled to the Big Easy to face the struggling Saints, who were 0–3 and desperate for their first victory.

This wasn't exactly what the NBC producers had in mind for their *Sunday Night Football* coverage. The Cowboys were without Tony Romo and Dez Bryant, and it wasn't certain until moments before kickoff if Saints' All-Pro quarterback, Drew Brees, would play with his ailing shoulder.

But to the Cowboys' nation, this was a chance to catch their team on their local NBC affiliate, whether they lived in Dallas' popular uptown district or in Virginia, which oddly enough ranks in the top five among U.S. states in traffic for the team's website, DallasCowboys.com, behind Florida, New York, California, and of course, Texas.

And for this game, many Cowboys fans were getting another infrequent treat—watching their team in their favorite uniform. Since the Cowboys are one of the few home teams in the NFL to regularly wear white jerseys at home, fans rarely get to see their team in the blue road jerseys, outlined with silver pants that match the silver helmets.

The strong consensus of Cowboys fans suggests they actually favor the blue jersey the best, maybe because it's only worn once or twice a season if that. But such as the case with teams like the Yankees and Cubs in baseball, or even the Lakers and Celtics in the NBA, the Cowboys don't often mess with changing the uniform. Owner Jerry Jones is considered cavalier about many things, but changing the historic look of the Cowboys' uniform is something he knows is a sensitive subject to a fan base that doesn't like change. He tried it during the 1994 season, introducing a new white jersey that had blue stars on the shoulder pads. Had the Cowboys not been tripped up by the 49ers in the NFC Championship Game that year, spoiling their quest for a third straight Super Bowl title, Jones and the Cowboys might have kept that jersey around longer. Instead, it was shelved by the next year, and the Cowboys have kept the traditional whites for all non-Thanksgiving games.

Longtime general manager, Tex Schramm, who is often considered the architect to many of the historic traditions associated with the Cowboys, decided years ago to put his team in white jerseys at home, offering the Dallas fans a chance to see different colors each week. Instead of always seeing opponents in white, he thought it would give a different, refreshing look to see the Eagles' green or the red jerseys of the Cardinals or the Giants wearing blue.

That's one thing Jerry Jones hasn't changed, although the Cowboys have tinkered with a different Thanksgiving uniform at times and ended up wearing blue the last couple of seasons.

And to be precise, the road uniform is a navy color, and has been since after the 1980 season. That's when Schramm decided to alter the royal blue road jerseys for a darker look. Current assistant equipment manager, Bucky Buchanan, whose dad, "Buck," was the longtime Cowboys' equipment boss for twenty-five years (1973–1998), recalls a telephone call from Schramm that triggered the change.

"Tex called the house one day in the early eighties, right around 1981," Buchanan said. "He wanted to talk to Dad and said he wanted us to match the San Diego Chargers uniform. They had a navy jersey they had just switched to, and so he got Dad to find that exact color and that's what we switched to."

And that's been the Cowboys' road jersey ever since—although it's rarely used on the road.

But on this night, the Saints had chosen to wear white at home, but it had nothing to do with their 0–3 record. The NFL requires all teams to turn in their uniform assignments before the season. Actually this year, the Cowboys had already worn the navy jerseys once in Philadelphia and would wear them in consecutive weeks in November against the Bucs and Dolphins.

Under the bright Superdome lights in New Orleans, the silver and blue seemed to gloss even brighter.

Wide receiver Terrance Williams seemed to think so, as he trotted out to the field during pregame warm-ups. "Let's go, fellas. We're looking good. If you look good, you play good."

Earlier in the week, Williams stood in front of his locker back at the Valley Ranch headquarters and told media reporters the receivers, including himself, needed to step up and help Brandon Weeden better than they did a week ago.

"It's our job as receivers to make it quarterback-friendly like we do for Tony (Romo)," said Williams, who cited a critical dropped pass late in the Falcons game. "That's not going to happen again. No excuses. When he comes my way, I'm going to catch it."

For the second straight game, the Cowboys tried to take the pressure off of Weeden with a strong running attack. Versatile quick back Lance Dunbar had an impressive 45-yard run early in the game, displaying a dose of speed that had been missing in the offense, especially with Dez Bryant still banged up.

Early in the second quarter, Weeden moved the offense down to the Saints' 1 for a first-and-goal. Joseph Randle again got the call, and once again, decided to leap over the top of the pile. This time, making matters worse, he held the ball out with one arm to cross the goal line. Almost instantaneously, Randle was met by a Saints defender who jarred the ball loose, and New Orleans recovered for what seemed to be a turnover.

This was just seven days after Randle flew over the top and scored and was told after that play, and then several times during the week in team meetings, not to stretch the ball over and expose it to defenders. The play was called on the field as a fumble, so when Randle went to the bench, he was met by a furious coaching staff, including his position coach, Gary Brown, who had already kicked over the metal benches.

But since all turnovers are reviewed by instant replay, the officials went under the hood to check the play, and it was determined that Randle actually put the ball a few inches over the goal line before it was knocked out. The play was reversed, and the Cowboys were awarded a touchdown.

Randle, who had been hearing it on the sidelines from several coaches during the three-minute review, stood up with his hands in the air after the touchdown was announced, and he expected to get some apologies from the staff and his teammates. It didn't happen, which set him off even more. That's when Randle fired back and had to be restrained by a couple of players on the sidelines.

To Randle, he didn't understand the problem. Sure, he wasn't supposed to hold the ball out and fumble. But he scored. He didn't fumble—so why all the fuss?

The Cowboys actually benched Randle for the next two series, and it might have been for longer had another season-ending injury not occurred. Dunbar opted to return a kickoff eight yards deep from his inside and got his knee caught in the field turf under him as he was knocked backward. As the trainers rushed toward him, Dunbar could only lie there, knowing he had likely torn his ACL in his knee, which would end his season.

That's exactly what occurred for the fourth-year tailback, who was having a breakout season through four games.

Injuries kept piling up throughout the game at the worst times. Sean Lee, who probably would've been a three-time Pro Bowler by now in his career if he could have stayed healthy, got banged up again, suffering a concussion near the goal line, and he didn't return. Newly-acquired receiver Brice Butler, who was traded for to give the offense some speed, hauled in a 67-yard bomb from Weeden and was headed for a touchdown before he pulled up with a hamstring injury at the 10-yard line. The Cowboys didn't get a touchdown out of the drive, and Butler would miss seven of the next eight games.

Still, the Cowboys had a chance, trailing just 20–13 in the last four minutes. Weeden engineered a masterful drive that ended with a fourth-and-7 pass to Williams, who made good on his promise to come through in the clutch. Williams' diving touchdown catch in the corner of the end zone tied the game with 1:56 to play.

The Cowboys got a gift at the end of regulation; after Brees had carved up the defense and put the Saints in position to win, New Orleans kicker, Zack Hocker, clanged a 30-yard field goal off the left upright, sending the game into overtime.

"It's a new game, men," Garrett shouted on the sidelines. "It's a new game. Let's go win it."

The problem was, the Cowboys didn't win the coin toss. The Saints got the football first and on first down, backup linebacker Andrew Gachkar, who had been playing the entire second half with Lee out, had to limp off the field with a leg injury.

Scrambling, the Cowboys rushed rookie Damien Wilson onto the field, where he was quickly asking his teammates where to line up and whom he needed to cover.

Meanwhile, Brees saw all of this. He knew he hadn't seen 57 (Wilson) in the game, so he motioned running back C.J. Spiller out to the flat and changed the play to a wheel route. Wilson looked back toward the defense when the ball was snapped and never had a chance. Spiller ran right by him, hauled in Brees' perfect pass, and raced eighty yards to victory. It just so happened to be Brees' four-hundredth career touchdown pass.

Just like that, the Saints had won in what became the shortest regular-season overtime victory in NFL history, lasting just 13 seconds.

Just two weeks earlier, the Cowboys had boarded a plane in Philadelphia, riding the wave of a 2–0 start, despite the injuries to two key offensive players. Still, there was never-ending support as the fans, and even media pundits, thought this could be the early making of a dream season.

Now, they hopped on the American Airlines charters with a 2–2 record, and even more injuries added to the mix. And now, it wasn't just the media bagging on the Cowboys, but their own state representatives.

Texas Governor Greg Abbott took to Twitter immediately following the game, posting:

"*#%>! @Cowboys defense. More porous than the Texas border."

Uncalled-for shots by political figures or not, the Cowboys boarded the plane at 11:55 p.m. When they landed around 1:45 a.m., it officially was the start of Week 5 in the NFL. And with that, defensive help was about to be on the way.

Of course, they were going to need all the help they could get, because the defending champions and their future Hall of Fame quarterback were about to be on the way, too.

Chapter 7

MISMATCHED

Friday

Senior quarterback Matt Keys woke up Saturday morning just hoping that the night before was a bad dream. Losing to rival Plano West in the final seconds despite being down inside the 5-yard line with a chance to tie the game was bad enough. But now he had an injured right hand that could be broken.

When he went to bed, the frustrated and heartbroken eighteen-year-old wanted it all to be over. But by the next day, the ultracompetitive, always-smiling senior was back to his usual self. He knew he needed to see the Plano training staff about his hand, but it was starting to feel much better, and he was happy about that.

"When I got up Saturday, I was ready to get into it again," Keys said. "The trainers told me the swelling had gone down, and it was going to be okay. I was relieved. I wanted to finish this season strong. We knew we still had a chance to get into the playoffs, but we had to win."

The Wildcats' rivalry with the Plano East Panthers might not be as intense for the current players, who live closer to and have more cross-over with their West peers, but to the alumni and older fan base, the East game is always THE game.

As many as 15,000 fans would pack John Clark Field when the two high schools started their rivalry, one that surprisingly got rather competitive in a hurry. After Plano won the first three meetings from 1982 to 1984, the 1985 Plano East squad finally beat the Wildcats for the first time. One of the Panthers' varsity players then was Joey McCullough, now the head coach of Plano East and the younger brother of the current Plano coach, Jaydon McCullough.

Joey was also an assistant on the 1994 Panthers squad, the same year Jaydon was in his first season on the Wildcats' staff. While Plano East won the game, 28–7, both teams would remember that season for much different reasons.

Plano East went on to play in one of the most famous high school games in sports history. Trailing by 24 with 3:03 remaining in the fourth quarter of a playoff game at Texas Stadium against John Tyler High School, the Panthers made an epic comeback, using three successful onside kicks to eventually grab a 44–41 lead with twenty-four seconds left. However, on the ensuing kickoff, John Tyler returned the ball ninety-seven yards for a touchdown, spoiling what could've been the greatest comeback in high school football history. John Tyler would go on to win the Class 5A Division II state title.

Meanwhile, the Wildcats cruised through the playoffs in the 5A Division I bracket and claimed their seventh state championship in that same 1994 season.

Plano East would later win eight consecutive games in the rivalry (1997–2004), but the Wildcats had since turned the tide, winning three straight after a 34–6 victory in 2014, the first "McCullough Bowl" in the rivalry.

Always trying to deflect attention away from himself or his family, Jaydon winces when he hears the "McCullough Bowl" reference.

"We really try not to make it about us," Jaydon said. "He's my brother, but it's not me against him. Plano versus Plano East is much bigger than that. I always support him and he supports me. We really never try to make it personal between us. It's really about the kids."

During the week, Jaydon said he didn't have much contact "at all" with his younger brother, whom he had always called his best friend. Head coaches typically don't chat throughout the week, and this was no exception.

Jaydon knew his younger brother had one of his better teams in a while. The Plano assistants, especially the defensive ones, couldn't believe the talent the Panthers had on offense.

"When you look at their skill guys," defensive backs coach, Chris Fisher, said, "they're just as good, if not better, than Allen. They've got two really big playmaking receivers and a quarterback who is probably as good as we've faced all year. They've got a lot of guys to worry about."

Plano's offense had a few things to worry about as well. Keys' right hand was sore all week, but by game time, he was gripping the ball well enough to function. He knew, though, that if he took a few hits to his hand, it could become a problem.

What he didn't know was that the first such hit would come from his own player. On Plano's opening possession, the Wildcats had a third-and-5 and called for a run to Brandon Stephens. Nate Browne, a sophomore just called up, was in the game at fullback and making his varsity debut. But as Keys turned to hand the ball off, he collided with Browne, who took the wrong angle for his block. The ball fumbled to the ground, and while the Wildcats were able to recover, they wasted a chance for a first down. Keys also took an unnecessary shot to his hand, perhaps signaling what kind of night this would be.

Thanks to two long punt returns by the Panthers, Plano East had built a 17–0 lead by halftime. The Wildcats once again couldn't get Stephens going as the offensive line struggled to create space. Meanwhile, Keys had little time to throw, getting hit early and often, spending what seemed like most of the first half on his back.

At the break, Jaydon McCullough is usually the last one up the tunnel because of the quick radio interview he does with a sideline reporter. But as he was hustling up the ramp, he caught up to a few slow-moving players who had their heads down as if there weren't two more quarters to play.

"Let's go hustle in," McCullough said briskly. "Get your heads up. We're not out of this game."

The Plano coach carried the same message into the locker room.

"Men, we've come back from leads like this before," McCullough said. "And we've had leads like this and seen other teams come back on us. We have to play twenty-four more minutes and fight to the end. That's all we can do. I know we haven't played our best. We are better than that. Let's go show everyone what type of team we can be."

All of a sudden, McCullough had the visitor's locker room fired up again. Once every season, Plano finds itself as the visiting team at John Clark Field, something that never seems to sit right with the players and coaches.

"It's just weird being over there," Keys said. "It's like a totally different stadium when you're in the other locker room."

As the Wildcats came down the tunnel, Stephens ran past a familiar face in Stanford running backs coach Lance Taylor, who was one of the Plano running back's key recruiters. While Stephens had already committed to the Cardinal earlier in the season, Taylor was on hand to get a closer look at what he believed to be a future member of the squad.

The Wildcats got the ball in the second half and engineered their best offensive drive of the game: a 13-play jaunt that was highlighted by a fourth-down conversion by Keys. Down by the goal line, Stephens appeared to have turned the corner for a touchdown, but was jolted by Plano East linebacker Anthony Hines, who sent the running back flying nearly four yards out of bounds. Not only that, the vicious shot pressed Stephens' helmet into his right ear, causing a huge gash down the side of his face. While Stephens was getting looked at by Plano head trainer, Chris Reynolds, McCullough immediately thought the running back had broken one of his team rules.

"Are you wearing an earring?" he asked, figuring that's what caused the cut.

Both Stephens and Reynolds assured him that wasn't the case, although in reality, McCullough's main concern was when his best running back would be able to return to the field. So concerned that his offense couldn't punch it in without its star ball carrier, the head coach took off down the sideline, trying to get the attention of the side judge, who was standing at the 1-yard line.

But just before McCullough could get a timeout, Keys snapped the ball, calling his own number. And sure enough, standing in his way was Hines. But this time, Plano got the best of the matchup, as Keys wouldn't be denied the goal line, capping off the drive with the Wildcats' first touchdown of the night.

"I couldn't believe I won that battle," Keys said of Hines, a junior with hundreds of Division-I scholarship offers. "I just knew we had to score, and I wasn't going to be stopped."

For a moment, it appeared the Wildcats had a shot to rally. Alas, it wasn't meant to be as the Panthers broke loose for two long fourth-quarter touchdown runs to pull away, cruising in the second half to a 32–15 win.

As he walked off the field, Keys knew he had to be the vocal leader for his teammates. But inside, he was anything but confident.

"What started out so great, winning games and getting all kinds of attention, turned out to be not very fun," Keys said. "I was taking a physical beating. People were starting to question me as a quarterback. I just wasn't having any fun."

But it wasn't like others around him were partying it up, either. McCullough had just lost two city games in consecutive weeks, including a 17-point defeat at the hands of his younger brother. Afterward, he once again refused to acknowledge the family ties.

"It's about us and Plano East, and they were the better team tonight," McCullough said just before getting on one of the waiting buses that would take the team back to the school. "They are well coached, and they have great players. I give them a lot of credit. They've got a good team. There are a lot of good teams in this district."

But now, with a 1–4 record and only three games left to play, McCullough had to wonder if his team was considered one of them.

Saturday

Baylor football fans were used to these types of games. Only twenty years ago, and for more than a decade after that, the shoe was on the other foot.

When the Bears joined the Big 12 conference in 1996, they were instantly the punching bag of the league, taking everyone's best haymakers without delivering any return shot of their own.

These current players weren't around for the gloomy Baylor days that saw them win only eleven conference games in their first twelve seasons in the Big 12. But the fans still remembered the feeling of entering a game expected to lose by as much as fifty points.

Now, Baylor was on the other side, heading into their matchup with Kansas.

As a father of three, Art Briles knows better than to say he has favorites. The same goes for his players and his coaching staff as well.

Now, considering his own son, Kendal, has been on staff with him at Baylor since 2008, you'd like to think he takes the top spot. And his running backs coach, Jeff Lebby, is now his son-in-law and someone he's known since birth after he coached with his dad, Mike, back in Sweetwater, Texas.

But family members aside, there's no way Baylor strength coach Kaz Kazadi would be too far down any list for Briles, who has tried to instill hard work, dedication, energy, and toughness into all of his football teams.

No one has been able to epitomize Briles' message at Baylor better than Kazadi, who might be the most intimidating person walking around the campus these days. Now, those who know him say he's got a softer side with a big smile and a bigger heart; but make no mistake, when it's time to get to work, no one can be more demanding on the players than Kazadi. Just his scowl alone can be menacing, although he enhances that with a rock-solid physique that once helped him play five seasons of pro football, including a short time with the San Francisco 49ers, with stops in both the Canadian Football League and NFL Europe.

Kazadi's true calling, though, has been in athletic performance training, which began with a two-year stint working for the Kansas City Chiefs and then the University of South Florida before becoming one of Briles' first full-time hires in 2007, when he became the Bears' head coach. At the time, Kazadi was one of just four full-time strength coaches at Baylor, overseeing all sports. Now, with his help and a greater emphasis being placed on conditioning, Kazadi runs a department with nine full-time strength coaches and six more student assistants.

While Kazadi does work with other sports on occasion, his first priority is the football team, and his job goes far beyond making sure they're in good shape physically. The mental advantage he brings is something that is hard to duplicate.

On the sidelines, his look is quite intimidating. Built like a chiseled rock, the bald-headed Kazadi matches that menacing appearance with a piercing glare that could seemingly burn a hole inside the weak-minded.

Kazadi has obviously never taken a snap for the Bears, but his hard-nosed intensity has undoubtedly given the football team an edge. If nothing else, he's slowly helped change the image Baylor had as being a Baptist-school pushover that couldn't compete with the big boys in the Big 12.

Of course, none of Kazadi's in-your-face antics would garner any attention if the Bears hadn't improved on the field as well. But Briles doesn't just *think* it all goes hand-in-hand. He *knows* it.

"When I first met Kaz, I knew he was the right person for this job because we shared the same goals and the same approach," Briles said. "He's tough, he's creative, and he knows how to train people both mentally and physically. We want our kids to be tough on the field, but also tough-minded."

As the Bears hit the road—through the air for the first time all season—it could've been rather easy to overlook their next opponent, a Kansas team that not only hadn't won a game all year, but had lost to these Bears by a combined score of 160–42 in the last three seasons.

But it was four years ago that Briles still remembered.

"We have always had a lot of respect for Kansas after what happened to us in 2011," said Briles, who still considers Baylor's dramatic 31–30 win in Lawrence, Kansas, to be one of his favorite games as a coach—on any level.

Down 24–3 early in the fourth quarter, a Robert Griffin–led offense finally got on track, scoring three times in the final ten minutes to not only tie the game, but also give Briles and his staff an idea of just how explosive the offense could be. In overtime, the Bears scored first and then stopped a two-point conversion to grab their sixth win of the season, making them bowl-eligible for the second straight year.

Since then, Briles has made sure the Bears realize how dangerous the Jayhawks can be. The guy who helps him do just that is Kazadi, who has a unique way of being both a cheerleader and an ass-kicker.

When Baylor is at home, all the players, coaches, and support staff take a "Bear Walk," trekking through thousands of fans who make a narrow path of more than five hundred yards from the buses to the stadium. But on the road, Kazadi and his troops do their best to simulate the "walk," albeit with just a dozen or so staffers.

With each player he greets, Kazadi usually has some kind of unique message. For 400-pound tight end LaQuan McGowan, he'll say something like "It's your day, big fella!" or to linebacker Taylor Young, an undersized but tougher-than-nails defender, it's "Play fast. Play physical."

Quick, blunt messages, but they get the job done.

Games like these are when Briles relies on Kazadi more than ever. Sure, his team had no problem getting up for last week's shootout against rival Texas Tech. Or in a couple of weeks when nationally ranked Oklahoma comes to town, the players won't need any added motivation.

But these 11 a.m. kickoffs, which call for the team to wake up at 7, meet, have breakfast, and hop on the buses to play in an older, half-full stadium against a winless team, can be a challenge for even the most motivated eighteen- and nineteen-year-olds.

Questioning the toughness of any testosterone-filled young man is always a good start.

"They say we're not tough enough!" Kazadi yelled during the pregame stretch. "They say we don't play anyone. Well, let's show them who's tough today. Burn hot! Burn hot! Burn hot!"

Anything and everything that could get under his players' skin, Kazadi uses it, bringing a passionate but fierce demeanor that will get anyone's attention.

Whether it was that intensity, or the fact that Las Vegas oddsmakers had Baylor as 45-point favorites, the Bears came out and dominated Kansas in every aspect of the game during the first half. A touchdown on the first drive extended Baylor's streak to five straight games with a score on the opening possession as Corey Coleman reached the end zone twice in the first quarter.

The defense got into the act as well with three turnovers, including one fumble return for a touchdown by cornerback Xavien Howard. But the main highlight news stations used for this game featured Baylor's biggest scorer of the day.

The "big fella," as Kazadi called McGowan before the game, actually played small—like an agile receiver. Quarterback Seth Russell dumped off a pass to his tight end, who stepped over a safety (not so willing to tackle a four hundred pounder) and into the end zone for the second touchdown of his career.

"I was getting real anxious, but I knew it was coming," McGowan said after the game. "I always try to keep you on your heels. On one play, I might run up and hit you in the face. On the next play, I might slip right past you and catch a touchdown."

If any other player had found the end zone for a 38–7 second-quarter lead, it likely wouldn't have gotten the defensive players off the bench, but McGowan wasn't just a phenomenon to the outside world. He also excited his teammates.

"Big guys love when big guys do things," Briles said. "He's just a loveable guy. And when it's his turn to make a play, he's ready. He just adds a little flavor to the dessert."

McGowan burst onto the scene in the 2015 Cotton Bowl the previous January with a similar touchdown catch against Michigan State. The video that went viral also included former receiver Antwan Goodley attempting to hoist the big guy in the air like Baylor's linemen do to the skill players. But McGowan maybe got an inch off the ground.

This time around, though, All-America tackle Spencer Drango tried his hand, or hands, at lifting the big guy. With some success, Drango managed to get McGowan a couple of feet in the air, which created another viral video and thankfully not torn triceps in the process.

The ironic part of McGowan's touchdown was really his own availability for the game. On Thursday night before the team departed on Friday, the tight ends got together for dinner, a customary tradition for position groups to congregate at their position coach's house. But later that evening, all of the players who ate dinner ended up sick to their stomachs. From Gus Penning to Jordan Feuerbacher to redshirt freshman Sam Tecklenburg, all of them found themselves hugging toilet seats that night, leaving them questionable to play in two days.

Only one tight end didn't make it over that night—McGowan, who certainly isn't afraid to put away some food and easily could've been right there with the rest of the sick unit. By game time, Penning was able to play, but the Bears had to mostly use a four-receiver set throughout the game.

Typically, even in the biggest of blowouts, Briles will put his starters in for at least one third-quarter series before pulling them from the game. But with a 52–7 lead at halftime, he didn't want to risk any more injuries, so when the team came out for the third quarter, most of the offensive starters had their shoulder pads off. Russell, Coleman, KD Cannon, Shock Linwood, the entire starting offensive line, and even McGowan got the star treatment.

The defensive starters stayed in for a couple of third-quarter series, which turned out to be record-breaking for Oakman. He got the sixteenth sack of his career, setting a new all-time Baylor mark.

With the coaches all out of the booth and on the sidelines, the only issue now was to just stay healthy. The Bears were so banged up at running back coming into the matchup, unsure if both Devin Chafin and Linwood could even finish the game with lingering injuries, that they brought along redshirt freshman JaMycal Hasty, who hadn't taken a snap all year, but would've been ready to burn his redshirt tag if needed. Fortunately, Baylor was able to run Terence Williams for the bulk of the second half.

Freshman quarterback Jarrett Stidham, who was called "Steedham" for most of the Fox television broadcast by college announcer Tim Brando, continued to shine, throwing two more touchdowns as the Bears cruised to victory.

Baylor went to 5–0, and more importantly, got out of the game without any more injuries, the Bears continuing to dominate a team that hadn't beaten them during the Art Briles era. Up next, however, was an opponent that not only had their number, but just twelve months earlier had prevented Baylor from playing for the national championship.

The players didn't need a reminder of who was next on the schedule, although in the coming week, you could bet Kazadi and his staff weren't about to let them forget.

Sunday

At 10 a.m., two security guards wearing AT&T Stadium badges carefully lifted two barricades to open up the Lot 4 parking lot, which is actually across the street, but still only a few hundred yards away from the doors of the stadium.

On this morning, the early risers had stacked up lines all across the stadium in anticipation for this game and for the some five hours of preparation. For games like this, with the defending champion Patriots and their star quarterback, Tom Brady, the tailgating can't start quick enough.

In high school and college football, most teams never get to face the greatest players across the country. With fixed schedules years in advance, and the majority of the opponents immovable because of district and conference affiliations, it's rare when they get to square off against the elite players.

In the NFL, the matchups are infrequent, especially the inter-conference battles between AFC and NFC teams, but they will play every four years and visit all thirty-two teams at least every eight years. And that's exactly how long it had been since Brady's last game in Dallas, which was played at the old Texas Stadium that was imploded soon after AT&T Stadium was built in Arlington.

Brady's first, and possibly only, game at the place known as "Jerry World" nearly didn't happen, as he was initially suspended five games for his involvement in the deflated footballs that surfaced in the 2014 AFC Championship Game against the Colts. Brady vehemently denied any wrongdoing but after a lengthy investigation by the NFL, Commissioner Roger Goodell handed down the suspension for Brady and wiped out the Patriots' first-round pick in 2016. Brady contested there was never enough evidence to support these claims and after the U.S. district courts ruled that Goodell went too far in his punishment, Brady eventually won his case and the suspension was lifted.

Ironically enough, it was first believed that Brady would miss the game against Tony Romo's Cowboys. Now, it was Romo out of the lineup and Brady getting the chance to lead his Patriots to a 5–0 record.

While the Cowboys' main focus was to stop 12 in navy, there were plenty of 12 jerseys roaming the exterior of the stadium, hours before kickoff. Much has changed in the NFL in the last twenty years, but attendance by road-team fans nears the top of the list.

In fact, even in the last three years, ticket brokers such as StubHub say out-of-region fans account for 40 percent of NFL tickets sold. In 2012, it was just 26 percent and in the 1990s, it was around 12 percent.

Technology has made things easier for fans out of market to follow their team. If a job supplants a family from Dallas to the Tampa area, no longer is the avid football fan forced to adopt a new team, because that team is what they read about in the local paper and see on the evening news. With the Internet, smart phones, ESPN highlights, the NFL Network, and cable packages such as DirecTV, fans can remain loyal to their teams, even when their area codes change.

Opposing fans often come from the opposing city, especially against the Cowboys. Since Dallas is a centrally located city with an accessible airport that takes flights from hundreds of U.S. cities, many fan bases from other teams pick Dallas as a destination to attend a game each year.

So the thousands of Patriots fans in attendance for this game likely came from the Boston or northeast region, especially since it was their first trip to the Cowboys' new stadium, which wasn't so new anymore, having opened in 2009.

Ironically enough, the last time the Patriots played in Dallas, Brady's backup was none other than Matt Cassel, who was just in his third season and had only attempted thirty-nine passes and had yet to start a game. Cassel's opportunity occurred in 2008 when Brady suffered a torn ACL in the first game of the season, opening the door for him to start the remaining fifteen games. While the Patriots did go 11–5, they missed the playoffs, which remains the only season since 2003 that New England has been home for the postseason.

Cassel still parlayed that season into a contract with the Chiefs and later the Vikings and Bills before winding up in Dallas. Through the first two weeks, Cassel remained the backup to Weeden, but despite the Cowboys' 0–2 record since Romo's injury, a change in the rotation was not in the cards—at least not yet.

So the Cassel vs. Brady matchup had to wait as the Cowboys stuck with Weeden, although owner Jerry Jones made some interesting remarks following the Saints game when he said Weeden had too many "limitations" in his game to be compared to a quarterback such as Brees, who had won a Super Bowl. And to think Weeden was about to face Brady and his four rings.

But for the first time in a month, the primary focus for the Cowboys didn't center on the quarterback position. They had Greg Hardy to thank for that.

The Cowboys welcomed back two defensive starters who came off the NFL suspension list in both Hardy and Rolando McClain, who had violated the league's substance abuse policy and was given four games. Hardy's original 10-game suspension—for his involvement in a domestic violence charge that was later dropped when his ex-girlfriend failed to appear in court—was reduced to four.

Since he had signed with the Cowboys in March, the team's public relations department had not made Hardy available for interviews, as he politely declined repeated requests both at training camp and after preseason games. But with his suspension lifted and his preparing to face the Patriots in his first game, Hardy met reporters for the first time on Wednesday. He stood in front of his locker with perhaps thirty media members crammed around him, including ten cameramen, all making sure they didn't miss the defensive end's first official statements as a member of the Cowboys.

For the first few minutes, it was rather tame, as he talked about his excitement to get back on the field. But over time, Hardy couldn't help himself, using references such as "guns blazing" when describing how he expects to play Sunday.

Had Jason Witten said that—no problem. But one of the things Hardy's ex-girlfriend accused him of doing was throwing her onto a bed filled with assault rifles. Hardy also tried to make the media session playful when he said Tom Brady was "cool as crap" and then referenced his Brazilian fashion-model wife, Gisele Bündchen, asking reporters, "Have you seen his wife? I hope she comes to the game."

Nationally, columnists and reporters, most of which weren't in attendance, had a field day roasting Hardy even more, suggesting his attempts at humor came across as unapologetic and lacking in remorse for the reasons he was suspended. One female reporter from USA Today ripped the Cowboys fans and the expectation that they would cheer for him on Sunday.

Yet, they cheered, simply because Hardy gave them reason to. Like it or not, the Cowboys fans, desperate to see their team end a two-game losing streak, wanted to see success. And right away, Hardy made a difference, as did McClain, who teamed up for a sack on the first series. Hardy had two more sacks in the first half, as the Cowboys' defense flew around the ball and knocked Brady on his rear, dropping him five times before halftime.

Hardy wasn't playing like someone making his Cowboys debut, and he wasn't sounding like one on the sidelines, remaining vocal in between every series. He was offering encouragement to the younger players such as Jack Crawford, saying "Jack, Jack . . . more son! More son. More son. We need to take everything they've got." And with that, Crawford sacked Brady on the ensuing possession.

However, the Cowboys' offense had little success, managing just two field goals for the entire game. Joseph Randle regained his starting post at running back, but gained only sixty yards on fifteen attempts. Weeden's numbers were stagnant, as he threw for just 188 yards and one interception and was sacked three times.

And in the second half, Brady and his group figured it out, torching the Cowboys' secondary with big plays, eventually pulling away for what looked like a comfortable 34–6 victory to remain unbeaten.

The Cowboys, meanwhile, were winless without Romo, falling to 2–3 with a third straight loss. But that didn't seem to waver the confidence of the injured quarterback. In the middle of the field after the game, Romo and Brady met for a quick but standard handshake that has become a customary ritual for the quarterback fraternity to pay respects to their equals. Only Romo provided some semi-serious humor.

"See you in February," Romo said as he patted Brady on the chest, referring to a possible Super Bowl matchup in Arizona. Brady just laughed it off, knowing that his team would more than likely have a legitimate chance to be there and defend its title. The Cowboys, meanwhile, had lost three straight games and would play at least five more without Romo in the lineup.

In the locker room, reporters again huddled around Hardy, hoping for yet another headline-enticing quote. But when asked to grade himself and his performance, the menacing defensive end stared for seemingly three seconds at a reporter before his answer.

"F—, we lost," Hardy said. "Any other questions?"

Oh, there were plenty of questions for Hardy, for the quarterback position, and for several other aspects of this team that had lost three straight games.

The problem was, the Cowboys were quickly running out of answers.

Chapter 8
BRING IT HOME

Friday

No matter the size of the school, from the powerhouse 6A teams down to small-town six-man squads, and no matter the won-loss record, one annual event is synonymous throughout high school football:

Homecoming.

Teams can be undefeated and eyeing a state title, while others could be winless and just trying to keep games close. Either way, excitement always fills homecoming week, and for the Wildcats, it's no exception.

In fact, given Plano's longstanding tradition, homecoming week is likely a much bigger deal to that community than in other places. The Thursday night homecoming parade brings out thousands of people, who line up across the streets of Parkhaven Drive and Westside Drive, which leads right to the gymnasium of the school.

The traditional homecoming floats are a big hit, but the parade also includes a variety of organizational groups, including other sports teams such as soccer, volleyball, and even lacrosse. They unite, wear the team colors, and are supported throughout the community as featured members of the parade.

"To me, this is what being a part of Plano Senior High School is all about," Jaydon McCullough said just moments after this year's parade and before the annual homecoming pep rally. "The support we get from the community is amazing. Every year, it seems like more people show up than the previous year."

The turnout this time around particularly impressed McCullough, considering the team's 3–4 overall record. Plano was also just 1–4 in the District 6–6A standings and had to win its remaining three games to even have a chance to sneak into the playoffs, including their homecoming matchup with Boyd High School from nearby McKinney, Texas, another growing suburb north of Dallas.

But on this night, these fans didn't seem to care about the team's struggles. And for a little bit of the evening, the players didn't either.

Some of the seniors paired up with Plano's cheerleaders for a dance-off skit. Seeing bulky linemen such as Darion Foster dance to Katy Perry songs and cartwheel across the gym was always a fan favorite for young and old alike.

Homecoming is a school-wide event for every student organization, but in Texas, it's primarily associated with and honored through the football team. At halftime of Friday's game, the king and queen would be announced, along with similar honors for the underclassmen.

This year's homecoming court included two football players: quarterback Matt Keys and tight end Conley McCabe. That meant the pair not only would miss some of the halftime adjustments during the game in order to be involved in the homecoming festivities, but would also be absent for part of Wednesday's practice.

"The coaches are never happy about when you have to miss," Keys said. "But they understand, I think."

For this team, homecoming came at the perfect time, providing a much-needed lift for the Wildcats, who had just lost two straight city games to rivals Plano West and Plano East.

If it sounded like more of a buzz was circulating throughout John Clark Field on this night, it was probably just the plethora of mums being worn in the stands. Mums come in all shapes and sizes, and literally include a variety of bells and whistles. The latter actually would cause a problem in the first half of the game as a few students stopped the action on the field before a snap by blowing their whistles from the stands.

Just before kickoff, the nearly full home side gave a standing ovation to the members of Plano's 1965 state championship team, who were honored before the game. Led by Coach John Clark, the same man for whom the stadium is named, the Plano alumni waved to the crowd while donning their jerseys and the numbers they wore when they gave the city its first-ever championship with a 20–17 win over Edna High School.

Given the heightened anticipation that comes with homecoming, the Plano coaches were hoping the energy would generate improved play on the field. With the Plano student section in a frenzy, the older fans excited about reliving some of their glory years, and the players on the field knowing their backs were against the wall, the Wildcats seemed destined to have a fast start.

However, after a couple of first downs to begin the game, Plano's offense stalled when Keys was picked off and the interception was returned just across midfield into Wildcat territory. On Boyd's third play from scrimmage, the Broncos then grabbed a 7–0 lead on a 45-yard touchdown pass that stunned the Plano faithful.

The Wildcats, though, had an answer, putting together a lengthy fifteen-play drive that included five first downs. Keys was finally able to muscle his way into the end zone off a 1-yard run to tie the score.

As he came off the field, the quarterback looked up at his peers in the student section and gave the biggest fist pump he could muster, letting them know he was not only hearing their constant enthusiasm, but it was working.

Sadly for the Wildcats, that would be their last score of the game.

At halftime, Keys and McCabe ran out of the locker room to join their parents and respective dates for the Homecoming ceremonies. But in what would turn out to be somewhat of an ongoing theme for the night, both players came up short in their quest for the title of homecoming king.

In the third quarter, Boyd grabbed a 14–7 lead, but midway through the fourth quarter, the Wildcats were knocking on the door yet again with a chance to tie. Here they were in an eerily similar situation to their last home game against Plano West—trailing by the same 14–7 margin and trying to score down in the stadium's north end zone. The Wildcats fell short on a fourth-and-goal that night, and now faced another fourth-and-goal from the 1-yard line with about eight minutes to play.

"We went to our bread-and-butter," McCullough said. "It's a play we've run over and over and had success with it."

The Wildcats hurried to the line hoping to catch the Broncos off guard and loaded the right side of their formation with two tight ends and a fullback shaded to the right of Keys in the backfield. Running back Brandon Stephens lined up in the I formation.

Unfortunately, though, Boyd stacked that side of the field as well with defenders, and even though many eyes went with Stephens, there were enough Boyd players to stick with Keys, who kept the ball on a speed-option run. He was stopped for a 3-yard loss.

"There was just nowhere to go," Keys recalled. "They stacked the line, and I just ran it right into them. I felt right then, that was the game. We had to score and we didn't."

Plano's defense didn't help matters, allowing the Broncos to then march ninety-six yards for a touchdown and an insurmountable 21–7 lead.

With the game out of reach, Keys had a "what could've been" moment when he barked out a play and was stopped in mid-sentence by Stephens.

"He said, 'Hey, just give me the ball. I've got this one,'" Keys said of Stephens, who hadn't been able to break loose all game. "And so we change the play and he takes it and breaks about five tackles for twenty-five yards. Right then, I remember thinking how great he was. I felt bad for him because he was such a great player and the blocking just wasn't there for him. He rarely called for the ball, but he did on that play."

It wasn't enough, as the Wildcats lost their third straight game, which officially eliminated them from the playoffs for the first time in four years; none of these seniors had ever experienced a year at Plano without the postseason.

And don't think that was taken lightly.

When defensive backs coach, Chris Fisher, got home later that evening, he was met quickly by Foster, his live-in nephew who views "Uncle Chris" more like his father. At home, the two usually try to maintain a family atmosphere, leaving the coach-and-player relationship at the school. But on this night, there was no avoiding the reality.

With tears rolling down his cheeks, the young eighteen-year-old just collapsed in his uncle's arms, bawling his eyes out.

"Uncle Chris, I'm sorry," he said with a trembling voice. "I'm sorry we didn't get it done. I'm sorry we didn't have what it takes to win."

Fisher felt the same as his nephew, but still, seeing the agony right in his own living room was hard to take.

"You want him to have that chance to play (in the state finals) and have that success," Fisher said. "That's our standard. And he felt like he let me down. He knows we're judged as coaches. For some kids, they get upset. But for a coach's kid, they realize the ramifications of not making the playoffs. That was so hard on him."

Meanwhile, Stephens had a similar moment in his own living room. Leaned on all season, he was expected to carry the Wildcats not only into the postseason, but perhaps deep into the playoffs. Instead, following a much-needed bye week, his senior year had just two games left.

While he wanted to relive each play from the game and wonder how things could've been different, Stephens knew he had to get some rest.

In some eight hours he was about to put a different set of skills to the test—literally.

Saturday

By NCAA rules, football programs can only give out eighty-five scholarships in a school year. That might sound like more than enough, considering only twenty-two players are deemed starters. But when you account for redshirted players, injuries, and having adequate depth to make it through a season, scholarships are precious and coaches never seem to have enough.

At the end of spring practice, the Baylor staff had a heart-to-heart talk with senior defensive tackle Trevor Clemons-Valdez, who had been with the team for four years and had finished his undergraduate degree. He was working on his master's in sports management and had another year of eligibility, but the writing on the wall was clear: he would likely only be a special teams player, and his scholarship would be better suited for somebody younger.

Like the team player he'd been throughout his time with the Bears, Clemons-Valdez, or "Chubber" as his teammates and coaches called him, agreed to hang up the cleats. But he wanted to stay close to the team and so asked to be a defensive intern, helping out the program even while paying his own way.

All summer and during fall practices, Clemons-Valdez charted plays, helped cut up videotape, and did any other grunt work the coaches needed. But during Baylor's bye week, he was hunting with some of his buddies when an idea popped into his head. Knowing the team had just dismissed starting tight end, Tre'Von Armstead, for disciplinary reasons, Clemons-Valdez wondered if he could simply walk on again and help out as a blocking tight end, a position he hadn't played since high school in Copperas Cove, Texas.

"Knowing we needed help at the position, he asked me if he could come back," Art Briles said. "We loved him for doing that and helping us. He's always been a really unselfish player. He's one of those people who plays the game for the right reason—and that's for everyone else in the room."

For Clemons-Valdez, he was just happy to be back in the room once again. Mostly a reserve defensive tackle, who did get seven starts during his career, Chubber had lost about twenty pounds over the summer since he didn't figure he would continue playing. It wasn't long, though, before he was back in shape. He made his return against Texas Tech and saw limited action at Kansas, but couldn't have been happier to be on the field to face West Virginia, the team that handed Baylor its only regular-season loss in 2014, essentially knocking them out of playoff contention.

To the Mountaineers' credit, they surprised Baylor that day, running a brand-new defense, designed strictly for the Bears. West Virginia ran a "Cover 0" scheme, freeing up a defender to blitz on every snap. The way to combat that, for Baylor's offense, was to allow the quarterback to run the ball, something that wasn't exactly Bryce Petty's strong suit.

This time around, the Bears knew Seth Russell had the ability to really run, but hadn't had to yet. If West Virginia came out with the same approach, the coaching staff was confident that the results would be different.

When the game started, one thing was clear: Baylor knew exactly who had defeated them in the 2014 regular season. On the second play of the game, Russell and the Bears sent a message—by air—to the Mountaineers that this year was indeed going to be different. Russell threw one of his best passes of the season, heaving a throw that traveled nearly half the football field before landing perfectly in Corey Coleman's arms for a 50-yard gain to the West Virginia 15.

Another indication of what was to come that day was also revealed on the play, or just after it. Coleman got up and immediately traded verbal jabs with West Virginia cornerback Daryl Worley. It was foreshadowing at its best, as Coleman and the Bears would drop bombs on the field and from their mouths all afternoon.

Two plays later, Baylor got the look it expected, allowing Russell to have a huge lane on the left side for an easy touchdown run. The Bears took a 7–0 lead just fifty-eight seconds into the game, prompting sophomore receiver KD Cannon to yell to his teammates as he came to the sideline, "All damn day! All damn day and don't let up. They can't stop us."

For the most part, Cannon was correct, but it took a bit longer than just one drive to get there.

While the quick touchdown continued the team's streak of scoring on the opening drive of the game, the Baylor defense kept another discouraging trend up as well. West Virginia became the fifth opponent to score on its first possession against the Bears. West Virginia's Shelton Gibson was wide open right in front of the Baylor bench and scooted across the field untouched for a 70-yard touchdown to temporarily quiet the raucous McLane Stadium crowd.

"Be disciplined!" Phil Bennett screamed in the direction of safeties Chance Waz and Travon Blanchard as they walked off the field. "What are we doing out there? You guys have to pay attention."

Bennett had always been a fiery complement to Briles, and the head coach again kept things positive with some cool confidence that his offense would return the favor.

"That's all right. Get it back, O. We're going to go right down and score," Briles said to center Kyle Fuller and the rest of his offensive-line compadres as they strapped on their helmets again.

Briles knew his team well, especially the offense. Baylor answered right away, making Fox Sports television announcer Gus Johnson sound like a prophet. Just as he finished raving about Coleman, calling him a "freakish athlete," the junior receiver made another dynamic catch-and-run over the middle for a gain of forty-two, nearly giving him a 100-yard day less than four minutes into the game. Coleman finished off the drive with one of the easiest slant patterns he'd ever gotten, catching a 2-yard touchdown pass, which prompted him to immediately turn back at Worley and continue their jawing match, one that wouldn't stop until the final gun.

While his celebrating teammates corralled him on the sideline, the always-intense Kaz Kazadi kept him grounded.

"Keep eating, 'C,' " he barked. "Stay hungry! Let's go."

But perhaps Coleman didn't get the message so clearly. After the defense "held serve," as the coaching staff likes to call it, using a tennis reference, the offense didn't cash in as expected. On a third-and-11 play near midfield, Coleman was supposed to run to the sticks and stop on a hitch route. Instead, he somewhat weaved down the field and barely got a hand on the pass, which would've been on target and enough for a first down.

Knowing what a two-score lead can do to the psyche of Baylor's opponents, Kendal Briles nearly lost it on the sideline. His cap went flying, as did a few verbal pleasantries. As the receivers got back to the bench, Kendal circled the wagons for a moment trying to cool off, but he couldn't help himself.

He lit into Coleman, explaining the expected route over and over. When a couple of head nods by the receiver didn't stop his coach's tirade, Coleman finally barked back.

"Coach, I fucked up, coach. I got it."

That seemed to finally calm Kendal down. He knows Coleman is his most explosive player, and like the receiver just said, he knows Coleman "gets it" more often than not.

More sideline fireworks occurred after Baylor's next drive, one that again didn't lead to a touchdown. Jay Lee was open on the right side of the end zone, but Russell's pass was in the corner, forcing the senior receiver to torque his body at the last moment. In doing so, he couldn't get two hands on the pass.

While Baylor settled for a field goal, Lee didn't like one of the younger running backs telling him, "You gotta catch that!" Lee went off and had to be held back. He was literally pushed backward to a seat on the bench.

The temperatures were hot enough in Waco, and even hotter on the turf. But only a 10-point lead with a couple of failed offensive drives had things boiling even more.

In the second quarter, West Virginia trimmed the advantage to 17–14 before Russell and Coleman went to work again. Russell's 46-yard run right up the middle of the defense moved Baylor to the Mountaineers' 11.

McGowan and his teammates hurried to the line of scrimmage before Baylor changed its personnel package and sent the tight end back to the sideline.

"Stay here, big guy," Art Briles said to his winded 400-pounder. "We're going to need you here in a second. Get ready. Get a quick drink of wa . . . touchdown!"

Briles couldn't even finish his sentence. The offense didn't need more than one play for Russell to find Coleman in the end zone for this third touchdown, a record-breaking one at that.

Just six games into the schedule and the junior receiver had already set Baylor's single-season record for touchdown catches, surpassing Kendall Wright, who had fourteen in his senior year of 2011, which helped him become a first-round draft pick the following spring.

And even though it was still halfway through the year, Briles already knew there was a better than good chance that Coleman would be heading to the NFL as well. Games like this one against West Virginia certainly didn't hurt his draft stock.

In the second half, the Bears could virtually do whatever they wanted to offensively. The Mountaineers' defense had been softened up by the run, so now Russell could pick apart the secondary.

Coleman added another highlight-reel touchdown grab, showing once again his ability to stop and start better than anyone. After catching a slant over the middle, the electrifying receiver stopped in the middle of the field, letting the cornerback fly past him, and then switched directions and outraced the remaining defenders to the end zone.

"You breakin' dem ankles, CC," shouted one of the freshman receivers who practiced with Coleman every day.

But it wasn't just Coleman making plays. Lee was having some fun as well. He caught two third-quarter scores to push the margin out to twenty-four, giving Baylor some breathing room heading into the final frame.

Coming off the field after his second touchdown, Lee was met by an amped-up Kendal Briles, who gave him a friendly slap to the facemask. "That's how you finish!"

Lee then got a hug from a former player in street clothes. "I see you, four. Way to wear the four," said David Gettis, who was a wide receiver for Baylor from 2006 to 2009 and obviously had worn that jersey as well.

The only negative for the Bears in the second half was an ankle injury to star defensive tackle Andrew Billings, who had to be taken to the

locker room. After missing one series, he returned to the field in uniform, but with the help of crutches.

"I can go," Billings said to the training staff. "Let me try it and see."

Billings tried it, going back into the game at his regular nose tackle
spot. One of the strongest players on the team—he was a state power lifter
in high school—Billings had no leverage with his legs and was pancaked
to the ground. Just like that, he was out of the game and didn't return.

"That's all right, 'Bill,' " Art Briles said to him as he walked off. "Get
off your feet. We'll get you ready for next week."

West Virginia kept scoring, but the Bears did as well. Late in the
fourth quarter, with freshman quarterback Jarrett Stidham in the game,
Baylor was down in the red zone once again, knocking on the door. From
the 9-yard line, Stidham faked a run and pulled back to throw, finding a wide open . . . intern? Formerly yes, but currently Clemons-Valdez,
sporting the 98 jersey he had worn for the last three years, was waiting
in the end zone and hauled in the pass for his first collegiate touchdown.
He barely even had the ball tucked under his left arm before he was fist
pumping with his right.

"Boys, our defensive intern just scored him a touchdown!" receivers
coach, Tate Wallis, yelled out, causing quite a laugh among the coaches.
Chubber was greeted on the sideline by just about every player and coach;
but with the ball still tucked under his arm, he made his way through his
teammates with one destination in mind.

Clemons-Valdez went straight to the first row in the stands and
handed the ball to his mother, who had a 35mm camera in one hand and
now a game ball in the other.

"Here's a guy who wasn't going to play, and he just wanted to be around
the team in any way he could," said running backs coach, Jeff Lebby. "So
he frees us up a scholarship, then walks back on because he knew we
needed help. It's the greatest example of a teammate that there is."

One would think a touchdown with 1:21 left in a 31-point game would
be the final fireworks, but Baylor had to kick off and, with mostly the
second-team coverage unit on the field, allowed a 100-yard return for

a score, giving the coaches for the kicking units something to chew on for another week. However, they nearly matched it on the next kickoff as redshirt freshman Chris Platt, one of the fastest players on the team, returned the kick ninety-two yards before getting tackled at the West Virginia 3 with fifty seconds remaining. Baylor ran one offensive play but was stopped short of the end zone, and an injury to a West Virginia player then led to an automatic timeout with thirty seconds left.

On the sidelines, with Kendal in his ear wanting to run another play and several thousand giddy fans behind him urging for the same, the head coach just smiled at his freshman quarterback, who looked rather eager to punch it in the end zone himself.

"I've dealt with peer pressure my whole life," Briles said. "Are we going to give in to it now? Are we going to give in to peer pressure or do what's right? Let's do what's right. Just let it run out."

So the clock ran out as Briles ran to the middle of the field to shake hands with Dana Holgorsen, who was on staff with him nearly fifteen years earlier when the two were assistants at Texas Tech. Holgorsen not only gave Briles and his team high praise, but also called attention to a specific player.

"That number one (referring to Coleman's jersey) is the best player in the country," he said.

"Well, coach, don't tell anyone else that," Briles said with a chuckle. "I'm trying to get him to stay for another year."

"Ha, good luck with that," said Holgorsen, who likely would have loved nothing more than to see Coleman enter the NFL Draft early and not have to face him again.

In the locker room, the postgame celebration was a little rowdier than normal. One might think becoming bowl-eligible with a sixth win wasn't worthy of a raucous celebration for the number-five team in the country, but Briles always made a point to announce it to his team.

"Guys, it's hard to win in this league. It's hard to win," he told the players. "We don't know what bowl we're going to, but we know we're going somewhere."

Obviously, the national championship was still the ultimate goal, and the best way to get there was to be undefeated, something Baylor couldn't claim after the last time they faced West Virginia.

Sunday

The most loyal of football fans not only know their beloved team inside and out, but also share a true understanding of the mindset of the players and coaches.

On the flip side, a team knows that much of its success relies on having these crazed fans, feeling their passion, and sometimes living off that enthusiasm when its back is against the wall.

For the most part, teams and fans are on the same page. But if there is one thing that many of them disagree on, it's the timing of the bye week.

Players not only love it, but they need it. Their bodies have been getting banged around since late July and a weekend away from the grind can be rehabilitating for both the body and mind. For the coaches, the mental grind never goes away, but at least for a few days, they have a chance to breathe, and in the Cowboys' case, possibly regroup with a chance to right the ship that seemed to be sinking fast.

For the fans, good luck finding one that truly loves the off week. What makes them so passionate is that they rarely can get enough. When their team wins a big game, the avid fan can barely wait another seven days to keep up the momentum. And after a loss, or maybe a few losses in a row, that wretched taste that sits in their mouths for a full week just lingers until game day arrives again. That's when seven days between games can feel like a month.

So imagine how the Dallas fans must have felt after losing to the Patriots at home for a third consecutive loss, knowing there would be two full weeks before getting the chance to return to the win column.

A season that began with so much promise, a 2–0 start with wins over division rivals New York and Philadelphia, had now turned into a 2–3 record with both Tony Romo and Dez Bryant out for significant time. Sure, there was time to turn things around, but it was clear to the coaching staff that changes needed to be made.

Usually, Jason Garrett isn't one for revealing anything about the current game plan, especially when it comes to personnel. He's always rather reserved with the media when asked about injuries and when it comes to lineup changes. Garrett's philosophy is to hold as much information back as possible, abiding by the "knowledge is power" mantra and keeping his opponents in the dark when it comes to what to expect from his team.

But with the Cowboys limping toward the bye week, Garrett uncharacteristically announced a change in the plans—some ten days before the game—announcing that Matt Cassel would replace Brandon Weeden in the starting lineup.

The only surprise was the timing of the announcement, but Garrett sensed that his team needed a spark during the week off; so he figured this could be a resounding message the players would respond to in a positive way. Well, at least most of the players.

For Weeden, it was one of the worst birthdays he could ever recall. He walked into the Valley Ranch complex Wednesday morning, and the now thirty-two-year-old was summoned to Garrett's office, where he was informed of the move. All last season, Weeden had backed up Romo as the number-two quarterback and now after three games—and three losses—he was sent back to that role.

To no one's surprise, he wasn't happy about it.

Weeden held nothing back when approached by reporters at his locker at Valley Ranch, which was only about thirty feet away from where Cassel was still meeting with reporters about his promotion.

"Obviously, I'm pissed," said a stone-faced Weeden, who had quickly become a favorite among the media members for not only his willingness to conduct interviews when requested, but his generally candid responses. "It's the nature of the business. I have to be ready again. I'm back in that position—one play away again. But they know I'm pissed. But I'm a pro. What else can I say?"

Even Weeden understood that a 0–3 record as the starting quarterback wasn't acceptable. But what chapped him the most was a game plan that limited his ability to throw the ball down the field. What got him to the NFL was a strong arm that earned him a second-round selection in the Major League Baseball draft as a pitcher back in 2002 with the Yankees. He spent four years in the minors before opting to play football at Oklahoma State, where he threw a few passes to Dez Bryant early in their college careers.

Weeden could definitely throw the ball, but felt like the offensive plan centered more on his managing the game than trying to win it. And after three losses, instead of switching up the plan, they just switched quarterbacks.

The Cowboys went from a player who was 0–4 as a starter in Dallas and 5–19 as a career starter to Cassel, who was at least closer to .500 with a 34–38 record, including a victory earlier this season with the Bills.

Cassel stood in front of about twenty-five reporters and answered every question with class and humility but also a sense of confidence.

If there is a physical prototype of what NFL quarterbacks look like, Cassel fits it. At 6–5, 230 pounds, he sports a light-bronze tan that seems rather constant from his days of growing up in California and attending Southern Cal. With dark brown hair, bright blue eyes, and a square jaw, Cassel is the poster boy for the All-American look. Obviously, the Cowboys and their fans were concerned a little more with how that right arm of his could help dig this team out of a hole.

Oddly enough, the California-born, traveled veteran of the NFL said playing for the Cowboys was a "dream come true," having growing up following the Cowboys along with his father, who grew up in Lubbock, Texas—about six hours west of Dallas.

"We always supported the blue star," Cassel said. "So growing up a Cowboys fan, I think it's huge that I'm in position to be the starter. We're all kind of pinching ourselves right now."

While Cassel stood in front of the media, beaming with excitement and confidence, he knew he was being called upon to deliver in the figurative sense. Literally, his wife, Lauren, was getting close to delivering as well, some thirty-eight weeks pregnant with the family's fourth child.

Cassel actually conducted the entire interview with his cell phone in his right hand, making sure he had his phone with him at all times.

"She might have called right now," Cassel joked with reporters. "I keep my phone nearby in case she calls. I'm staying ready."

While the rest of Cassel's teammates were taking their NFL-mandated four days away from the complex during the bye week, the Cowboys' new quarterback spent his weekend in a Dallas hospital. As it turned out, the timing of Lauren and Matt's baby boy couldn't have been better. Born on Saturday of the bye weekend, Clayton Cassel now gave the family two sons and two daughters.

Fearful that the birth would cause him to miss precious practice time or perhaps even threaten his availability for the next week's game, Cassel had cleared that hurdle.

Now, it was time to get his new team back in the race.

Chapter 9

MORE PAIN THAN RAIN

Friday

In Plano, Texas, as well as just about every town throughout the Lone Star State, and even in most places across the nation, lasting memories are made on Friday nights in the fall.

But there's always one Saturday morning for nearly all high school students, whether they wear a uniform or not, that can have a lasting impact on their future.

It's not the same Saturday for everyone, and in some cases it can be taken on a different day, but rest assured, there are classrooms full on Saturdays across the state with nervous seventeen- and eighteen-year-olds holding nothing but a sharpened number-two pencil.

On this Saturday morning in mid-October, Brandon Stephens was among several students from all over the area who were ready to take the SAT. The standardized test, along with the ACT, is a widely used examination that colleges use to determine admissions for prospective students, along with their grades in the classroom.

When compared to football, daily tests and quizzes are like practices. Report cards are equal to a Friday night game. But the SAT is the state championship game of tests.

With the enormous implications of this exam, Stephens was doing his best to focus. As the star running back of a Plano team that was just eliminated from playoff contention the night before, he was crushed inside. As a senior and one of the team leaders, Stephens dreamed of finishing his stellar prep career in the playoffs, possibly even at AT&T Stadium in Arlington or NRG Stadium in Houston in the state championship. Instead, he knew he had just two more games left as a high school player.

But like many of his teammates, Stephens was so much more than just a football player. For him, the phrase "student-athlete" was indeed in the right order because he dedicated as much time and energy to his schoolwork and grades as he did to football, if not more. And his parents, Tim and Charlotte, certainly wouldn't have had it any other way.

In fact, during Stephens' junior season, he brought home an uncharacteristic C on his report card.

"That didn't go well," he recalled. "My family doesn't do Cs."

And even though Stephens had a battle with an advanced placement history course during the fall of his senior season, and at one point worried that he was going down the path of another C, he pulled through and managed to record a high B.

Now, as he sat in a classroom full of other students from various local high schools preparing for the test, Stephens seemingly might have had less pressure than his peers who were still waiting for acceptance to their college of choice. Stephens had already verbally committed to Stanford back in early September on a full athletic scholarship.

But Stanford is considered by many to be the "Ivy League" of the West Coast, so the pressure to deliver high marks was likely no different, if not even greater, than the pressure Stephens felt to carry his team to victories on Friday nights.

"I studied my tail off for the SAT," Stephens recalled. "In the middle of the season, and we've got our own classes, but I found time to study for that. It's not easy to prepare for, but I was confident, and I was ready for it."

Even at this point in the year, quarterback Matt Keys was still undecided about where he would go to college. He entered the season still hopeful that a successful effort on the field might lead to a football scholarship—but only at a bigger school that met his academic requirements.

With his eyes on the Ivy League, or potentially schools such as Vanderbilt or Stanford, Keys had a solid fallback plan of attending the business program at the University of Texas in Austin. So playing football for just any small school that offered him a scholarship wasn't going to be a viable option for him. Keys knew more than likely his football career would end the very second the curtain fell on Plano's 2015 season, but he still wasn't about to close the door on anything.

Keys had already taken the ACT and scored "very well," which wasn't a surprise to the usually straight-A student. Other than a "high B" in a calculus class, a course the quarterback said "easily could've been an A," his grades didn't change much at all during his senior year.

This was Keys' first and only season as the starting quarterback, though, which did alter some of his time management, especially in the mornings.

On Tuesdays and Wednesdays at 6:30 a.m. each week, Keys had a film-room session with quarterbacks coach, Carson Meger, and selected offensive players. On Thursday mornings, Keys attended a bible study at the school and then led a Fellowship of Christian Athletes meeting on Friday mornings, which made for long days with the game later that night.

So finding time to study during weeknights was challenging.

"I was always so tired," Keys admitted. "Football is my top priority. I would come home beat and do homework, but during the season, just finding time to sleep was the biggest problem."

And that's one of the reasons Keys welcomed the bye week with open arms. While he certainly caught up on his sleep, especially on the weekend with no game, the quarterback also adopted a different attitude for the final two outings of his high school, and most likely his football, career.

"For me, it was always about figuring out what I'm playing for," he said. "We thought we were going to be a playoff team, but it didn't happen. So when the bye week hit, I really tried to refocus myself. I wanted to just soak up the time in my last two or three weeks of football that I'd ever have. I put so much time and effort into it, and my family has been there with me the entire way. I just wanted to make the most of it. But, the week off was really nice."

Actually, the week off was good timing for other reasons. As it turned out, many games in the Dallas-Fort Worth area that weekend were either postponed or even cancelled because of torrential downpours that flooded some areas.

So with the week off, the Wildcats avoided what likely would've been a night of lightning delays and certainly an evening of relentless rain. The players probably would've loved it, slipping and sliding around the sloshy elements reminiscent of the days when they played football in the backyard. The parents, meanwhile, probably were just fine with how the schedule played out.

As for the coaches, during the bye week they might have taken a slight pause in their daily rigors, but not much of one. The combination of not having a game on Friday night and being eliminated from the playoffs certainly didn't change the mood or the schedule of Jaydon McCullough. If anything, his nights were even longer during the break, as he and the staff dug deeper in the film room, trying to figure out ways to finish the season on the right foot.

With two games to play, McCullough tried to balance the present and the future. There were some players on the junior varsity and freshman teams who were being considered for promotion up to varsity by the coaches.

"But the main focus is our seniors," McCullough said that week. "We've got a bunch of seniors who have done everything we've asked of them for four years. They've got two games left, and we're going to make sure we do everything we can to send them off the right way."

And by saying that, what might have been a week to catch their breath, turned into just another week in the grind . . . without the game, of course.

Saturday

The figurative dark cloud that hung over the football program just before the start of the season seemed to be slowly fading away. Even with the ongoing Pepper Hamilton investigators coming and going from time to time with sporadic interviews and requests, the public focus was certainly shifting away from those storylines and more onto the field of play, which so far was flawless. With an undefeated 6–0 record, things had literally brightened up for the Bears—as in nothing but sunshine.

Five of the six games began with clear skies and few clouds. The lone exception was an indoor matchup against Texas Tech at AT&T Stadium, where the windows in both end zones even allowed some sunrays to flood the field during the second half.

But all of that came to a sloshy end against Iowa State. Not only did the rain come down, it never stopped on this Saturday, the Waco area totaling nine inches in a 24-hour span. To make matters worse, the rain was a slippery sign of foreshadowing that would follow the Baylor team for the remainder of the season.

For starters, the rain completely washed away the majority of Baylor's homecoming activities, including the annual parade, a 25-block march through the downtown streets of Waco that began in 1909. The Friday night bonfire was also cancelled with the pep rally moved indoors to the Waco Convention Center.

Local weather reports were predicting "substantial" rainfall beginning that Friday night and continuing all day Saturday, and on this occasion, the meteorologists couldn't have been more on point.

While there was some discussion between the schools and the Big 12 conference about moving the game to later in the day on Saturday, the notion was dismissed because of television scheduling. The game was set for an 11 a.m. kickoff on ESPN, and the number-two-ranked Bears were too big of a draw now to shuffle the deck around.

One person who wouldn't have minded a later start was Baylor passing game coordinator, Jeff Lebby, who lived about twenty-five minutes from the school on the outskirts of Waco. His route to the city included more than a few flooded streets that even his three-quarter-ton Dodge diesel pickup had trouble navigating.

On his way to pick up Kendal Briles—a tradition for home games—Lebby called him to not only explain why it was taking a bit longer, but also for some advice on how to maneuver through the standing water on the road to Briles' house.

"He said, 'Throw it in four-wheel drive and just stay on the phone with me,'" Lebby recalled. "So I drive it all the way to the right side, which should be the most shallow part of the road, and it ends up throwing me all the way to the left bank of the road. But I managed to get out of that and then ended up picking up Kendal. What usually took me eight minutes to get him, took me twenty-four."

By then, they knew they were going to be late for their 7 a.m. game-day meeting. Art Briles, who was understanding during events such as these, told them both to simply be careful and make it in safely.

When they arrived at the school, though, both realized that Lebby's truck didn't go completely unscathed as his front license plate was ripped off and hanging by just one screw—perhaps another case of foreshadowing for the day.

Once the players arrived at the stadium, it was determined that All–Big 12 defensive tackle Andrew Billings would not be able to play after battling a high-ankle sprain suffered the week before. Billings spent the first three days in a walking boot before switching to a protective shoe brace on Wednesday. Art Briles had reiterated all week that Baylor's being favored by as much as thirty-seven points over the Cyclones had no bearing on the decision not to play Billings, nor did the upcoming bye week that would follow this game.

"We don't think past Saturday," Briles said. "If he can go, he'll go. But right now, he's very limited."

When Saturday rolled around, Billings was far from being 100 percent and the rain, along with the slippery turf, wasn't a good combination to risk playing him. After a couple of minutes on the field with his teammates, he quickly went to the locker room, looking for the biggest rain suit the Baylor equipment staff could provide. He knew that would be his uniform for the day.

For those who were playing, the pregame warm-ups at least gave both teams an idea of what was in store. Several of the defensive backs went back inside to the locker room to switch shoes after slipping and sliding on the turf. Footing was an issue for everyone, while catching the ball was even tougher for the receivers.

Freshman Ishmael Zamora, a backup receiver who looks more like a defensive end with his 6–4, 220-pound frame, was a player that the coaching staff believed could be one of the next great receivers in a program that has been self-proclaimed as "Wide Receiver U." The coaches loved his freakish skill set, but just six games into his playing career, Zamora was still trying to figure out his role within the offense. But on this day, he was just trying to figure out how to catch the ball in a monsoon.

Zamora came out for the warm-ups wearing his standard Nike receiver gloves, but it wasn't long before he switched them out for a different pair with more adhesiveness in the palms. He found out that was even worse in the rain, so took the gloves off completely and finished his pregame routine by catching passes with his bare hands, albeit constantly drying them off on a towel, which, of course, wasn't so dry itself.

But as the Bears prepared to receive the opening kickoff, featuring Zamora as one of the two returners, he couldn't help himself. He broke the special-teams huddle and went looking for his gloves again, quickly putting them on before rushing onto the field. As it turned out, Zamora wouldn't catch a pass all afternoon, despite three targeted in his direction.

In the stands, the school's marketing plan for a Green & Gold "Stripe Out" was taking a huge hit. What has become a popular one-game promotion each year has fans wearing the two colors in alternating sections to create a dynamic "striped" stadium visual.

T-shirts and jackets are rather easy to find around Waco in both green and gold. However, ponchos and raingear are a different story. While there were some fans who tried to cooperate and wear the appropriate color, others just made sure they stayed dry in the midst of the torrential downpour.

Far from a sellout crowd, the attendance of 45,512 was better than expected, and the student section was in full force with many of the exuberant young fans reveling in the rain. And early on, the fans had plenty to get excited about.

After scoring a touchdown on its opening drive in the first six games, Baylor had to work to extend the streak to seven. Quarterback Seth Russell was nearly intercepted twice, including one that easily would've been returned for a touchdown. Instead, the potential turnover was dropped by the Cyclones' cornerback. On the next play, Russell went right back to that side and hit Corey Coleman for a 33-yard touchdown, the ball just fluttering through the rain and right into the wide receiver's stomach as he fell backward in the end zone.

The drive wasn't pretty, but that didn't seem to bother anyone on the Bears' sideline.

"Let's win ugly!" strength coach Kaz Kazadi screamed to his players as Baylor prepared for its first kickoff. "Anyone can win when it's pretty. Let's win when it's ugly."

That's what the Bears proceeded to do, steamrolling the Cyclones in one of their fastest starts to a game all season. With Russell running and passing, and running back Shock Linwood juking and jiving, the offense had built a 35–0 lead midway through the second quarter.

While Baylor was having little trouble with the downpour, Iowa State had all sorts of problems with fumbles and dropped passes left and right. The Cyclones were sliding around on defense and continuously missing tackles.

But they did find some momentum after a 42-yard run by Joshua Thomas set up Iowa State's first touchdown. That entire drive featured several runs up the middle, as the Cyclones seemed to find a spark rushing inside, especially with Billings not in the game.

In fact, the Bears had to use Trevor Clemons-Valdez at defensive tackle, a position he had played the previous three seasons before agreeing to give up his scholarship and become a defensive intern. With a need at tight end, Clemons-Valdez rejoined the team in late September to help the offense, but now he was back in the rotation on the defensive side of the ball. Needless to say, he certainly wasn't able to fill the void left by Billings, one of Baylor's strongest players.

Trailing 35–7, Iowa State continued to rally in the second half. The Cyclones not only moved the ball on offense, but also figured out a way to slow down the Bears as well. Baylor was shut out in the third quarter and didn't score in the fourth until the team, leading 35–20, managed to get down inside the Iowa State 30-yard line with just more than five minutes remaining.

When it was 35–0, offensive stars such as Russell and Coleman never dreamed the Cyclones would still be in the game at this point. But now up by just two scores, Baylor needed to convert a third-and-5 at the 21-yard line to push the lead back over twenty.

On the ensuing play, Russell faked an inside handoff and kept the ball in an attempt to get around the corner, but was met by two defenders. Knowing he needed to reach the 16-yard line to move the sticks, he lowered his head and collided with Iowa State cornerback Jomal Wiltz. Russell was wrapped up and stopped a few inches short of the first down.

Usually, on fourth-and-1 at any spot on the field, the offensive players get up and motion toward the sideline to go for the first down. In fact, center Kyle Fuller and running back Devin Chafin did just that, expressing their desire to run another play. However, Briles saw something else that immediately got his attention.

"Seth was calling a timeout," Briles said. "He would never do that. But he was looking over at us and trying to call a timeout. I knew something wasn't right."

When Russell got to the sideline, he didn't have to say anything specific. The coaches and trainers just knew the quarterback was hurting, even before he told them that he had a sharp pain in his neck.

"If you look at a guy's eyes, you can see how serious it is," Briles said. "He was concerned. Nobody knows a body better than yourself. He knew something wasn't right."

Indeed, Russell knew. He went to the sideline and was surrounded by a handful of medical personnel who were asking him all sorts of questions. Not only were they testing him for a possible concussion, they were also trying to figure out specifically where the pain was.

Meanwhile, Baylor kicked a field goal, making it a three-score advantage and getting the ball back moments later after a fumble. Freshman quarterback Jarrett Stidham, who was telling bystanders just a few minutes earlier that the game was starting to appear like it would be his first not to play, was now thrown into action yet again. And he showed some playmaking and improvisational skills, buying some time with a rollout before finding Coleman in the end zone for a touchdown.

The score was the thirty-first of Coleman's career, which surpassed four-year standout Kendall Wright to set a new Baylor record. Coleman, who was already generating buzz about leaving early for the NFL, was still midway through his junior season.

Thanks to Coleman's record-setting touchdown, it was looking like a blowout again with Baylor now up 45–20. The Cyclones did respond with a late touchdown, but the Bears still enjoyed a 45–27 victory.

Coach Briles didn't care so much about the final score. In fact, deep down he knew his team needed a "grinding" game like this, especially considering the average winning margin of the previous six wins was thirty-nine points. What did concern him, though, was the health of his quarterback.

For a while, he did a good job of hiding it. The postgame celebration was normal, with Briles doing his usual chant where he rhetorically asks his players, "Whose house?"

"Our house!" They chant in unison.

"I said, whose house?"

"Our house!"

"Whose house?"

"Our house!"

"I said, whooooooose house?" Briles howled, showing he could still reach a high-pitched decibel when he wanted to.

"Our house!!!" the players responded one last time before the entire locker room erupted with another raucous cheer.

Business as usual it seemed, but inside Briles knew his starting quarterback was hurting. In the postgame press conference, it took three minutes before there was any question from the media about Russell's neck. Briles said that Russell would be evaluated over the next few days, and then answered a follow-up question with a nervous chuckle, saying, "We're always concerned about a player's health."

A few minutes later, a longtime local radio reporter, David Smoak, one of the featured hosts at the ESPN affiliate in Waco, pressed Briles specifically on the matter.

"If the game was on the line, would he have continued to be able to play today?" asked Smoak.

"No . . . no," Briles said with a deafening pause. "And, the game is always on the line, but no."

Some of the media members in the room caught it. Others didn't. The ones reading between the lines raised their eyebrows and looked at each other. Now they were catching on to what the head coach and a just few others already knew.

Something was really wrong with Seth Russell. And at this point in the season, that seemed to be about the only thing that could slow down the Bears, who were starting to look every bit the part of being one of the best teams in the country.

Sunday

When it comes to traveling for road trips, every coach stresses the importance of keeping a routine.

Even if the bus rides are longer from one place to another, or there is a shorter flight for this game than the last, at least the players and coaches have a general idea of what to expect in terms of the process each week of packing up a football team and heading out on the road.

In high school and college, sticking with the schedule is vital, considering the players are still classified as student-athletes. When they're not playing football, they're attending classes and studying to maintain their grades.

In the NFL, there is more flexibility with their schedules simply because these players are now getting paid hundreds of thousands of dollars, and some in the millions, to play this kid's game. Plus, they're also adults who should be able to adjust to whatever is thrown their way.

With the Cowboys coming off a bye week and staring a three-game losing streak in the face, head coach Jason Garrett tossed them a curveball a few days before returning to the field.

For as long as any player, coach, or staff member could recall, the Cowboys have always traveled just one day before a road game, staying the night at the team hotel and then returning home immediately following the game.

But when you play for the Dallas Cowboys, you have to be ready for all kinds of schedule changes, some of which are expected, such as playing on Thanksgiving just four days after the previous Sunday. Altering the schedule is a common occurrence for the Cowboys, so Garrett didn't feel as if this change would be too drastic. Plus, he thought it was definitely worth any inconvenience.

Instead of sending his team to New York on Saturday as is the regular routine, he decided to take the entire squad up a day earlier and have them visit the One World Observatory on the top floors of the One World Trade Center in Manhattan, which opened earlier in the year to honor the victims and families affected by the horrific tragedy of September 11, 2001.

Garrett and his wife, Brill, who were living in New York at the time of 9–11, visited the memorial during the off-season, and he knew instantly that he had to figure out a way to take his team there.

So, much like he did a few months earlier at the end of training camp,

Garrett tried to keep the switch in routine as low-key as possible, only telling the operations crew of the plan. As expected, however, word eventually got out and by Tuesday of that week, everyone in the team's travel party seemed to know of the early departure time.

The Cowboys had quite an adventure just getting to the airport on that Friday, as a heavy downpour continued to hit the Dallas-Fort Worth area. The rain had been a factor all week, forcing the team to move its practice to a local high school that had an indoor facility.

At one time, the Cowboys did have a tension structure that allowed for indoor workouts, but the building collapsed in 2009 during a strong storm in the middle of a May practice, severely injuring a couple of staff members, including current scout Rich Behm, who had been paralyzed from the waist down since the accident. Instead of rebuilding, the Cowboys chose to either use their stadium in Arlington or just find a local high school in the area when the need arose to practice indoors.

Longtime equipment staffer, Bucky Buchanan, also serves as the team's unofficial meteorologist and will keep Garrett up to speed on the forecasts. On this day, he told the head coach that the weather would hold off in time to get in a practice outside at Valley Ranch before they headed to the airport. But the storm was much stronger than anticipated and just before the start of the workout, rain was coming down in buckets. By then, the Cowboys had already cancelled the buses that would've taken them to a practice facility nearby, so the new plan forced the players to carpool and drive themselves over to Coppell High School, which was about nine minutes away.

The real problem, though, was back at Valley Ranch, as the storm had knocked out all power. By the time some twenty carloads of players had returned, there was still no electricity in the building. The players, coaches, and the entire travel party needed to shower, change, and get dressed for their trip to New York.

With the Cowboys' operations crew scrambling to find generators and some portable lights for the bathrooms so the players could get ready, the team managed to be only a few minutes late to the scheduled 2 p.m. charter flight that afternoon.

For the most part, the consensus among the travelers was more just being annoyed about the shortened week. Friday is one of the few nights that the players get to relax because they're typically out of the building early in the afternoon. For veterans with families, such as tight end Jason Witten, Friday night is the one evening during the season that they get to spend the most time with their wives and children.

So leaving early for New York wasn't exactly received with open arms initially. But once the players got to the Big Apple, hopped on the ferry that took them into the city, and started to see and experience their surroundings, what was once considered to be an inconvenience seemed to all be forgotten.

Decked out in suits and ties, a group of about one hundred people, including players, coaches, equipment managers, trainers, video staff, and some in-house media members, toured the breathtaking memorial at Ground Zero.

Some of the rookies on the team, like receiver Lucky Whitehead, were just eight years old when the Twin Towers fell. Still, players young and old all paid their respects during the tour. Whether it was a video display inside the elevators that changed with each floor level, or the powerful "Voices" tribute that showed some of the survivors telling their own personal stories of that unforgettable day, the night was powerful in many ways to many people.

Yet, none of them really knew the purpose for the event.

Sensing that, Garrett grabbed the microphone following the team's private dinner, which was held inside the observatory, and provided the reason . . . and much more.

"The question is . . . why are we here? My wife, Brill, and I came here this summer in July. I wasn't here ten minutes, I was standing in front of the Voices video, and I said, 'We've got to take our team here.' It was one of the great tragedies in our country's history—September 11, 2001. This memorial is to commemorate that; it's

impossible to do it better. So simple and elegant and really, really well done . . .

"That's not why we're here.

"I know it's impossible to do the elevators any better. You stand in, look forward, and you're going to go up and they're going to give you the history of New York City in forty-two seconds. You're going to see buildings go up and go down. It's the most amazing thing I've seen in my life . . .

"That's not why we're here.

"The view, three hundred sixty degrees around this unbelievable city. There's no better view on the planet than this view. One hundred and two stories up, looking at New York City from every angle . . .

"That's not why we're here.

"When we came here in July, I went into that Voices area, and I think it's meant for people to just walk through it. I took about three steps and I stopped. I watched it again and again and again. I couldn't move.

"The reason we're here is those voices and what those people said. I stood there and thought about us and thought about our football team. The expression I use with you guys all the time is 'mental toughness; be your best regardless of circumstance.' There was some circumstance that day.

"As I stood there for twelve minutes, and then watched them again for twenty-four minutes, I thought about this night and those voices. I think about the people. That's why we're here. This place is incredible. The elevators are incredible, the view is incredible, but think about the voices and think about the people.

"The foundation of this place is bedrock, but really the foundation is people. Just remember why we're here. And live it."

Bone-chilling speeches like that have become a trademark for Garrett. His postgame words, after both victories and defeats, are part of the reason his players say the coach they know is vastly different than the often poker-faced persona that the public sees on the sideline.

The human element of Garrett comes out from time to time, and he put it on display during this Friday night in New York. No, it's unlikely his players could possibly feel the connection he has to the city and the 9–11 tragedy, but that wasn't his point.

On this night, Garrett wanted his team to realize that it's not about physical things or surroundings, but rather the people. He didn't want them to play for money or play for accomplishment. He wanted them to play for each other.

Clearly, the head coach was pulling out all the stops here. Not only did he make a change at quarterback, but sending his entire team up a day early to experience the memorial was another way Garrett was trying to motivate his troops.

And for a while on Sunday afternoon, it seemed to work. The offense was a bit more productive behind Matt Cassel, but not appreciably better. Joseph Randle ripped off two impressive rushes for twenty-four yards before suffering what appeared to be a rib injury, prompting the running back to take himself out of the game. Surprisingly enough, while the initial issue didn't seem to be that serious, Randle never returned.

Not then, not ever.

The Cowboys didn't miss him, though, as Darren McFadden not only took over, but with a blend of speed and power, showed some glimpses of last year's sensational season by DeMarco Murray. McFadden went for 152 yards rushing, but still the offense was showing its warts.

Cassel threw three interceptions, including one returned for a touchdown in the second half. Still, the veteran managed to tie the game midway through the fourth quarter on a pass in the end zone to a diving Devin Street, evening the score at twenty.

Unfortunately, the game stayed tied for only about twelve seconds. That's how long it took for former Cowboys' return specialist, Dwayne Harris, to show his old squad why they should've re-signed him in free agency just a few months earlier. Harris was a do-it-all special teams ace who could return kicks, cover kicks, and even play wide receiver on offense. Instead, Dallas decided to keep Cole Beasley, giving him a contract worth $3.4 million per season. Beasley's rapport with Tony Romo was well documented, but with the starting quarterback out, Beasley's numbers had dipped in 2015.

Enacting his revenge, Harris broke the game open with a 100-yard kickoff return for what proved to be the winning touchdown.

This Cowboys defense, which had stopped quarterback Eli Manning and his Giants all night, now saw their efforts wasted by a special teams gaffe. That didn't sit well with many of the club's defensive players, yet only Greg Hardy actually said something, walking into the Cowboys' special teams huddle as they prepared for the ensuing kickoff return.

With fire in his eyes, Hardy exploded, trying to encourage the unit to perhaps return the favor. But the intrusion wasn't welcomed, especially considering that he had approached players who were still pissed off after allowing a touchdown.

Special teams coach, Rich Bisaccia, isn't the biggest of men, standing only around 5–7, but he's afraid of no one. He told the 6–4 Hardy in no uncertain terms to get out of his huddle, prompting Hardy to slap a clipboard out of the coach's hands.

That's when Dez Bryant, who was missing his fifth straight game with a foot injury, tried to intervene and hold Hardy back. In reality, it was two aggressive, animated players in each other's face, trying to out-yell the other one to get a point across. But it came across on television as another heated and embarrassing incident for two players who looked like they were fighting.

What the Fox TV cameras didn't see, however, was Hardy approaching Bryant just a few minutes later with a slap on the back, gesturing a thank you for helping him avoid an even bigger media firestorm.

Most importantly, of course, the Cowboys couldn't overcome the late touchdown. The offense turned the ball over on downs in the final two minutes and then Beasley fumbled away a punt, adding salt to the wound for Cowboys fans, who had to be wondering just why the team chose to keep Beasley over Harris back in the off-season.

When the game ended, Garrett shook hands with Giants head coach,

Tom Coughlin, at midfield, but had little interest in meeting with anyone else. Head down, stone-faced as usual, Garrett made the slow, methodical walk to the team's dressing room.

He had switched quarterbacks. He had altered the travel routine. He had tried to inspire his players with a message about team, unity, and an importance of purpose.

Nothing was working, the Cowboys having just lost their fourth straight game. But what Garrett couldn't fathom was that before things would get better, they were going to get much worse.

Chapter 10

COMING UP SHORT

Friday

Rest can be nurturing for the body and mind. But after too much time away from their craft, even football players and coaches can get a little stir crazy.

That's why when Jaydon McCullough was informed on Sunday evening, October 25, that his next game would be moved up from Friday to Thursday due to weather concerns, it didn't faze him much. In fact, the ever-intense, ready-to-battle head coach actually preferred the schedule change.

"Our kids need to get back out there," McCullough said. "We've had a week off. We're rested. We didn't mind the move."

Now, had the Wildcats not had a bye week leading up to this change, and/or been fighting for a playoff spot, his mindset might have been different. Regardless, the change in schedule called for an altered practice regimen, speeding up the preparation process and cutting into some of the team's workout time.

But there was another change on the practice field that week, and for the players, it was music to their ears. Literally.

The Plano coaching staff pumped music through the speakers of the indoor facility in attempt to lighten the mood during practice and possibly break up the monotony of normal sessions that include nothing but whistles, coach-speak, and regular player chatter.

While the tunes didn't drown out the coaches entirely, the range of music, which was handled by Chris Fisher, gave the players a chance to get back into the groove, so to speak.

Fisher is an extreme music buff with an uncanny ability to recite a wide range of lyrics—from Merle Haggard and Willie Nelson of the country western era long before he was born in 1975, to Tupac Shakur and Snoop Dogg from his high school and college days, to even today's teenybopper hits from Justin Bieber and Taylor Swift. The latter might have something to do with him having three daughters, but without question, Fisher was the right coach for the task, as he controlled the music using the hundreds of songs in his iPod.

"I make sure we've got the clean versions out there, of course," Fisher said. "But, we mix it up. A lot of the guys like rap, but I'll throw in some 1980s hair band groups like Def Leppard and Van Halen. The kids give some weird looks to the eighties stuff, but the coaches love it. And really, it's a great bond sometimes between the players and coaches."

Nonetheless, the players welcomed the change, and according to the coaches, they had crisp, intense practices that week. Some of the assistants were fearful the music might be more of a distraction, but in this case, it had the opposite effect.

Even twenty years ago, changes to a football schedule just four days before would have been more difficult to announce. Before the Internet and long before social media, the simple method of "word of mouth" might not have been enough to spread the message that a game was being moved up one day.

In today's world of cell phones, text messages, Twitter, and Facebook, such scheduling changes can be posted in minutes. That's why the stands on Plano's visiting side looked as strong as ever, despite the recent change, playing on a school night, and the team's elimination from playoff contention.

Then again, this is Plano, where the Wildcats have been the fan favorite since 1900, when the first official high school team was formed in the city.

In fact, Plano had just as many, if not slightly more, fans than the home squad of Edward S. Marcus High School in Flower Mound, another area suburb, which not only owned an 8–1 record, but was playing its last regular-season game, having a bye week the following Friday. That meant it was also senior night on the other side. Still, the Wildcats' contingent of fans made the trek over from Plano, hopeful for an upset.

Running back Lopaka Yoro, who stands exactly five feet tall, certainly doesn't have big feet. But before the game, he had a rather big problem as he got to the visiting locker room and realized his cleats weren't in his equipment bag.

Quickly, he got on the phone to catch his parents before they made the 30- to 45-minute drive over, hopeful they could bring him a pair of size seven cleats for the game. Now, the team will have extra pairs of shoes for situations like this, but just not in Yoro's size.

About an hour before kickoff, the running back was nervously awaiting his parents' arrival when he spotted a pair of shoes sitting inside the locker that he was temporarily using. For most high school games, the visitors dress in a locker room used by the host school's JV or freshman squads. In the same locker assigned to Yoro sat a pair of cleats, probably from one of Marcus' freshman players, and they were a size seven, fitting Yoro perfectly.

Ethically, it might not have been the right thing to do, but kickoff was just minutes away. The odds that there were shoes in this locker room at all seemed unbelievable, much less finding ones that would fit his undersized feet. Thankfully for everyone, though, Yoro's parents arrived just in time with his regular cleats, and he was able to keep the random shoes in the locker in which he found them.

Unfortunately, when the game finally started, Plano's defenders looked as if they were wearing sandals, at least in the first quarter. Despite the week off, the rejuvenated attitudes of many of the seniors and the music in practice to invigorate their spirits, the Wildcats couldn't have looked any flatter at the start of the game.

Marcus jumped on Plano with two long touchdowns early, and then pushed the lead to 21–0 before all the fans had even arrived at Marauder Stadium.

The once-enthusiastic group of youngsters, who had had so much hope and optimism earlier, now sounded more like a Sunday morning congregation at church. There was little chatter, no fire, and no intensity. With so much time remaining, the game had all the makings of the Allen debacle from five weeks earlier that ended with a 65–0 loss.

However, against Allen, the Wildcats never got Brandon Stephens into the flow of the offense. That didn't happen this time around as Plano kept feeding the ball to their workhorse running back, and before too long, the Maroon and White had made a game of it, trimming the lead to 24–10 at halftime.

Still, Jaydon McCullough wasn't happy—with anyone. Not the players, not his assistants, and not even himself. Typically, the coaches wait outside the locker room for his initial halftime meeting with the players, but McCullough purposely had all of the coaches inside the walls for this speech.

"Guys, I've failed you," McCullough said with the same passion and intensity he regularly displays on the sidelines each week. "We, as coaches, didn't get you as prepared for this game as we should have. As the head coach, I'll take responsibility for that. But we're not playing as well as we can, either. We can play better. We can coach better. And that's exactly what we're going to do in the second half."

And that's exactly what they did. Thanks to the hardnosed running of Stephens, who finished with 236 rushing yards, the Wildcats clawed all the way back. Stephens' 25-yard touchdown run with 5:15 to play tied the score, 31–31.

But Stephens never got another carry. Marcus marched the length of the field and chewed up all but twenty-six seconds of the clock before kicking a 37-yard field goal that proved to be the game winner.

As the players and coaches walked off the field, the mood was different. There certainly wasn't joy or elation, but a sense of pride and accomplishment was definitely felt.

"We're not about moral victories," McCullough said on his postgame radio show before echoing similar words to his players. "But, I'm proud of the way they fought. Proud of the way they battled to the end. We played a very good team tonight and had our chances to win. We came up short, but I think we took a big step in the right direction."

Of course, this is the same guy who keeps a photo of himself with the Wildcats' three state championship–winning head coaches on a wall above his desk. It's not just a cool photo of him with Gerald Brence, Tom Kimbrough, and John Clark, but also a reminder of the standard that has been set at Plano.

McCullough hopped on the bus knowing his team's 3–6 record wasn't sitting well around the community and perhaps even within the higher-ups in the district.

So what would a 3–7 final record look like if we don't win next week against Lewisville?

McCullough wasn't sure about the answer to that question. And he certainly didn't want to find out.

Saturday

Art Briles is a man of many sayings and witty catchphrases, including quite a few that he gathered while growing up, going to school, and later beginning his coaching career in West Texas.

One that he uses often is "we don't apologize for winning."

He doesn't concern himself with style points, or covering the spread, or how the game unfolded. If his team won, he's happy—end of story.

So why on the Sunday morning following a 17-point victory over Iowa State did Briles have this pit in his stomach? The same feeling he had after a loss? Baylor might have seen its 35–0 lead trimmed to just a

15-point advantage midway through the fourth quarter, but it was still a convincing win.

What had Briles sick to his stomach was the thought of losing his quarterback, Seth Russell, for the rest of the season, if not longer.

He saw the look in Russell's eyes when he came to the sideline late in the game, moments after suffering a helmet-to-helmet shot that would leave him with a serious neck injury.

"You hate to see tough players hurt," Briles said. "I know he was hurting, and you're always concerned about that. Not just as a player, but as a person."

He knew Russell was getting further tests on Sunday and there would soon be several phone calls coming his way with updated information. Briles was just hoping for good news.

Technically, Baylor was beginning a bye week, but considering the next game would be the following Thursday, it wasn't exactly a full seven-day break. By Friday, the Bears would switch their routine around, practicing on Saturday and Sunday in an attempt to simulate what a regular workweek is like for the team leading up to a game.

But that still gave Briles time to hit the recruiting trail on Sunday and Monday at the beginning of the off week. He arrived in Dallas looking to catch up with a few players who had already committed to the Bears, but were waiting until the February 3 signing day to ink the dotted line.

Before he even met with a single recruit, though, Briles got the phone call he was dreading.

Members of the Baylor medical staff informed him that his star quarterback, who was already garnering Heisman Trophy attention, had a broken bone in his neck and would be out for the remainder of the season. Russell planned on getting a second and perhaps even a third opinion, which would include a visit to Dallas himself to see Dr. Andrew Dossett, an orthopedic surgeon. But that appointment would have to wait until Monday because Dossett was one of the Cowboys' team doctors and was with the club in New York for the Sunday game against the Giants.

While news started trickling out about Russell's neck injury on Sunday, it wasn't until Tuesday when Baylor officially announced that he would need surgery to repair his damaged cervical vertebra.

"It was devastating—not for our football team, but for him," Briles said. "We're talking about a young man who has been with us for four years. He's grown up with us and has given his whole life to prepare and get ready for this opportunity to perform. He was playing well and then, all of a sudden, everything changes. I hated it for him."

When Briles returned to Waco, he immediately visited with his fallen quarterback, who was wearing a protective brace around his neck.

"I just remember his spirit," the coach said. "You're not going to find many players in that situation who have the faith and the strength he had. He just said, 'Go get 'em' and that he was going to do everything he could to come back strong."

For Baylor to move forward, it meant the reins would be temporarily passed on to Jarrett Stidham, the true freshman quarterback who had played in all seven games of the season thus far. But Stidham's talent was the real reason why Briles wasn't too concerned about a drop-off in his team's play, and not because he already had some experience under his belt.

"No, it was because he was good," Briles said. "You can play and still be bad. He was good. He's probably the smartest young quarterback I've ever had. He just understands the game, and he's got all the tools. He hadn't been playing like a freshman, so we knew once he got in there that he would be surrounded by some great players who would help him. I really wasn't concerned. You can win with him."

If there was ever a good time to lose your starting quarterback for the season and be forced to turn to a freshman, it would be during a bye week with ten days to prepare.

Stidham spent even more hours in the office of Kendal Briles, Baylor's offensive coordinator, and watched as much film as he could. He was already becoming a regular in the film room, but for this upcoming matchup he wanted to make sure he watched just about every Kansas

State game the school had played this season, as well as the Wildcats'
2014 meeting with Baylor.

"You can't be too prepared," said the nineteen-year-old. "I felt comfortable with the offense and the players around me, but I just wanted to
soak it all in."

The Bears were 7–0 and ranked number two in the country, but it
didn't take a professor to know the meat of the schedule was coming up.
A road trip to Kansas State was first before key games against Oklahoma,
Oklahoma State, Texas, and, of course, Baylor's most intense rival, TCU.

Nevertheless, Briles' team wasn't looking ahead to anyone other than
the Wildcats. The same, however, couldn't be said for the rest of the conference.

At the end of the Thursday night game in Fort Worth between Big
12 opponents TCU and West Virginia, Horned Frogs head coach, Gary
Patterson, made it clear what was on his mind after his eighth-ranked
team beat the Mountaineers, 40–10.

During the postgame handshake with West Virginia head coach,
Dana Holgorsen, who opened the dialogue with the standard, "Congrat-
ulations, coach," Patterson wasted little time in getting to the point.

"Thanks, so what do you think our chances are against Baylor?" he
asked. "What do you think?"

"You'll win," Holgorsen quickly fired back. "You're the more complete
team."

And that was it. Obviously, that was the answer Patterson wanted to
hear, especially from a coach that had just played both teams in the last
few weeks.

What it really showed was just how much Patterson was thinking
about his matchup on November 27 against the Bears, which was still
four weeks away. Some might have thought he would've asked the West
Virginia coach about Oklahoma State, a team that not only had already
faced and beaten the Mountaineers, but was the next opponent on TCU's
slate.

When asked later about his question to Holgorsen, Patterson didn't retreat, even saying he had asked other coaches the same question about Baylor earlier in the season. "You'd be surprised how much that goes on," Patterson said.

Baylor and TCU were undoubtedly on a collision course. The media had been hyping it up since last year's 61–58 thriller that saw Baylor rally from twenty-one down in the fourth quarter to win. But now it seemed apparent that at least one of the head coaches was already thinking about this year's showdown as well.

Who knows if Briles was doing the same? For now, he was just trying to get a freshman ready for another team in purple.

Sunday

In the early months of 1979, Bob Ryan at NFL Films was trying to write a unique opening for each team's highlight video of the previous season. After watching clips upon clips of the Cowboys, two things became evident to the former editor-in-chief. Not only did the Cowboys have some of the NFL's most recognizable players, but their fans extended far beyond the city limits of Dallas and even Texas.

The opening script for the Cowboys' 1978 highlight film, voiced by the legendary John Facenda, got straight to the point:

> *"They appear on television so often that their faces are as familiar to the public as presidents and movie stars. They are the Dallas Cowboys, America's Team."*

With that, the ever-popular moniker, "America's Team," was born. It wasn't created by the Cowboys, but of course the franchise didn't hide from the distinction and actually embraced it.

Nearly forty years later, the 2015 version of the Cowboys still featured two of the main aspects of the created nickname. The fans had since expanded from being national to now being global, as the Cowboys were one of the world's most popular teams with dominating fan bases in nearby countries such as Mexico and a strong presence in places like England, Brazil, and Germany as well.

As for those familiar figures, that hasn't changed either. From "Dandy" Don Meredith to Roger Staubach, Tony Dorsett, Thomas "Hollywood" Henderson, and Drew Pearson to Michael Irvin, Deion Sanders, and later Terrell Owens, the Cowboys have always had some of the most recognizable players and faces in the game.

This year's team also wasn't lacking for name power. And as the Cowboys positioned themselves for a showdown with the two-time defending NFC Champion Seahawks, a team Dallas upset a year ago up in Seattle, it was those same high-profile players garnering the headlines in the week leading up to the game.

It started the Sunday before in New York, when after a disappointing loss to the Giants, Jerry Jones, whose celebrity status outweighed all but a handful of his players, created a buzz when he called Greg Hardy "one of the real leaders" on the team. Hardy had just gotten into a sideline spat with both a coach and then teammate Dez Bryant, who was trying to corral the lightning rod. Hardy was playing in just his second game with the Cowboys after serving a 4-game suspension, and his off-the-field behavior had dominated NFL headlines for the last year.

Jones and the Cowboys had received all sorts of criticism for even signing Hardy in the first place. And just two weeks after being reinstated to the team, it was believed that Hardy showed little remorse for the actions that had caused him to be suspended, especially after his tongue-and-cheek gun reference. More recently, it looked like the Cowboys' *other* high-strung player had restrained Hardy from violent behavior.

When Dez Bryant was the one trying to calm the situation, it was quite a show.

So once Jones called Hardy one of the team's "leaders," it just allowed more national media pundits to go on the attack against the Cowboys in general as well as Jones personally for enabling Hardy and giving him such as platform.

With the quote quickly spreading across the Internet, most of the media members were writing their weekly columns based on hearsay from the handful of reporters who had actually sat around Jones when he made the statement. And yes, the owner had called Hardy a "leader," but the context wasn't as generic as the quote was portrayed.

The actual question centered on Hardy's practice habits and his work ethic. Jones called him one of the leaders because when it came to setting the right kind of tempo in practice, Hardy did, in fact, lead by example. For the most part, that clarification was never mentioned, and Jones to this day still gets heat for calling one of his more controversial players a team leader.

But by Wednesday of that week, Hardy's outburst in the previous game or his status as one of the locker room leaders were a moot point.

True to form in the life of the Dallas Cowboys, another storyline had trumped Hardy's news. Running back Joseph Randle, who had injured his midsection during the loss to the Giants, only to watch Darren McFadden step in and rush for 152 yards, was still nursing the injury heading into the Seattle game. While his status for the Sunday showdown was unclear, his role on the depth chart was more definite.

Even though Jason Garrett had said in his press conference that McFadden "absolutely" earned more carries and would get more touches in the game, and Jerry Jones had also said on his radio show that McFadden would likely start, the news didn't sit well with Randle once it became official. In fact, after the coaches informed him that McFadden would take over as the starter, Randle took off.

He stormed out of the Cowboys' practice facility at Valley Ranch, sending team officials scurrying to locate him. For about thirty minutes, Randle wasn't responding to calls or texts, including some left by Bryant, a "big brother" to Randle considering that they both had gone to Oklahoma State and actually had worn the same number 1 jersey for the Orange and Black.

Randle never came back to the facility that Wednesday, but did return the next day for treatment and a few closed-door meetings, one of which was with Jason Garrett. This wasn't the first time in even recent history that a player had left the complex after learning of his demotion. Cornerback Morris Claiborne made a similar exit back in 2014 when Orlando Scandrick replaced him as the starter.

Like Randle, Claiborne came back the next day. But unlike Randle, Claiborne would eventually get back in the good graces of the coaching staff and play again.

Randle's season, and life, was spiraling downward. And ironically, it was all occurring just two weeks after he returned from a bye week where he said he gained a "new perspective on life" after watching his eleven-year-old nephew play running back in his home state of Kansas. Randle said watching that game helped him realize not only his "love for the game," but also how much of a "blessing it is to be playing for the NFL, with so many kids looking up to me."

Now, things were fading fast for Randle, and there was nothing he could do about it.

Meanwhile, the defending NFC champions were coming to town. There weren't many NFL cities in 2015 where playing the Seahawks was secondary news, but with the Hardy and Randle situations, plus the return to action of Bryant after he missed six games due to injury, the actual matchup with Seattle wasn't the biggest storyline.

That might have been because the Seahawks were also struggling somewhat. With a 3–4 record, Seattle was just one game ahead of the Cowboys, who had now lost four straight games after a 2–0 start.

During the pregame warm-ups, Bryant was shown on the Cowboys' gigantic video board several times, and whether he was running a route, catching a pass, or singing along with the music in the stadium, the roar of the crowd was deafening each and every time they saw him. This team and this fan base had missed Bryant's passion, his energy, and his play on the field.

But the ones who expected Bryant to simply return as the dominating receiver who set a franchise record with sixteen touchdown catches in 2014 were vastly disappointed. Bryant's rust was apparent, although it didn't help that he also had to face Seattle's All-Pro cornerback, Richard Sherman.

The Cowboys struggled to move the ball all game long, but the only reason they weren't blown out was because of their own tenacious defense. Dallas was flying around the ball defensively, which was only fitting considering the team was honoring former safety Darren Woodson at halftime of the game.

Woodson became the twenty-first member of the illustrious Ring of Honor, which is the Cowboys' Hall of Fame, an exclusive group led by a one-man committee of Jerry Jones. Woodson was a quiet, but always steady defensive force for the 1990s teams that featured Emmitt Smith, Troy Aikman, Michael Irvin, and a dominating offensive line.

One of the hardest-hitting players in Cowboys' history and the team's all-time leading tackler, Woodson no doubt appreciated what he was watching on the field as both teams were trading big hits. There was, though, a scary moment just before halftime during a special teams play when Cowboys safety Jeff Heath caught Seattle receiver Ricardo Lockette with a big block that sent Lockette to the ground, where he lay motionless for about ten minutes.

Heath was flagged on the play for a blind side block, but wasn't fined later in the week after NFL officials reviewed the play. However, some of Lockette's teammates took offense and tried to come after Heath for what they perceived to be a dirty hit.

Whenever there was any confrontation, Bryant was usually in the middle of it. However, as Lockette remained on the ground, Bryant had a rather heated conversation with the officials, and the Fox TV cameras showed him mouthing the words, "that's what he gets." By the time halftime rolled around, social media had taken over. Screen shots and Vines taken off the TV screen were posted, and reposted, and quickly went viral, insinuating that Bryant was talking about Lockette, an assumption that Bryant made sure to address when the game was over.

As for the rest of the game, Hardy got himself involved in the third quarter, batting a pass from Russell Wilson up in the air and then catching it for an interception deep in Seattle territory. The play was expected to lead to a touchdown, but even with Bryant back in the lineup, quarterback Matt Cassel and the offense couldn't find the end zone against the always-stingy Seattle defense.

Still, the Cowboys managed four field goals from kicker Dan Bailey, which late in the fourth quarter was enough for a 12–10 lead. But in the end, Wilson showed some poise and calmly drove the Seahawks into field goal range for a game-winning kick, giving Seattle the 13–12 victory.

No matter if the Cowboys hung in there longer than the experts predicted. No matter if the defense turned in one of its best games of the season. The bottom line was simple: this once 2–0 football team was now 2–5 and had two more games remaining before their starting quarterback, Tony Romo, could return.

The frustration was felt in the locker room afterward. Just a week after he had played peacemaker on the sidelines with Hardy and the special teams huddle, and a few days after he had tried to convince Randle to get to the facility after storming out, Bryant now took his turn to go off.

This time, the media got the wrath, although the person who initially put the Vine video together was a Fox TV reporter from another city.

By the time Bryant was back in the locker room, obviously frustrated with another loss and catching just two passes for twelve yards, the receiver chastised the reporters for wrongly accusing him of "trash talking" Lockette, when he was actually talking to the referees, which isn't exactly a preferred practice either.

"I won't ever, ever, ever, ever wish bad on a player that's been knocked down," Bryant yelled, standing near his locker deep within the bowels of AT&T Stadium. "C'mon man. Stop with the bullshit. Don't put clips together and do that. (The conversation) didn't have nothing to do with (Lockette). I swear on my daughter's soul I would never in my life do that to anybody."

Bryant's rant was genuine and certainly believable. Again, he was just talking to the wrong group because these reporters were mainly standing around his locker room trying to ask him about returning to the field for the first time in six weeks, not something that was floating around the Internet.

Unfortunately for many of those media members, it wouldn't be the last time—that month—they'd get caught in the middle of a Bryant rant.

Chapter 11
HELLO & GOODBYE

Friday

In high school football, especially in Texas, there is no such thing as coasting to the end of a season—at least not in the mind of a football coach.

For 355 days in each year, there are countless hours of preparation, meeting, strategizing, practicing, and training that all leads to ten Friday nights of action. And if they're fortunate, some teams get to do it for a few more weeks in the playoffs.

But if nothing else, everyone is guaranteed ten games, and even if the postseason is not an option, a football coach will make sure his team doesn't take its foot off the gas for any reason.

No, Plano wasn't headed to the playoffs, but rest assured, its coaching staff spent just as much time, if not more, getting ready for its Week 10 showdown against Lewisville High School.

Sure, other teams might have been playing for a spot in the postseason, or perhaps even a district title. For those on the Plano staff, they were coaching for their jobs.

On the Saturday morning before the final week of the season, in their regular meeting held at the high school, Jaydon McCullough didn't sugarcoat the situation. Maybe the head coach was going off a real conversation he had with Plano athletic officials at the district, or perhaps he was just sensing a vibe. There was even a possibility he was just trying to use a scare tactic on his coaches that he hoped might trickle down to the players.

In any sense, McCullough told his staff that the Wildcats needed to win their final game of the season.

Or else? Well, that's the tricky part, especially with high school coaches who are considered teachers first. In fact, the high school level is actually somewhat opposite of the college and professional ranks, where the guys on the bottom of the totem pole are safer than the ones at the top.

At most high schools, including Plano, the head coach's contract is tied in with the offensive and defensive coordinators. So if a school district decides to remove its head coach, the OC and DC can be out as well. But the other coaches have teaching jobs either at the school or nearby elementary and middle schools, making it more difficult to remove them.

However, with a new head coach, nothing would be guaranteed. Those on the staff might not lose their jobs as teachers, but could be reassigned as varsity coaches.

Needless to say, this next matchup against Lewisville was vital for the Wildcats coaches, not to mention the seniors, who had all week to prepare for their last high school game. And for all but maybe a handful, this would be the final football game of their lives.

While many of the seniors probably would've preferred their final game be held at John Clark Stadium in Plano, where they'd played the majority of their home outings over the years, running back Brandon Stephens didn't seem to mind the game being played just down the road at Tom Kimbrough Stadium.

There are times when each of the three district schools—Plano East, Plano West, and Plano—must travel about fifteen miles north to Kimbrough, which is actually in Murphy, Texas. Stephens, though, saw the irony in the fact that unlike many of his fellow seniors, he actually suited up as a freshman in the 2012 season opener, which just so happened to be against Lewisville. Oh, and it was played at Kimbrough as well.

"For me to start and finish my career against the same team, and in the same stadium, was pretty neat," Stephens said. "I remember I had some good runs in that first game."

Stephens would have even more in his last one.

As the players rolled up to the stadium, the reality of playing their final game in a Wildcats uniform was starting to sink in. Quarterback Matt Keys admitted his senior year was a rollercoaster of emotions that went from him at first thinking he might land a football scholarship to eventually calling a loss to Plano West the worst night of his life. That defeat, coupled with concerns that his wrist could be broken, had him briefly wanting the season to be over.

But with his high school career coming closer to its end, Keys spent the bus ride to the stadium and part of the pregame warm-ups just trying to reflect on his entire journey—from playing on the freshman team to breaking his collarbone in a scrimmage just before his junior year to then this entire season, which had been an unpredictable ride of ups and downs along with the disappointing reality of missing the playoffs.

As game time approached, however, he set all that aside. Keys went around to just about every player he could find, whether they were seniors or maybe even a freshman who had just been moved up to varsity, and told them to make this last one count.

A senior tradition at Plano, and most high schools for that matter, is to introduce every player who is suiting up for his final home game. A few minutes before kickoff, the nearly thirty seniors lined up single-file in the south end zone with Chris Fisher standing nearby, waiting to greet them.

Fisher didn't have the title of coordinator, but when it came to moments like this, he was certainly the right person for the job. The players had always related to "Coach Fish" as someone who not only had been in their shoes, having played high-level high school football and even a couple of seasons in college, but also as a rather hip, down-to-earth thirty-nine-year-old with probably more rap songs on his iPod than many of his students realized.

To each of the seniors, Fisher gave his own quick, personal message. For the defensive guys he coached, particularly defensive backs such as T.J. Lee, he might have held them a bit longer or tighter before a final pat on the back as they headed through the line of cheerleaders and drill team members, where Jaydon McCullough was waiting on the other end to give his own words.

Between Coach Fish and Coach McCullough, the seniors were given a final emotional send-off before going to battle one last time.

With the players lining up in numerical order, Stephens stood first, donning his 2 jersey, which he had switched to after wearing 33 during his freshman year. Stephens was met by Fisher, who gave him a strong hug with a couple of helmet slaps before telling him he was a great player and an even better young man.

Stephens went through the line and got to McCullough, who told him something he won't ever forget.

"He just said, 'I love you,'" Stephens recalled. "That meant a lot to me. He didn't have a lot of time to say anything, but he said that, and I knew he really meant it."

Stephens jogged toward the sideline where the underclassmen were waiting. Not far behind him was 28. Matt Keys shared a quick hug with Fisher, who had always admired the quarterback's toughness and grit; but like Stephens, Keys mostly remembered meeting up with McCullough at the end of the line.

"It all worked out, didn't it, Matt?"

"Yes, sir, Coach."

But honestly, Keys didn't know what he meant at first.

"At first I was like, 'We're 3–6, Coach. How did it work out?'" Keys said. "But now I know what he meant. He was talking about all of it. From when I was a skinny freshman to a sophomore killing it on JV and then moving up to varsity. I broke my collarbone in a scrimmage where the quarterbacks aren't supposed to get hit and missed my junior year, and then came back this year and learned from the experiences. All the lessons I'll take away from having to bounce back after a loss and sticking it out with the guys even though we were hurting, that's really what Coach meant. I appreciate him for saying that.

"I really love Coach McCullough because he gets more out of seeing the men he coaches become something and watching them grow than he does watching them win. And if you're going to coach high school, that's the way it should be."

Coaches aren't supposed to have favorites, and if they do, they're not supposed to admit it. But in 2015, Fisher had no problem revealing his true feelings.

Darion Foster, wearing 35, was not only Fisher's favorite player on this team, but was in reality his favorite player of any team he had ever coached.

As Darion made his way up to the front of the line, he knew it was going to be hard to see his uncle. For a moment, Fisher lost track of the numbers, trying to give each kid a proper and genuine send-off. As he gave a strong hug and backslap to 33, Thimayya Washington, Fisher turned back toward the line and stretched out his hand to grab the next guy.

The next guy was Darion. The baby-faced nephew who he affectionately called "numb-nuts" for years was no longer the skinny ball boy running on the sidelines. He wasn't that late-blossoming teenager who had yet to grow into his body. As he stood before him, Fisher saw a man, one who grew up under his roof.

Fisher's tongue came out in an attempt to keep from crying. He then grabbed Darion by the neck, put his face right by his ear, and gave him five seconds that his nephew won't ever forget.

"This is your time. Show 'em what you can do tonight! Go out there and play your fucking heart out. I love you!"

Plano coaches don't cuss on the football field. It's more than just frowned upon. It's simply not allowed, especially toward the kids. But there are always exceptions, and in this case, Fisher wasn't talking to *any* player. At that point in time, he wasn't talking to Darion Foster, the football player, or even his nephew. That was his son, the son that he and his wife, Janna, helped to raise.

Fisher held on to Darion a bit longer than the other players and actually walked a few yards with him before finally letting him go. With that, he turned back around, put his hand out, and greeted the next senior.

Yes, the emotions were running high. And not a single snap had been played.

Once the game began, the coaches were pleased to learn that their pregame scouting reports were indeed correct—their team was better. That statement couldn't be made often in 2015, but against the Farmers of Lewisville, Plano had more skill and, frankly, just more passion and excitement.

The Wildcats pulled away in the fourth quarter, thanks in large part to Stephens, who looked every bit like the player headed to the Pac-12. Just as he did a week earlier against Flower Mound Marcus, the running back weaved through defenders, showing speed, power, and some open-field jukes as well.

With Plano leading 24–17 midway through the fourth quarter, Stephens took a handoff around the right side, found some daylight, and rushed thirty yards for a touchdown, not only putting the game out of reach, but also pushing him over the 200-yard plateau in his high school finale.

The score put a finishing bow on Stephens' illustrious career, one that began with a long run out of the south end zone and concluded with a touchdown jaunt into the north end zone—with an entertaining four seasons of football in between.

When Stephens returned to the sideline, his quarterback had just one word for his fellow senior.

"Stud!" Keys shouted as he affectionately punched Stephens in the chest. "Stud!"

As the minutes trickled down to seconds, it was becoming obvious that the Wildcats were going to finish the year like they started—in the victory column. What happened throughout the course of the season seemed irrelevant in the final seconds. In fact, any focus on the past was replaced by perhaps a glimpse of the future.

Freshman tailback Kyron Cumby entered the game in the final minutes and dashed through the middle of Lewisville's defense for a 31-yard touchdown run that sent the entire bench into a frenzy, as if the game were on the line. Cumby had been dazzling all year on Plano's tenth grade squad, and it was only a matter of time before he got his chance to shine with the varsity.

With one run in the final game of the season, it felt like a true passing of the torch from Stephens to Cumby.

Not every player was on the sideline cheering, though. Keys didn't wait until the end of the game to find his family. While he would've liked to take the last snap, he was fine with the backup getting a couple of reps. Plus, it gave Keys a chance to share an emotional hug with his parents, in particular, his mother.

With tears rolling down their cheeks, the moment was one of joy and a little relief. Keys had the picture of him hugging his mother on the sideline framed and gave it to her for Christmas some eight weeks later.

Just like McCullough told him before the game—it all worked out.

And not just for Keys, but the entire Wildcats team, which wrapped up the season on a triumphant note. At Plano, winning the final game is expected to mean winning the state title, something that had happened seven times in the school's past.

But judging from the smiles, the hugs, the tears, and the pure joy that encompassed everyone that poured onto the field after the game, Plano celebrated like it was indeed a championship.

Obviously, this town knew the difference between being the best in the state and a 4–6 record. But 2015 was a journey, a topsy-turvy one that had its share of potholes as well as twists and turns. In the end, the Plano Wildcats survived and made it to the finish line.

"This is what high school football is all about," McCullough said, as he hugged his wife and friends.

The Plano Senior High Wildcats have won seven state championships and are always hungry for that eighth title. *(Photo by Big Lou Goodrum)*

Despite an unproven quarterback in Seth Russell (17), Baylor still had high hopes for 2015 after producing forty wins in the previous four years. *(Photo courtesy of the Dallas Cowboys)*

After nearly advancing to the NFC Championship in 2014, the Cowboys had no reason to think they couldn't and wouldn't take the next step in 2015. *(L to R: Jason Witten, Terrance Williams and Darren McFadden; Photo courtesy of the Dallas Cowboys / Jeremiah Jhass)*

When it rained, it certainly poured on both Tony Romo and the Cowboys in 2015, both literally and figuratively. *(Photo courtesy of the Dallas Cowboys / Jeremiah Jhass)*

The Wildcats get ready for the season-opening kickoff against Tyler John Tyler at John Clark Stadium. *(Photo by Big Lou Goodrum)*

r_andon Stephens _cored a touchdown _n his first carry of his _enior season, leading _he Wildcats past John _yler. *(Photo by Big Lou _oodrum)*

After his first win as Plano's starting quarterback in the season opener, Matt Keys (28) was able to celebrate with his fellow teammates. *(Photo by Big Lou Goodrum)*

K.D. Cannon makes a juggling touchdown catch in the first quarter of a blowout win over Texas Tech a AT&T Stadium. *(Photo courtesy of the Dallas Cowboys)*

Easily the biggest tight end in the country, 400-pound LaQuan McGowan (80) caught a couple of touchdowns during the season but was used mostly as a blocker. *(Photo courtesy of the Dallas Cowboys)*

Johnny Jefferson an the Baylor offense had plenty of clear paths to the end zone in a 66-7 win over Kansas. *(Photo courtesy of Baylor Athletics.)*

At AT&T Stadium, Dez Bryant and his teammates are met by adoring Cowboys fans long before they ever make it to the field. *(Photo courtesy the Dallas Cowboys / Jeremiah Jhass)*

For entirely different reasons, neither Tony Romo nor Joseph Randle took as many snaps as expected before the season began. *(Photo courtesy the Dallas Cowboys / Jeremiah Jhass)*

For the second time of the season, Romo went down with a broken clavicle in the Thanksgiving Day loss to the Panthers, and this time, didn't come back. *(Photo courtesy the Dallas Cowboys / Jeremiah Jhass)*

Jaydon McCullough played for Plano Senior High in the early 1980s, won a state championship ring as an assistant, and now looks to guide the Wildcats to another state crown. *(Photo by Big Lou Goodrum)*

In what would become his final game at Baylor, Art Briles and his staff put together an impressive game plan in the Russell Athletic Bowl win over North Carolina. *(Photo courtesy of Baylor Athletics)*

Jason Garrett, who trails only Tom Landry for regular-season victories in franchise history, is the only former Cowboy player to become head coach of the team. *(Photo courtesy the Dallas Cowboys / Jeremiah Jhass)*

ano students always
nite on Friday nights,
it for this October
me, they show their
ie colors in support
Breast Cancer
vareness Month.
hoto by Big Lou
oodrum)

Brandon Stephens more than just carried the flag out before Plano games; the team's best player often carried the entire offense. *(Photo courtesy of the author)*

Chris Fisher joined the Plano ISD as a middle school coach in 2002 and worked his way up to being one the team's top assistants by 2015. *(Photo by Big Lou Goodrum)*

Freshman Jarrett Stidham was on his way to a career performance against undefeated Oklahom State when a foot injury wiped out his season. *(Photo courte of Baylor Athletics)*

After starting the season as a tight end, Chris Johnson stole the show in Stillwater, leading Baylor to an upset road win over the nationally ranked Cowboys. *(Photo courtesy of Baylor Athletics)*

Art Briles (wearin black) had plenty of top assistants around him, including his son Kendal (in front) and son-in-law Jef Lebby (far left). *(Photo courtesy of Baylor Athletics)*

Plano takes the field against defending champion Allen, led by seniors Darion Foster (35), Brandon Stephens (2), and Matt Keys (28). *(Photo by Big Lou Goodrum)*

A former Plano ballboy, Darion Foster (35) had a few breathtaking moments during his 2015 senior season, his first and only year on the varsity. *(Photo by Big Lou Goodrum)*

The Baylor-TCU matchup was the most anticipated game of the season, but Mother Nature had other plans, dumping buckets of rain from start to finish. *(Photo courtesy of Baylor Athletics)*

Andrew Billings (75) and his Baylor teammates had trouble getting their footing as much as corralling TCU star QB Trevone Boykin. *(Photo courtesy of Baylor Athletics)*

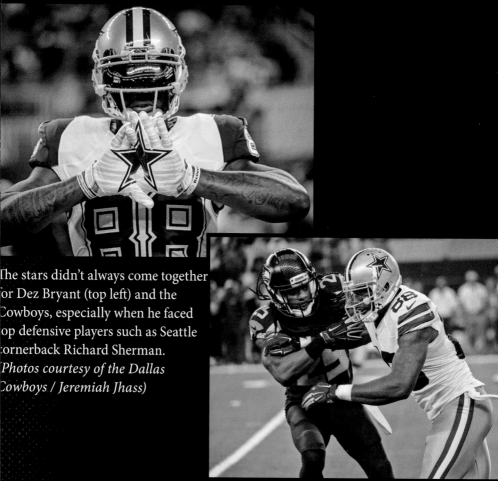

The stars didn't always come together for Dez Bryant (top left) and the Cowboys, especially when he faced top defensive players such as Seattle cornerback Richard Sherman. *(Photos courtesy of the Dallas Cowboys / Jeremiah Jhass)*

Veterans such as Jason Witten get ready for the Thanksgiving Day matchup against the undefeated Carolina Panthers at AT&T Stadium. *(Photo courtesy of the Dallas Cowboys/Jeremiah*

Chris Fisher, a defensive back in his playing days, still celebrates all interceptions with his players. (Photo by Bruce Walpole)

Chris Fisher was more than just a live-in uncle to Darion Foster (35). (Photo courtesy of Fisher family.)

In a surprise move, Brandon Stephens picked UCLA on National Signing Day (Photo by Big Lou Goodrum)

The excitement of Friday night is never higher than minutes before kickoff when the Wildcats are about to take the field. (Photo courtesy of the autho

Seth Russell and Johnny Jefferson had no problems carving up Texas Tech in a game played at the Cowboys' house of AT&T Stadium. *(Photo courtesy of Baylor Athletics)*

..D. Cannon and his
ellow receivers played
 huge role in leading
 aylor past West
 irginia, avenging
 heir only 2014 regular-
 eason loss. *(Photo
 ourtesy of Baylor
 thletics)*

By the time the Cowboys made it to historic Lambeau Field in mid-December, chances of making the playoffs were more than slim. *(Photo courtesy of the Dallas Cowboys/ Jeremiah Jhass)*

Plano had no answers for rival Allen, who dominated early and often and handed the Wildcats a demoralizing 65-0 defeat. *(Photo by Big Lou Goodrum)*

Battered and bruised all season, Plano quarterback Matt Keys called losing to Plano West "the worst night of his life." *(Photo by Big Lou Goodrum)*

Brandon Stephens could barely move after missing a game-tying pass in the final seconds against rival Plano West. *(Photo by Big Lou Goodrum)*

Down three quarterbacks, all Baylor could do in the Russell Athletic Bowl was run the ball. And they did just that, thanks to help from "snap-catchers" such as Devin Chafin. *(Photo courtesy of Baylor Athletics)*

The hero of the night in Orlando was Johnny Jefferson, who ran for a Baylor bowl record 299 yards, giving him an even 1,000 for the season. *(Photo courtesy of Baylor Athletics)*

Chris Fisher conducts his first intra-squad scrimmage as the new head coach of his alma mater, Palo Duro High School in Amarillo, Texas. *(Photo courtesy of the Fisher family)*

Despite the unexpected turn of events in the offseason, Baylor Nation will remain united, eager to stay near the top of the college football mountain. *(Photo courtesy of Baylor Athletics)*

The Cowboys never saw a 4-12 season coming but that will only force the team to stick closer together for the 2016 season. *(Photo courtesy of the Dallas Cowboys / Jeremiah Jhass)*

Doing interviews after the game is customary, but the head coach wasn't real interested this time around. This was a moment for his staff, his players, and his community. He was soaking it all in.

As was Darion, whose mother, Heather, had made the trek down from Amarillo along with about twenty-five of his family members. With tears rolling down his cheeks, Darion stood there and took picture after picture with different family members who wanted to share in the moment. Some of the shots included Coach Fisher, who himself was in a blur, having a hard time realizing he wouldn't be coaching his nephew anymore.

The two hugged again on the field, both telling how much they loved each other.

When the team finally made it to the locker room, McCullough thanked the players and the coaches for their efforts, not just in the game but throughout the entire year.

"I don't care if the season is over or not," he told them. "I couldn't have been any prouder of a group of young men than I am of you guys. You never stopped fighting. You never quit. And that's all we can ever ask from you."

As Fisher walked toward the bus to head back to the school, he pulled out his phone, which now had about fifty more photos on it from the postgame celebration. But he went to Twitter to check in on other high schools, most notably his own alma mater. He knew coming into the game that Palo Duro High School in Amarillo was 0–9, but was ecstatic to see that his Dons had avoided the goose egg and picked up a victory, beating Hereford High School to finish 1–9.

A few tweets later, he also learned that Palo Duro head coach, Steve Parr, had told his players after the game that he would be retiring after thirteen seasons at the helm.

To Fisher, this wasn't just any job, but *the* job he had always dreamed of having. When he decided to get into coaching just two years removed from his business degree, Fisher told his close friends that he aspired to become the head coach of Palo Duro High School one day.

Since then, the position had only been open once, and Fisher wasn't even a varsity coach at the time. But now the job was about to become available again, and this time he knew he was prepared to go for it.

As he rode back to the school, Fisher was surrounded by players who knew they had just played their last game for Plano.

He could only wonder if he had coached his final one for the Wildcats as well.

Saturday

There are nineteen Greek fraternities on the campus at Baylor. Most of the football players just consider the team as their own frat, but some have joined outside groups.

Quarterback Seth Russell wasn't officially in a fraternity, but lying in a hospital bed at the West Virginia Spine Center, the junior realized he had a strong group of brothers surrounding him, watching over him and caring for him. And some of them didn't even attend the school anymore.

Just days after undergoing successful surgery on his neck, Russell was more than a little surprised to see former Baylor quarterback Robert Griffin III, the 2011 Heisman Trophy winner and then-quarterback of the Redskins, pay him a visit during Washington's bye week.

Russell enrolled at Baylor in the fall of 2012, the same time Griffin was beginning his rookie season in the NFL. While they were never teammates, Russell and Griffin had met on several occasions when the former All-American returned to Waco in the off-season for workouts or made sideline visits at Bears games when his schedule allowed.

More than anything, they both played quarterback at Baylor. Because of that, they would always be fraternity brothers.

"He was such a warrior through the entire process," Griffin said. "He kept his faith the entire time. I'm just glad I could be there for him."

Meanwhile, the Bears were in the process of initiating a new quarterback into the exclusive club as freshman Jarrett Stidham prepared for his first career start in what was expected to be the toughest test on Baylor's schedule to date. After winning seven games by an average margin of thirty-six points per contest, the Bears now had to travel to usually hostile Kansas State, a place where in 2013, their last visit to Manhattan, Kansas, they'd won for the first time in school history. But even that game forced Baylor to rally in the fourth quarter for a 10-point victory, 35–25.

This Thursday night matchup, televised as the featured game on ESPN, called for some changes in the travel schedule, as it was one of the rare occasions during the school year when the football players had to miss class. In other sports, particularly basketball and baseball, Baylor student-athletes miss class regularly due to midweek games and long road trips to places such as Morgantown, West Virginia, and Ames, Iowa. But the flight to Manhattan was only a little more than an hour for the Bears, who left at 3 p.m. on Wednesday.

When they arrived at their hotel around 6 p.m., they were greeted with welcome signs, green and gold balloons, and a few dozen fans, mostly players' parents who had made the trip to see the game.

Following a team meeting and then brief sessions with each position group and its coach, the players headed to dinner, a prepared meal in one of the larger ballrooms. After that, many players were free for the next few hours before a 10:30 p.m. bed check. If they had family in town, it was a good time to visit, while others just hung out with teammates in one of the hotel rooms and listened to music or watched TV to pass the time.

It wasn't as much fun, though, for a handful of student-athletes who had to be reminded about the "student" part of the equation. As it was a Wednesday night, ten players had to take tests for classes they either had missed that day or for which they would be absent Thursday morning. Baylor travels with a rather large support staff, but particularly so when games fall during the week and extra administrators are needed for schoolwork. A separate meeting room in the hotel had been cleared just for test-taking purposes.

"Gotta hit those books!" junior defensive back Patrick Levels said as he rushed down from his hotel room and into the makeshift classroom.

The players had about an hour to get their work done, although there would be even more time Thursday morning before they had to prepare for that night's game.

Just outside the room, a group of Baylor fans were meeting with some of the players. Among them was Stidham, who didn't look like a freshman about to make his first start—on national television, no less. Even though he was in Manhattan, Kansas, or the "Little Apple" as they call it in the Midwest town, Stidham was feeling right at home, especially after he saw a couple of familiar faces from where he grew up in Stephenville, Texas.

Brothers Matt and Mitch Copeland had known Stidham nearly his entire life, as their father, Mike, has been a longtime football coach on the Stephenville staff. But the Copelands weren't just there to support Stidham. They were even closer to the Briles family. Both Matt and Mitch played for Art at Stephenville. Matt was Briles' first quarterback for the Yellow Jackets while Mitch won two state titles in 1993 and 1994, and was considered one of the best defensive players ever to suit up for Stephenville. Mike had been the defensive coordinator for all twelve of Briles' seasons in Stephenville and had been on the sidelines with the Yellow Jackets in some capacity for forty years.

The owners of a highly successful apparel franchise, Barefoot Athletics, which originated in Stephenville but had since branched out to several college cities, Matt and Mitch were actually visiting both the University of Missouri and the University of Kansas the day before, and couldn't believe it worked out so perfectly to come back through Manhattan for this game.

Also in attendance was past NFL starter and another standout Yellow Jacket quarterback, Kevin Kolb, who brought his entire family along for the game. Like the Copelands, he was also a Briles supporter, having played four years for him at the University of Houston.

With three former Stephenville passers all huddled around a table, the talk shifted to a friendly debate on who was the best quarterback in the school's history. Different answers were offered, but it was believed by more than a couple that the best of the best was actually Kendal Briles, the Bears' offensive coordinator who also led Stephenville to a state championship in 1999.

These discussions helped take Stidham's mind off the upcoming game. Before he headed up to his hotel room, he was asking friends and other Baylor staff members for a good movie recommendation before he went to bed. He'd been studying Kansas State's defense religiously for nearly two weeks now, so it was time for a change. He decided on the 1997 film *Good Will Hunting,* featuring Matt Damon and Robin Williams. After saying goodbye to his hometown friends, he tucked his iPad under his arm and went upstairs.

"He's ready," Kolb said with a confident head nod. "This kid is special. He'll show everyone tomorrow night."

The next morning before the game, as the buses loaded up in the parking lot of the hotel, the operations staff in charge of the itinerary couldn't stress enough the importance of getting there early. If they knew anything about Briles, it was that he had never been described as the most patient of human beings. When it was time to go, it was time to go, even if it was a few minutes before the scheduled departure.

Once during a road trip to the University of Texas-El Paso, while Briles was still the head coach at Houston, after all of the players had boarded the buses at the hotel, the head coach told the driver, "Let's go," even after being informed that three others hadn't made it on just yet. "That's fine. We need to go."

As for his wife, Jan, and daughters, Jancy and Staley—they were left to take a cab to the game instead.

That story seemingly got told every road trip, and so no one usually even came close to missing a bus on game day. As the team rolled into Bill Snyder Family Stadium, Briles was stopped by an ESPN reporter for a quick interview that made it on *SportsCenter* before the game. One of the first questions he was asked concerned Stidham and how the coach expected him to play.

"Well, we'll see when he gets out there, but we have confidence in him," Briles said. "He's just good. He's prepared. I think he's ready. But, we're about to find out."

Just before kickoff, the Bears ran out of the tunnel to their sideline and were met by thousands of raucous KSU students who were positioned just behind the bench. In the first row, one fan was rather proud of his homemade sign that read "Baylor Traded its Integrity For Victories," an obvious reference to the story back in August that had put the school and Briles under fire. But the sign also acknowledged the Bears' sudden success, and when a few of the offensive linemen gazed up, one of them yelled back.

"Yeah, and we're going to get another one of the victories right here."

All they needed was for Stidham to keep the train on the tracks. Just before taking the field for his first snap, Briles leaned in with one last word of encouragement.

"Hey, go show the world what we already know."

On the first drive, it couldn't have gone any better, thanks to the play calling. All three of Stidham's completions were short screen passes, letting the playmaking receivers and running backs do the work. But the young quarterback finished the drive by scoring on a 1-yard run for the game's first score, taking less than two minutes off the clock to gain a 7–0 lead.

"Just like that," Kendal Briles said to Stidham as he went to the sideline. "Beautiful! Now, let's do it again."

And so he did. Stidham's next pass was also a touchdown—a 55-yard strike to KD Cannon that gave Baylor a 14–7 advantage.

Midway through the second quarter, after a Baylor interception, Stidham stood on the sideline during a timeout. Showing just how loose this nineteen-year-old was, he tapped one of the Bears' administrators on the shoulder, but then slid to the side so that when she turned around, she didn't see him or anyone there. It was an elementary joke, of course, but typically didn't occur just before someone is going out to perform during a nationally televised college football game. Stidham laughed it off, buckled his chinstrap, and headed out onto the field.

On the first play of the drive, he launched a perfectly thrown ball to Corey Coleman for an 81-yard touchdown and a 21–7 lead. He might have been just a kid, but he was showing the world he was a kid with a great arm.

Baylor likely should've blown the game wide open and nearly did so early in the fourth quarter, but the offense settled for a field goal and just a 31–10 lead. That opened the door for Kansas State to score twice in the final frame, trimming the score to 31–24 with 4:07 to play.

Just like that, the game was on the line again, but in trying to protect the lead, Baylor didn't coddle its freshman quarterback. Instead, they let him do what he does best.

On first down, Stidham went to throw and fired a ball in between defenders to Cannon for a 40-yard gain. The Bears nearly scored a touchdown, but a penalty stalled the drive, and they eventually missed a field goal. Baylor would hold on after a late interception by safety Terrell Burt, escaping Manhattan with a win and giving Stidham his first victory as a starter.

As he met with reporters following the game, Stidham didn't seem concerned with his 23-of-33 passing for 419 yards, three touchdowns, and no interceptions.

"Hey, we just got the win, and that's what we came here to do," Stidham said with black smudges still on his cheeks. "Our defense got some big stops for us. I thought we moved the ball well. It was a great team win. I'm just excited to be a part of it."

When it was Briles' turn on the mic, he sat down with a little more attitude than usual, perhaps understandable considering he had just won a road conference game behind a freshman quarterback.

"I thought it was a powerful win," he said. "I don't know what anyone else thinks and don't really care, but we think we're a football team full of survivors. We've been through a lot. You can slap us around, talk bad about us, whatever you want, but when you look up here in November, we're still around. We're going to be a tough out, and we're going to fight and find a way to win."

When asked about Stidham, Briles chuckled and gave an "I-told-you-so" response.

"He played like we knew he would," Briles said. "The guy is really good. I thought he was unbelievable tonight. If you have talent, you don't need confidence. You all saw what we've been seeing. Our hearts and souls are with Seth right now. We hate that he's not with us. Seth did a great job of getting us going and putting us in position. Now it's time for Jarrett to trust his instincts and take over."

Briles showed some surliness, likely stemming from a sloppy fourth quarter that saw Kansas State rally and make it closer than it should've been. He was also looking to make a louder statement to the College Football Playoff Selection Committee that had introduced its first poll two days earlier, placing his team sixth despite a number-two ranking in the Associated Press poll.

"I still think we're the new kids on the block," Briles said. "If you're over the age of thirty, I doubt people say, 'Hey, let me tell you about the history of Baylor football.' That's just the reality. But it's our job to win. That's all we can do."

And through the first eight games of the season, that is all they had done.

Sunday

Every football coach in America, whether it's Pee Wee ball, the high school ranks, or even in the NFL, has to toe the line between success and duty.

Most coaches will admit it's their duty, or responsibility, to not only teach young men the X's and O's of football, but to also mold young men into upstanding citizens in the community and even to prepare them for life after football.

But coaches also have a commitment to winning games, or else they won't have a job—simple as that.

So every coach comes to a crossroads a few times during the season when they must make those tough decisions, ones that might hurt the overall success of the football team, but are needed to enforce discipline and accountability among the ranks.

All coaches want to win. And sometimes coaches will give players a second, third, fourth, and maybe even fifth chance to turn their lives around and fix whatever issue is holding them back.

But in some sad cases, enough is enough.

Heading into the eighth game of the season, the Cowboys had finally had enough of Joseph Randle and decided to part ways with the talented running back.

When most players are released, someone—usually from the football operations department—seeks out the player and tells him the head coach wants to meet with him. The term "bring your playbook" is the catchphrase no player wants to hear, knowing a meeting with the coach *and* being asked to bring the playbook is a sure sign for getting released.

Randle met first with Jason Garrett and then Jerry Jones on Tuesday in their respective offices at Valley Ranch. Despite all the issues and trouble he had found himself in during the last two years, those who were nearby Randle as he cleaned out his locker say he was "stunned" at the news.

Ironically enough, Randle was released just five days before the one game that was supposed to be his chance to shine. Sure, the Cowboys had already faced DeMarco Murray and the Eagles back in Week 2, but with Murray making his first return trip to Dallas, where he had ripped off a franchise-best 1,845 rushing yards just a year ago, this was the national stage that Randle coveted. He was the one who said Murray left "meat on the bone" in 2014 and vowed to not only replace Murray as the starter, but also improve the running game.

However, he never made it to the halfway point of the season.

"We just think it's time for him to not be on the roster," Jones said on his radio show that week on 105.3 The Fan. "That's the decision we made. But we stand ready to help him work through any of his other issues."

When a player gets cut in somewhat surprising fashion, especially when the team refuses to list a specific reason or instance, rumors will tend to surface. There was no exception with Randle, who was said to have had gambling issues or at least a debt with a casino. There were some reports the Cowboys were worried about Randle's mental health, but nothing of serious substance ever materialized.

Plain and simple, Randle wasn't released because of one major thing. There were several circumstances that kept piling up, forcing the Cowboys' hand to let him go.

Nearly a year earlier, Randle was arrested at a shopping mall for stealing cologne and boxers. While detained, police video caught Randle not only flirting with a female employee at the jail, but also trying to justify his mistake. "Dez didn't miss no games for slapping his mama," Randle said, referring to an incident in 2012 when Bryant and his mother had a domestic dispute, although no charges were filed. When word of those comments came back to Bryant, the receiver and Randle nearly got into a physical altercation on the practice field and had been separated by Jason Witten.

In the 2015 off-season, Randle was arrested on domestic violence and marijuana charges. While the authorities in Wichita, Kansas, decided not to pursue the allegations, the NFL wasn't about to turn its head. The league had been investigating all of Randle's situations, which included a visit back in August that forced him to miss the team's kickoff luncheon. But before he was issued a fine or suspension, or perhaps both, the Cowboys decided to wash their hands of the situation.

And by doing so, a message got sent throughout the locker room as well. Severing ties with a starting-caliber player also opened a few eyes, hammering home the point that each player must take care of his business on and off the field.

"The NFL is like life," said veteran defensive end Jeremy Mincey. "You're here one day and gone the next. It's the nature of the business. We wish him the best and hope everything works out for him."

Another vet with similar words was Darren McFadden, who now seemed to have a stranglehold on the starting running back spot.

McFadden said he sent a text message over to Randle to "keep his head up." But words of encouragement can only go so far, especially from ex-teammates who must keep their focus on the task at hand.

Now, it was McFadden vs. Murray in his return trip to AT&T Stadium, the game coming just seven weeks after Murray had rushed for a grand total of two yards on thirteen carries. And while he had started to find his groove somewhat in Philly's fast-paced offense since then, Murray never seemed to be a great fit for Chip Kelly's scheme.

Murray was able to tie the game with a second quarter touchdown, and also did his best to help out his defense at times. Sideline cameras caught the running back barking out some of the Cowboys' plays and tendencies.

In one instance, Murray was telling Eagles cornerback Nolan Carroll to "watch the hitch," and sure enough, Carroll was covering Bryant, who indeed ran a hitch route. Still, the Cowboys found a way to be productive, at least more so than in the previous week's loss to the Seahawks that saw them put up only four field goals. This time, Matt Cassel hooked up with Cole Beasley for a pair of touchdowns and was looking to break a 14–14 tie early in the fourth quarter when an unlikely nemesis popped up yet again.

Eagles linebacker Jordan Hicks, the same defender who fell on top of Tony Romo in Week 2 and broke the quarterback's collarbone, picked off a Cassel pass and raced sixty-eight yards for a go-ahead touchdown, sending many of the announced crowd of 91,827 back into their seats with a feeling of "here we go again."

However, the Cowboys made things interesting, thanks in large part to Bryant, who still wasn't 100 percent healthy in his second game back from a broken foot. Cassel had been with the team long enough to know that, if needed, he could just chunk it up to Bryant and hope for the best. And during a wild sequence in which the quarterback was about to be sacked, that's exactly what he did.

In what essentially became a "Hail Mary" pass, Bryant rose above a sea of hands and came down with a remarkable catch, tying the game and sending the crowd back into a raucous frenzy that the stadium hadn't experienced since the Week 1 comeback thriller to beat the Giants. In that season opener, safety J.J. Wilcox made a signature play early on when he smacked wide receiver Odell Beckham Jr. over the middle, jarring the ball loose and setting the tone for a physical night of football.

This time around, the Cowboys and Eagles would go into overtime, but on their first possession, Eagles quarterback Sam Bradford found a streaking Jordan Matthews over the middle for what appeared to be a big gain to around the home team's 25-yard line. Instead, Wilcox failed to come up with the big hit, or any hit for that matter, and let Matthews sneak past him for a game-winning 41-yard touchdown.

Just like that, the Cowboys' efforts once again were lost. Defensive end Greg Hardy, who was inches away from sacking Bradford on the final play, was so upset with the outcome that he took his helmet off and with two hands slammed it down on the turf, his mouthpiece, chinstrap, and any other particles that were attached to the helmet flying around in a mini-explosion.

Which was fitting because the Cowboys' season was exploding in front of their eyes, and it was happening in different ways. Sure, the offense was the main culprit with Tony Romo out, but this was another example of the defense failing to come through in the clutch. The defense allowed a game-winning touchdown in overtime against the Saints, allowed a last-minute drive by the Seahawks the week earlier, and had now given up another overtime loss. And two weeks prior, it was the special teams that surrendered what proved to be the game-winning touchdown on the road in New York.

Before the game, in the team huddle, Mincey had tried to rally the troops with a fiery pep talk, telling them, "It ain't about how you fall. It's about how you get back up. And today, I promise you, we're gonna get back up."

But this thing was bigger than any emotional speech could fix. The Cowboys didn't get back up. Instead, they kept falling, all the way to their sixth straight defeat.

Chapter 12
TWO KINDS OF TURNOVERS

Friday

In Texas, there are two distinct types of high school football programs every year: the ones that make the playoffs, and the ones that don't.

Each district in the state, even the ones with just six schools, will send four teams to the postseason. Of course at Plano, the treacherous nine-team district of 6-6A proved to be too lethal for the Wildcats to advance past the tenth game in 2015.

For just the second time since Jaydon McCullough had become the head coach at Plano in 2007, his Wildcats were not participants in the postseason. Life after football started in mid-November for a change.

For some of the players, it meant open afternoons with no practice. For others, it meant moving on to the next sport. That included the coaches, who often doubled and even tripled up by helping out with other sports at the high school.

So where did McCullough spend his next Friday night after the regular season was over? Well, that would be at a high school playoff game, naturally.

Now, don't think it wasn't somewhat painful for him to sit in the stands; but just like he preaches to the players on his own team, McCullough's life truly is "family first." And with his brother, Joey, head coaching archrival Plano East in the first round of the playoffs, McCullough was there when the Panthers traveled to Denton's C.H. Collins Athletic Complex, the home stadium of Billy Ryan High School.

Although in full support of his brother, McCullough was still no different than other coaches who let their minds wonder about, "What if this could've happened here?" or "What if the ball bounced our way there?" That was just part of being a coach and always wanting to compete.

While many who supported the maroon and white at Plano might have found some comfort in seeing Plano East fall to Ryan, 56–33, McCullough certainly didn't share the sentiment.

"I love my brother and always want him to win . . . except when he's playing us," Jaydon said with a big smile. "But I'm really proud of what he's doing over there."

Had Plano East made it all the way to states, it's likely McCullough would've been at every game, if his schedule permitted. And being the head coach of a team out of the playoffs, that's something he would've made work.

However, attending playoff matchups can't be easy on any coach whose program not only has been successful, but also is expected to be every year. Watching those games at neutral sites, and sometimes at venues such as AT&T Stadium only brought back more memories for McCullough. He took his Plano team five rounds deep in the playoffs during his first year as head coach, only to lose to eventual state champion Trinity High School from Euless, 30–27, in an epic game played at the now-demolished Texas Stadium.

Two years later, one of McCullough's fondest memories occurred after his team dropped to 2–6 following a 51–7 loss to Allen High School. The Wildcats won their last two outings to sneak into the playoffs and then defeated Duncanville High School in a game that saw them trailing 17–0 at the half before rallying to win 28–17, setting up a rematch with Euless Trinity, which had scored eighty-eight points the week earlier in their playoff win. With the game being played at the brand-new Cowboys Stadium, now AT&T, Plano again fell by three, 41–38, to the Trojans, which went on to claim another state title.

McCullough would've given anything to be back in the playoffs again, but all he could do now was focus on next year. And he was grateful for the opportunity to do that.

While he had told his assistants before the last game that beating Lewisville was important for everyone's job security, there was never any official statement from the higher-ups, which he chalked up to "no news is good news." Maybe there wouldn't have been any change regardless of the final game, but McCullough and his staff were certainly excited that they didn't have to find out.

However, one of his assistants had thoughts of leaving anyway. Not that Chris Fisher was unhappy, but like most assistant coaches, his dreams and vision included running his own program, especially one that he called home.

"BEING THE HEAD COACH of Palo Duro High School was the reason I got into coaching," said Fisher, an all-district cornerback at PDHS in 1993, when he was also one of the senior captains. "I didn't know if that would ever happen, but when I became a coach, that was a goal that I set out for."

A walk-on defensive back for two years at Midwestern State University in Wichita Falls, Texas, Fisher ended up quitting football so he could focus on his academics, and once worked three jobs in one semester to help pay his own way in his quest to become the first person in his family to graduate from college.

Earning his business degree in the fall of 1998 was a major accomplishment for Fisher, who moved to Dallas immediately and started working for Toyota Motor Credit. But it wasn't long before he got that football itch. And after seeing some of his former college buddies land teaching and coaching jobs in the Plano area, it piqued his interest. Within just a couple of years, Fisher got his teaching certificate and was working in the Plano ISD himself. By 2005, he was coaching varsity full-time and would wind up spending fourteen years at Plano.

Along the way, he had interviewed for five other head-coaching jobs, including Wichita Falls High School, Plano East, and R.L. Turner High School in nearby Carrollton. That's the one job Fisher thought he had locked up back in 2012.

"I walked away thinking I had nailed it," Fisher said. "I left the interview so confident that I was already making plans in my mind of who to bring with me."

But Fisher was passed over, just like he was for high school head-coaching positions in the towns of Salado and Dumas as well.

He never had played at any of those schools, though. Fisher had never walked the hallways at places such as "Old High" in Wichita Falls or worn the uniform at Plano East. He knew what it was like to be a Palo Duro Don, so when he put together his résumé packet for the sixth time, he just had a feeling this one would be different.

While Fisher was looking for a possible change, the same thoughts were starting to creep into the mind of Brandon Stephens, Plano's do-it-all running back who had committed to Stanford back in Week 2 of the regular season.

When the season ended, Stephens' verbal commitment was still strong, but the free time allowed him to at least consider some other options, even if it wasn't publicly. Recruiting services around the country are involved in a competitive business, with various websites and reporters always trying to gain the latest information. So Stephens was asked often, by both strangers and oftentimes classmates, if he was still going to Stanford.

Through November and into December, that answer never changed. But inside, he was starting to weigh his options again and even pulled out a few of the shiny, glossy brochures and letters he had received from other schools.

Again, Stanford was still the plan for Stephens, but with the season over, he knew his options—and eyes—were now open for any possibility.

Saturday

In most professions, especially in sports, some of the hardest-working members of the team are those behind the scenes who generally get no credit or praise for their work.

For nationally recognized college football programs, such is the life for the media relations directors, also known as sports information directors.

At Baylor, a school that has a rather strong group of media coordinators, the guy in charge of the day-to-day operation, especially with the football team, is Heath Nielsen, the associate athletic director for communications. When it comes to media requests for Art Briles and/or the Baylor players, media outlets both in Waco and nationally have to run through Nielsen, who joined the Bears' media staff in 2000. To say he has seen a drastic change in the way the university is now covered would be the biggest of understatements.

A school that once had to recruit reporters to come out to games now has to turn away credential requests, especially for big games against opponents such as Oklahoma, a matchup of two top-fifteen teams.

But there was no better sign that a program had reached elite status in the world of college football than to have the ultimate pregame show held in your own backyard. ESPN's *College GameDay*, which had been a weekly mainstay during the season since 1993, had reached epic proportions over the years, both for the viewers at home who used the three-hour show as their tour guide for a Saturday of action, and of course the fans who packed themselves behind the set to get their face and homemade signs on camera.

The signs are usually creatively witty, but often too over the top with sophomoric humor and trash talking. Still, it brings uniqueness to a show that always ends with a round of predictions. That includes wacky former coach, Lee Corso, who often makes his pick by wearing the head of a mascot, but has used other measures as well, such as shooting off rifles while at Texas Tech or bringing live animals on air like dogs or even a chicken once at South Carolina.

When Nielsen got the call the Sunday before the Oklahoma game that *GameDay* would be coming to town, he just took a deep breath, knowing what was in store for the upcoming Saturday.

"Well, it makes for a very long day with the show starting at eight a.m. and then the things we have to do to prepare for it, plus the game being at seven that night," he recalled. "But it's worth it because for our program, and our brand, it doesn't get any better than *College GameDay* coming to your campus. And so it's a huge thing for us, for recruiting. We were excited to be a part of it again."

In 2014, Baylor ended its regular season with a victory over Kansas State, an outcome that Corso didn't predict. He stunned the raucous Bears crowd back then by slapping on the Wildcats' mascot head, and made it worse by saying, "Today, the winners are wearing purple," which also referenced that rival TCU would likely claim the Big 12 title with a Baylor loss.

But the Bears were able to win the game, prove Corso wrong, and claim their second consecutive conference crown, a title they shared with the Horned Frogs even though Baylor had beaten TCU in their head-to-head battle.

This time around, the fans were eagerly awaiting Corso's pick, but were fired up by their own head coach, who made a rather unique entrance. He arrived by pontoon boat, which took him from the football offices straight to the set, where he visited with ESPN's sideline reporter, Samantha Ponder.

Needless to say, Briles got the crowd riled up. He deflected a question about national pundits doubting his team's 7–0 record because of a lack of quality opponents by pointing to the nearby fans.

"Can they doubt this?" he said, knowing it would generate a roar from the bright-eyed students who had made their way to the set at 5 a.m. that morning. "It's a great day. You can find criticism in anything you do, but what we go by is results. Our team has done everything it can do to make this a big game. If we don't take care of September and October, this isn't a big game today."

Knowing Briles is notorious for giving anyone and everyone around him nicknames, Ponder put him on the spot, asking him to do the same for the foursome on the set, including the host, Reece Davis, who was in his first year after Chris Fowler moved into the broadcast booth and was set to call the game later that evening for ABC. Briles had forgotten about that move, and so when he turned around to check out the group, he mistakenly called Davis "Chris Fowler," which prompted his partners to erupt in laughter. Briles playfully ribbed some of the guys, including Desmond Howard, telling the 1991 Heisman Trophy winner to "come up with a new pose."

After the interview, Davis playfully fired back, saying his new nickname for Briles would be "Gary Patterson," the TCU head coach, stirring the pot somewhat considering the intense rivalry that the Bears and Horned Frogs had recently formed.

At the end of the show, Corso went with the Baylor mascot, giving the fans what they wanted to hear and allowing them to walk away from the spectacle feeling as if it were the first of two expected victories that day.

But just like the previous game played at McLane Stadium three weeks earlier against Iowa State, kickoff was met with a steady rainfall that stuck around for most of the night. Despite the weather, one person who was likely happy to be on the field during pregame warm-ups and probably didn't feel a drop of rain was quarterback Seth Russell, who was on the sideline for his first game since his neck injury, one that had required surgery and an extended stay at a West Virginia hospital.

Russell's presence was a huge lift for the players, who all took a quick moment to step out of their pregame drills and come over to wish their fallen quarterback well. He didn't look the same, wearing an elaborate brace with a hard exterior that made sure his neck and upper back stayed compact.

"I was just so happy to be there and see the guys," Russell said. "Yeah, you want to play and be out there, but with everything that happened, I was just glad I could be there and support my team. It felt right to be down there with them."

Jarrett Stidham had won his first career start ten days earlier at Kansas State, but everyone knew this would be a stiffer challenge, despite playing at home where the Bears had won an NCAA-best twenty straight games.

As if Oklahoma's stingy defense wasn't enough to worry about, Briles had a couple of other things on his mind that weren't sitting well. Running game coordinator, Jeff Lebby, who also coached the running backs and was the most experienced assistant up in the press box during games, would miss the entire first half to serve the self-imposed suspension for Lebby's visit on the Tulsa sideline during a September game against Oklahoma.

Briles wasn't happy about the situation then, and his feelings had hardly changed since. He was still wondering how much any coach could gain by standing on the sideline, and now was just hoping the offense could function normally for a half.

The coach was also unsure how explosive Corey Coleman would be, the dynamic receiver having tweaked his groin during practice. While it wasn't reported at the time by any media outlet, Coleman revealed four months later that the injury occurred while he was taking reps as a cornerback for a new package Baylor was planning to use on third downs. The idea was to have him shadow always-dangerous wide receiver Sterling Shepherd, one of Oklahoma's top offensive weapons.

Not only did Coleman not play any defense, he wasn't the same on offense, either, being held to just three catches for fifty-one yards.

Early on, the Bears made a statement with a run-heavy attack that produced a touchdown on their first drive, which was aided by a 15-yard roughing the passer penalty on the Sooners. But Baylor paid a big price, as Stidham suffered a back injury that limited his mobility and arm strength throughout the rest of game.

And with that, matching up with Oklahoma quarterback Baker Mayfield became even tougher. A former Texas Tech starter, who used the national stage to showcase his talents, Mayfield had the Sooners in control for most of the game and led 34–20 midway through the third quarter.

Stidham engineered a rally and helped cut the lead to 37–34 early in the fourth, but the Baylor defense couldn't stop Mayfield when it needed to, a crucial late touchdown helping the Sooners regain a double-digit lead and capture a 44–34 win. That ended Baylor's home winning streak, which had included a perfect 10–0 record at the school's new McLane Stadium.

With the rain continuing to pour down on the Bears, the players had trouble keeping their heads up as they came to grips with the crushing loss. Walking through the tunnel, up the small flight of stairs, and then over to the locker room had been done several times before, but never with this feeling of defeat weighing on them.

For a season and a half, McLane Stadium had been a safe haven for winning. Even Nielsen felt the change, knowing he needed to ask some of his key players to come to the postgame media room to meet the press. That's when he saw a side of them that he hadn't seen before, and didn't prefer to see again, but still admired.

"It's easy when you're winning games and the guys are happy," Nielsen said. "My job is easy to get a few guys to come in and talk then. It's when you lose a tough one like we did to Oklahoma, and the guys are disappointed and they don't want to talk to anyone. I'm super impressed when the loss comes and the players have played up to their capabilities, but they still buck up and face the media when you know they don't want to.

"Sometimes the fans dehumanize these players they read about and see on TV and don't realize they're nineteen- and twenty-year-old kids with a mic in their face having to take tough questions from adults. But I always get really proud of the guys during a loss, and I was again after that game."

Whether it was All-America offensive tackle Spencer Drango or Stidham or even Briles, all of them uttered the same four words in their respective press briefings.

"Control our own destiny" was a popular phrase following the game, and the Bears' chances of winning at least a share of a third straight Big 12 title was obviously something about which the head coach had reminded his team in the locker room. With Oklahoma already losing once to Texas, Baylor could still finish 11–1 overall and 8–1 in the conference if the team won its next three games.

Controlling their own destiny and winning out would indeed give the Bears a piece of the Big 12 title, and perhaps could still put them in the discussion for the College Football Playoff, which included the top four ranked teams.

However, the road wouldn't get any easier, as the Bears were now headed to a place where they had never won in seventy-six years. That would then be followed by a trip to their rival's home field to face a squad that had nothing but revenge on its mind.

Games like this were just another example of Briles' favorite saying in reference to programs that turn the proverbial corner from "hunters to the hunted." For many years, Baylor was the team for which other schools felt sorry when they gave them 50-point beatings. Now, Oklahoma and its fans were parading around on the Bears' home field, pounding their chests in victory.

And two more conference foes were ready to pile on for more punishment.

Sunday

The bittersweet feeling in Jason Garrett's stomach during the Cowboys' Wednesday afternoon practice was overwhelmingly noticeable to the head coach.

After experiencing six straight losses without his starting quarterback, Garrett more than welcomed the sight of Tony Romo back on the field again. He was practicing with the first-team unit, throwing passes to all the receivers while also leading the position drills and directing traffic as always.

That was the good news. The bad news for Garrett and the rest of the Cowboys organization—as well as the fan base, for that matter—was that Romo still wasn't eligible to return to action. The NFL allows teams to place one player on an eight-week injured reserve list during each season, and Romo seemed an easy choice for the Cowboys after he broke his collarbone.

But the risks that came with moving him off the active roster and onto this list were for reasons just like this upcoming Tampa Bay game. Romo probably could've played, but since he had to sit out a full eight weeks, his return would have to wait.

And after losing six straight, the vibe surrounding this team was no matter who the quarterback was under center, if it wasn't Romo leading the charge, the Cowboys couldn't and wouldn't win.

Even against the Buccaneers, with rookie Jameis Winston taking the snaps? Surely the Cowboys could figure out a way to get past a 3–5 Tampa Bay team that featured the NFL's number-one overall pick at quarterback, although Winston still needed plenty of polishing midway through his first year.

For Dallas, the saving grace in this entire season was that no one in the NFC East was running away with the division. As bad as having a 2–6 record was, in reality the Cowboys never trailed any of their three division foes—the Giants, Eagles, or Redskins—by more than two games. And considering both wins to start the season were against NFC East opponents, the Cowboys still had a chance to sneak back in the race, especially if they could get some momentum going before they had to face their division rivals again.

At this point in the season, any win would do.

However, while the world was watching Dallas struggle on Sundays, especially in the fourth quarter of recent games, this team was fighting an uphill battle during the week as well.

The Cowboys didn't have just Sunday problems, but rather a seven-day cycle of issues. And for the most part, repeat offenders were the cause.

For different reasons, of course, Greg Hardy and Dez Bryant remained the top storylines in the week leading up to the Buccaneers game. Once again, Hardy's Twitter account was an issue, as he changed his bio in an attempt to declare his innocence in the domestic violence charges he had faced a year earlier. During the players' day off on Monday, Hardy decided to change the bio page to read:

Innocent until proven guilty-lack of knowledge and information is just ignorance-the unjust/prejudicial treatment of diff categories of people is discrimination.

Call it a coincidence, but just a few hours later, the national website Deadspin.com, a sports site that has somewhat of a cult following for its mixture of hard-hitting reporting with an oftentimes humorous slant, released a 126-page transcript of the hearing Hardy had with the NFL in March. Five days earlier, the website had released a full gallery of photos that showed the defensive end's former girlfriend, Nicole Holder, with severe bruises and cuts that she claimed were from Hardy.

By the end of the day, Hardy had removed his new Twitter bio, after yet another meeting with Garrett, who never reveals much of the details in what he calls "in-house matters." Back in May, the head coach and the Cowboys' support staff had its first issue with Hardy and his social media decisions when the defensive end made an insensitive reference to the "Twin Towers getting blown up," referring to the September 11 terrorist attacks when responding to a fan's tweet about Carolina Panthers' wide receivers Kelvin Benjamin and Devin Funchess.

During the week, the Cowboys' public relations staff did not make Hardy available for comment in an effort to diffuse the situation.

As for Bryant, he regularly makes his own decisions not to talk to reporters, but that doesn't keep him from engaging in banter with the media. On this day, the receiver was looking for veteran ESPN columnist Jean-Jacques Taylor, who had been a longtime Cowboys beat reporter for *The Dallas Morning News.* Bryant was upset with Taylor for a column he wrote suggesting that the receiver's two catches for twelve yards against Seattle two weeks earlier hadn't come close to resembling a player who was given a $70 million contract.

In the NFL, that's usually the easiest way to set off a player—publicly accuse him of being overpaid. So Bryant and Taylor, neither of whom is considered a locker room regular, had been looking for each other over the last week. When they finally talked, things got heated, and were then taken up several notches when wide receiver Devin Street walked into the fray and claimed that Taylor, who is African-American, used a racial slur against him, which Taylor profusely denied.

Sitting off to the side, an outside reporter who rarely visited Valley Ranch, was quietly observing. It was writer Robert Klemko of the website, The MMQB with Peter King, who quickly tweeted that "Dez Bryant just blew up on a reporter, went on a ten-minute rant."

Only the real blowup was about to happen to the author of the tweet.

Having calmed down after his argument with Taylor, Bryant went back to his locker, where he went straight to Twitter. That's when he noticed Klemko's tweet and immediately yelled his name out in the locker room to come forward. When the writer did, the two had to be separated by some of Bryant's teammates, and even Garrett made a rare appearance to try to calm the situation.

Bryant was so heated about what he felt was a one-sided tweet that painted him in a negative light that he yelled, "Don't single me out like that. If you're going to report something, report it right." He then turned his anger toward the Cowboys' PR staff, telling them to "Fix this shit!" Later in the day, he took to Twitter himself and offered up an explanation for his actions:

> "Now I guess I'm the bad person??? The media comes in our locker room with no restrictions . . . I guess they can say whatever and it's cool . . . let me remind all of you . . . WE ARE HUMANS AS WELL . . . WITH FAMILIES . . . we have to live with a lot of false talk about us . . . I chose to stand up for me and what I represent . . . I'm so sorry if a lot of you can't handle being talked to direct."

Needless to say, this losing streak was taking its toll on the team. While it might have been easy for outsiders to call it simply a six-game skid, the struggles were becoming a real issue inside the walls of Valley Ranch. Forget six games. How about fifty-three days? That's how long it had been between the Cowboys' last win and Bryant's latest locker-room blowup.

When losing streaks get this bad, the negativity is felt daily, not just on game day.

The Cowboys arrived in Tampa Bay with hopes of ending their downward spiral and creating a little momentum around the team before Romo returned the next week in Miami. But the Saturday night before the game, not all the players seemed on board. At least they certainly didn't all make the team meeting.

Hardy was a no-show for the defensive meeting at the hotel, which resulted in a fine, but not a suspension. He still started and had a solid game, although Fox TV cameras did catch him and fellow defensive end DeMarcus Lawrence having a heated verbal exchange on the sidelines. But those two were actually playing well for a unit that limited the Buccaneers to just a field goal for the first fifty-eight minutes of the game.

The problem was that Matt Cassel and the Cowboys' offense could muster only six points. And that seemed to be enough after safety Jeff Heath's second interception late in the fourth quarter. But on a crucial third-down play with a chance to perhaps seal the win, Bryant dropped a pass he normally catches, forcing Dallas to punt.

Clinging to a 6–3 lead, the Cowboys' defense once again failed to close out a game, allowing Winston to drive the Bucs to a go-ahead touchdown in the final minute. Dallas had actually forced and recovered a fumble two plays earlier, but a holding call on Heath gave Tampa Bay another chance, which Winston used to score the game winner.

On the Cowboys' final desperation drive, there was some hope when Cassel fired a deep ball to Bryant, who was streaking to the end zone against the Buccaneers' man coverage. But a slight push in the back by the defender moved the receiver off his course, and safety Bradley McDougald came up with the interception to win the game. Bryant was criticized heavily, including by Fox color analyst John Lynch, for giving up on the route and not making more of a fight to get the ball with the game on the line. Bryant had a reputation for a guy who would win the ball in the air. On this play, however, he wasn't even close.

And with that, the unthinkable came to an ugly reality. The Cowboys walked off the field while getting an earful of the cannons that were blasting from the life-size pirate ship in the end zone, knowing they had just completed seven straight games without their quarterback and couldn't manage to win a single one. Brandon Weeden tried his hand and lost three straight starts. Cassel relieved him and had now lost four.

But they were both about to step aside—one more so than the other—as Romo was finally ready to return to action.

Chapter 13

ROAD WARRIORS

Friday

Not many towns in Texas have a richer or longer tradition of successful football, especially at the highest level, than Plano.

While the Wildcats have won seven state titles, Plano East has had some powerhouse teams as well, and Plano West has been a formidable program in its first ten years of existence.

Yet, after just one week of the 2015 state playoffs, none of the P-Town schools were still playing football.

With East losing in the first round, and the other two schools failing to even make it out of the lethal District 6–6A, the season had officially come to a close for the city of Plano.

For Matt Keys, the end was bittersweet. Obviously, he was disappointed that his team didn't maintain the standards of Plano Senior High and make the playoffs, but the rollercoaster of his senior season was taxing. The hits certainly piled up over ten games.

Still undecided on where he would attend college, Keys wasn't even sure what his next move would be for the rest of his senior year. A gifted athlete, he likely could've run track or played baseball. He also thought about just relaxing and taking it easy.

He never could've imagined what the next *stage* of his life would be.

Keys had spent the last few months calling plays. Now, he was about to be in one.

About a week after the regular season ended, a couple of classmates from the theater department approached Keys in the hallway at school. At first he thought it was a joke, but he soon realized that they were serious in their attempts to get him to join the school's next play, a production of the musical *Legally Blonde.*

While an initial thought of "football players and musicals don't mix" ran though Keys' mind, he was somewhat flattered that he was even considered for the part. After he declined at first, Keys kept thinking about it. What had piqued his interest were the words "small role," as he would only have a couple of lines. The girls also told him he would only need to go to two rehearsals.

"Yeah, they lied to my face," said Keys, who soon learned after he agreed to take the part that his role was not as trivial as he first thought. "It turned out to be one of the leading characters. I'd say probably the third-most prominent role. I was in four scenes and had to do a choreographed dance in the middle of the stage."

He signed up to have a couple of lines, but ended up with nearly twenty-five as he was given the role of "Kyle," who is described as a fit, handsome UPS driver. That description alone might have helped Keys warm up to the idea.

"In about a week, I had swapped a head coach for a director," he joked. "At first I wanted it to be quiet. I didn't want people to find out that I was doing it."

Good luck with that. High school gossip has seemingly never taken too long to spread, and that was before texting and social media. Within two days, everyone knew Keys was in the play. And once he found out it could be beneficial for exposure and possibly ticket sales to tout the fact that the quarterback of the football team had a primary role, Keys didn't hide from it any longer.

He also didn't mind his friends jokingly calling him "Troy Bolton," the lead character played by actor Zac Efron in *High School Musical,* a pop-cultural trilogy of movies about a star basketball player who, in similar fashion, joins the school's play.

Not only did Keys start to warm up to the stage, but the rehearsals also gave him an opportunity to better know the people involved with the play. In addition to quarterbacking, Keys had run a Bible study for fellow players and classmates. He was also a member of the National Honor Society and Fellowship of Christian Athletes and was a part of the homecoming court. With just a couple of months to go in his senior year, he thought he knew everything there was to know about his school and peers.

"As it turned out, I think we learned a lot of lessons about judging people," Keys said. "I have so much appreciation now for those kids in theater. They're the most nonjudgmental and accepting people ever. They accepted me right away. I ended up having another locker room for a little bit."

But on *this* team, he wasn't the quarterback. No longer was he the one on whom everyone counted to save the day when the things got tough.

And after the season Keys had just endured, it was definitely a welcomed change.

Saturday

When it comes to rivalries, fans and the media typically play the biggest role in not only creating but also enhancing the drama between two teams. Usually, rivalries are simply geographical, pitting two of the state's top programs against each other. Or it could be driven by a connection of the coach and his former university. Sometimes, rivalries are formed by the fact that the two teams simply play incredibly close games.

Regardless, for one reason or another, Baylor had now gained a few rivals in the Big 12. From Texas Tech, a school where Art Briles had coached some fifteen years earlier, to the traditional state powers of Oklahoma and Texas, to the budding rivalry with TCU, the Bears and their fans had plenty of people to dislike, and vice versa.

But ask Briles and his coaches the same question about rivalries, and they'd answer it differently.

"Well, Oklahoma State is the team that has given us the most problems, especially up there," Briles said. "I don't know about all of that [rivalry] stuff. I just know the teams that have been hard for us to beat. That's what we focus on."

Since Briles and his staff had arrived in Waco, the Cowboys of OSU had been a thorn in their side, especially in Stillwater, where Baylor hadn't won since 1939. The Bears had only defeated Oklahoma State twice in their last seven meetings overall.

And, their most recent trip up to Boone Pickens Stadium saw Baylor's 2013 national championship bid come to an end after the Cowboys smashed the previously undefeated Bears, 49–17, in front of a national audience that was wondering at the time if the 9–0 Bears were legitimate title contenders.

Now, Baylor was getting a chance to return the favor.

After losing to Oklahoma in their previous game, the Bears had dropped to number ten in the latest playoff rankings, while Oklahoma State sat at number six with a perfect 10–0 record. The Cowboys knew if they could win their final two games—both at home against Baylor and Oklahoma—they would likely make the College Football Playoff as one of the four top-ranked teams in the country.

Once again, the world was watching as the two squared off in front of ABC's national television audience.

"Our guys were extremely confident—all week in practice, the night before, and in pregame warm-ups. Just very confident," said offensive coordinator, Kendal Briles. "For us having lost the last game to OU, and coming back on the road in a place we hadn't won at, the guys just came out very confident and focused. We didn't really have any pressure on us. Just go out there and perform."

From the very start, that's exactly what Baylor did. Quarterback Jarrett Stidham, who was still aching somewhat from a back injury he sustained early in the last game, showed no signs of any problems when he lofted a perfectly thrown pass to Corey Coleman on the first play from scrimmage. The 48-yard bomb set up an early touchdown.

Stidham then showed some improvisation on Baylor's next drive, scrambling around to give KD Cannon a chance to get downfield for yet another bomb. That 59-yard score put the Bears ahead 14–0, giving the few hundred Baylor fans who had traveled up from Texas reason to make their own noise in the southwest corner of the end zone.

But as expected, Oklahoma State rallied back, tying the game 14–14 before Baylor managed to surge ahead again before the half. The Bears should've been up by more than just ten points, having turned the ball over two times in the first half while also missing a field goal.

However, late in the second quarter, on a third-down play at the OSU 21-yard line, Stidham rolled to his right and was tackled by two defenders near the sideline.

"I knew right then that something was wrong," head coach Art Briles said about his freshman quarterback. "He went down right in front of us. That's just not a way for your foot to bend."

Stidham, who had passed for 258 yards in the first half alone, went out for one more series before halftime, but his lack of mobility was apparent as he stood in the pocket for too long before eventually fumbling. That would turn out to be his final play of the game . . . and season.

If this were a sports movie, some dramatic music would have played as the coaches huddled up in the locker room before deciding to turn the reins over to the backup, which would have been followed by a dramatic speech from the coach to the player about it being "his time to shine."

In reality, there was no time for all of that. Kendal Briles went over to Chris Johnson, who had started the season playing tight end and on special teams, and made it short and sweet.

"C.J., you're in."

And that was it.

Johnson, an imposing figure for a quarterback at 6–5 and 235 pounds, which was the same size as some of Baylor's defensive ends, figured he might get the call, especially when Stidham hobbled into the locker room. All week long, Johnson had practiced as the backup and had been mentally preparing himself to play.

Backup quarterbacks always talk about the "mental reps" of going over the plays time and time again just to visualize what happens if and when their number is called. But in reality, nothing can truly prepare a quarterback for the game except the game itself.

As OSU got the ball first to start the third quarter, Johnson could barely contain himself. His heart was pounding so hard that he wondered if people around him could see his 13 jersey twitching with every beat. But you couldn't tell he was nervous by looking at his face. He kept reminding himself about a saying Kaz Kazadi always preached to them: "Butterflies are normal, but don't let them control you. Control the butterflies."

And that's how Johnson remained cool and confident, even when he trotted onto the field for the first time with the Bears still leading by ten.

Not only was Stidham out for the game, but starting tailback Shock Linwood had injured his foot and was held out of action as well. Playing with its third-string quarterback and second-string tailback, Baylor called a run on first down, but let Johnson air it out on the next snap. He had Cannon deep, but the ball was just barely underthrown and OSU's defender made a great play to knock it down, forcing third down.

After sending in the play, Kendal Briles didn't like what he was seeing from the formation, so the Bears called timeout. That's when Kendal decided to draw up a new play. Literally.

On the headsets, he called up to Jeff Lebby.

"Kendal basically came up with a new play we had never done before," Lebby recalled. "He knew what he wanted to do, so we called for a spread formation and a QB zone play for Chris to keep it."

So during the timeout, the coaches discussed the play with the tight ends and linemen, telling them where to go while Johnson was getting instructions from Kendal.

"We just wanted him to get a little confidence," Kendal said. "We thought we could open a lane for him, and he's a good runner."

Indeed, the lane was opened and Johnson followed his blockers, not only picking up the first down, but also running over a defensive back in the process for a 10-yard gain.

And with that, Johnson was ready to fly.

"I think that play changed the entire game for us," Kendal said. "C.J. just took over and had a phenomenal game."

After his first-down pickup, Johnson finished off the drive with a beautifully thrown pass to Jay Lee for a touchdown, extending the lead to 31–14.

Pounding his chest with excitement, Johnson was mobbed by his teammates, who seemed more surprised than excited after watching his first career touchdown pass.

But what they didn't know was that Johnson was just getting started. On Baylor's next possession, he connected with Cannon, this time on a 71-yard bomb, stunning an OSU crowd that couldn't believe Baylor was whipping them with a backup quarterback.

As if this was his one-hundredth touchdown instead of his second, Johnson smoothly pointed toward the sky and walked off the field, only to be attacked even more by his ecstatic teammates.

When Johnson walked into the end zone later in the fourth quarter for a game-clinching touchdown run, most of the sideline coaches erupted with joy. But Art Briles didn't move. He just smiled and turned back toward his fellow staff with a look of joy and disbelief. Not to say that Briles didn't have confidence in his players, but for Johnson to step in and dominate the game in such a way was a pleasant surprise for all of them.

Meanwhile, the Baylor defense kept OSU at bay until the fourth quarter when the Cowboys added a couple of touchdowns. All that did was mask what was truly a blowout win for the Bears, who came away with a 45–35 victory, the school's first at Oklahoma State in seventy-six years.

In the locker room, Art Briles was in a dancing mood, knowing he had never left Stillwater with a smile on his face. This time he shared a few dance moves with his players before giving his normal "Our House" victory speech.

"We turned it into whose house?"

"Our house!"

"Whose house?"

"Our house!!"

"I said whoooooose house?"

"Our house!!!"

And Briles finished it off with a resounding, "Yes, sir!"

Seven days earlier, Briles had walked out of the locker-room huddle surrounded by players crying their eyes out after losing to Oklahoma. Now, they had just beaten an undefeated team on its home turf, and did it with a quarterback who had never played meaningful snaps.

During the Bears' return flight to Waco, the middle of the plane, which is where the bulk of the athletes sat, was jubilant, the aisle filled with joyous players who were proud of their accomplishment.

In the back, where the coaches were relaxing, the feeling was bittersweet. While his team was enjoying the moment, Art Briles and his staff really couldn't.

"When you play two conference road games in six days this late in the season, it's tough," Briles said. "We got back early Sunday morning, and we had to play on Friday. So we were already a day behind and now we knew Stidham was out. Chris played phenomenal, but we had to get him ready for another tough game against a tough opponent. And we had only six days to do it."

And this wasn't just *any* opponent, but rather Baylor's fiercest rival in TCU, which always posed a stout defense. There was just no way for Briles to get Johnson and his team prepared for the storm that was about to hit them in the next week.

Sunday

In the ever-changing world of technology, keeping up with your favorite sports team is easier than ever. While the daily newspaper and ten o'clock newscast still exist, today there are much quicker ways to get the latest news.

Social media not only provides fans much-needed information right at their literal fingertips, but players themselves now have a strong voice with their own social media accounts.

If Tony Romo wasn't the last NFL player to join Twitter, he had to be right up there when he finally did so in May of 2015. And once he did, he quickly gained more than 100,000 followers in just three days.

By the time Romo rejoined his team in late November after missing eight weeks with a broken collarbone, the Cowboys were more or less helpless, having lost all seven of their games to see their once 2–0 record vanish into a 2–7 mark. Although oddly enough, Dallas' NFC East rivals weren't faring much better, and considering that the Cowboys still had two games left against Washington to strengthen their division record, they remained in the hunt for the playoffs. But, they had no room for error.

Romo, who at this point had tweeted just eighteen times in seven months, again took to Twitter not only to show off his love for the 1980s, but to send a message as well.

He posted a video of a scene from the movie *Major League,* a baseball comedy about the Cleveland Indians, a club that began the season hopeless and destined for failure, but rallied to make a run to the playoffs. The scene shows a meeting where the lead actor, Tom Berenger, who plays a catcher and is considered the veteran spokesman, stands up to address his teammates:

> *"Well, I guess there's only left thing for us to do. Win the whole . . . fucking . . . thing!"*

In the movie, the pivotal scene brings the team together, and they then reel off the necessary wins to capture the American League East title.

While it's standard for some high-profile athletes and coaches to have others handle their social media accounts, Romo was asked in the locker room the next day if he indeed wrote the tweet.

"Oh, that was me," Romo said with his customary smirk. "No one else I know is that funny."

Could the Cowboys have a Hollywood ending as well? Romo has never been called cocky or arrogant, but like most quarterbacks, he doesn't lack confidence. In his mind, they were 2–0 with him as a starter, and he saw no reason why the Cowboys couldn't make another run now that he was back in the lineup.

Conversely, just as Dallas hadn't lost with Romo behind center, the team hadn't won a game since Greg Hardy had been reinstated by the league. Hardy had made a few plays on the field, but not only were they not impactful enough to help the Cowboys earn a win, they were all overshadowed by distractions that were either following him from his past or that he was now creating.

Heading into the week of the Dolphins game, the focus was obviously on Romo's return, but Jerry Jones decided it was time to speak up regarding Hardy. This was a player Jones had previously described as a leader for his work ethic in practice, a comment that drew national attention considering Hardy's troubled history. However, his past wasn't the main problem anymore.

The lack of remorse he showed for the alleged domestic violence incident rubbed his critics the wrong way, but he also didn't seem to be cherishing this second chance that the Cowboys, and most notably Jones, had given him. Hardy had missed a defensive meeting the week before in Tampa, and there had been a few times already in the season when he called the training staff early in the morning to tell them he was sick and couldn't make it in to practice. The definition of "sick" could mean a lot of things, but there was speculation going around Valley Ranch that Hardy was enjoying the Dallas nightlife a little too much, particularly on Wednesdays.

So Jones decided it was time to intervene, and he had a heart-to-heart talk with Hardy. Those close to the front office said it was a "shape up or ship out" type of meeting because the Cowboys were rather close to cutting ties with Hardy, whose antics were also starting to strain some of the team's relationships with its biggest corporate sponsors.

The Cowboys did lose a sponsorship in the middle of the season although it was never clear, or reported, if Hardy's presence was the reason. Another sponsor, American Airlines, admitted some concerns after the Deadspin pictures were revealed, but an AA spokesperson was quoted as saying, "American Airlines supports teams, not individual players."

In his meeting with the owner, Hardy obviously said enough of the right things to convince Jones not to make any personnel changes—at least not with Hardy.

To make room for Romo's reinstatement from injured reserve, the team waived the player that initially replaced him in the lineup. Brandon Weeden was shown the door as the Cowboys kept Matt Cassel as Romo's primary backup.

Weeden was visibly upset when he was demoted in favor of Cassel, and while he saw this move coming, he still wasn't happy as he left the facility for the final time. Weeden's biggest gripe, which seemed valid, was that he went 0–3 as a starter and didn't have Dez Bryant available, while Cassel was 0–4 with Bryant in the lineup for three of those games.

And Weeden's departure wasn't the only housecleaning the Cowboys did during the week of Romo's return. Running back Christine Michael and cornerback Corey White were both waived in somewhat surprising moves.

Ultimately, performance is the biggest factor in either keeping or cutting a player, but not following the team's protocols can sway a decision for removal as well. Michael and White did not adhere to the Cowboys' dress code on the previous trip to Tampa Bay. White told the website TMZ in an interview the next week that he wore a button-up shirt and slacks, but not a suit, and "they cut me."

Michael was brought over in a trade with Seattle, but took several weeks to grasp the offense and never contributed to the running game, despite the team cutting Joseph Randle three weeks earlier.

Defensive end Jeremy Mincey, one of the Cowboys' more vocal leaders said, "Sometimes you just have to make tough decisions. The NFL is a business. It's not always pretty. If you don't take care of your business on and off the field, you'll be gone."

However, cutting Michael and White only begged the question even more in regard to Hardy. Two guys were cut because they hadn't dressed up enough, and yet Hardy was still around even though he had missed meetings and reported late to others?

While Hardy remained on the team despite being in hot water, the entire squad found themselves in standing water an hour before the Cowboys' game in Miami, where an absolute monsoon had attacked Sun Life Stadium about an hour before kickoff. Although trying to see a few feet away was a challenge amidst the downpour, Jason Garrett did see something he liked.

"Our attitude in pregame was inspiring," Garrett said later. "They were like kids out there playing in the rain. You could just see their faces and the smiles. They weren't miserable or anything. They were having fun. I thought it might be a good sign for how we might play in the game."

As the team went back to the locker room one last time before kickoff, Hardy was met by arguably his biggest fan—super agent, Drew Rosenhaus, who gave his client a big hug even though the defensive end was drenched from the rain. Rosenhaus asked Hardy if he was going to be able to play through the weather.

"Come on, man, I'm the Kraken," Hardy said, referring to the mythical sea monster and his self-proclaimed nickname. "The Kraken lives in the water, bro. I'll be fine."

Once the game started, the rain was actually coming down harder than before. When Romo trotted out for the first series, the focus was certainly on both the weather and the quarterback.

Lost in the shuffle was Jason Witten's surpassing Bob Lilly's franchise record of 198 consecutive games played, which dated back to 2003, the tight end's rookie season. But Witten was used to being overshadowed, especially by Romo, who entered the league during that same year. Witten had never cared much about individual honors. Sure, the streak was a sign of toughness and dedication, but at this point in the season, he cared much more about just having Romo back than any personal record.

Ironically enough, Romo's first pass since Week 2 was—left-handed. Of course. Feeling a heavy pass rush, the savvy veteran switched the ball to his left and dumped a pass out to the running back to avoid a sack in the end zone.

Eventually the rain subsided and Romo calmed down as well, despite throwing an early interception. He later fired a touchdown strike to Terrance Williams, who made a leaping grab over two defenders. Earlier in the week, Garrett had personally challenged Williams about just such plays, telling him to "win the ball" when it's up for grabs.

Halftime in the NFL is usually just thirteen minutes, which is barely enough time to get everyone in the locker room and to make adjustments, much less to change clothes. However, because of the relentless rain, many of the players attempted to switch parts of their uniform, leaving equipment managers such as Bucky Buchanan scrambling, especially when it came to socks.

"Everyone wanted to get some dry socks," he said, "and I really didn't have enough."

As for Romo, he didn't just want new socks. He wanted everything new.

Removing a football uniform isn't a quick process, and it's even worse when the entire outfit is soaking wet. So Buchanan had to help Romo remove his jersey and pads and scramble to get an entirely new getup. Meanwhile, the big red-numbered clock in the locker room had reached under five minutes before the start of the third quarter.

Romo called another audible.

"Matt, you're going to have to start the third," Romo yelled at backup Matt Cassel. "I'm not going to be ready. We're getting the ball first, so you have to warm up."

Cassel thought it was a joke. This was, in fact, his first game in uniform alongside Romo. But he quickly figured out that Romo was serious, so he rushed to the nearest trashcan and scraped out a fresh dip of Copenhagen that he had inserted into his mouth only a few minutes earlier. Cassel spat out the dip, grabbed a football, and rushed out to the field to find some receivers to throw to.

Soon enough, the Cowboys were lining up for the kickoff return to begin the second half with Cassel looking for offensive coordinator, Scott Linehan, to go over the first series. Cassel was a 10-year veteran, but he hadn't expected this.

Just as the ball was about to be kicked off, though, Cassel got a tap on the shoulder. It was Romo, who just jogged right past him and said, "I'm good. I got it," as he ran on to the field.

With that, Cassel found his ball cap and resumed his backup duties. Crisis averted.

The Dolphins stayed close and tied the game late in the third quarter, but that's when Romo went to work. Facing a second-and-9 at the Dolphins 16-yard line, he checked into a play that would roll the safety away from the middle of the field, leaving Dez Bryant wide open for an easy touchdown, one that proved to be the game winner. Thanks in large part to a relentless defense that actually scored the day's first touchdown and produced five sacks, Dallas was finally back in the win column, beating Miami, 24–14.

After the game, the talk was obviously centered around Romo and his performance on Sunday, but many of his teammates said they were more inspired by him on Saturday. The night before the game, the quarterback uncharacteristically stood up in the team meeting and told them all how proud of them he was.

"It's been very inspirational to watch you guys," Romo said. "Even though we haven't won a game, I've seen a football team that never let up. We never quit. It's hard when you don't win each week because it gets tougher every time, but we're not done. We're going to keep fighting."

Romo's speech hit home with players such as Bryant, who said he "got chills" just thinking about it.

Mincey took it a step further, calling Romo a savior, who "just saved our season."

Still, the ship was anything but righted. At 3–7, there was no time to celebrate. Not only were the Cowboys facing a short week, but the best team in the NFL was coming to town.

Chapter 14

WHEN IT RAINS, IT STORMS

Friday

Now what?

That two-word question is one that every high school football player must answer at some point during the fall when the season comes to an end.

For the very successful teams, the answer is needed just a little before Christmas, meaning the football season lasted several rounds deep into the playoffs. But for the players on Plano's squad, the question was asked long before Thanksgiving.

And the answers obviously vary from person to person, depending on their skill set. Some jump straight into basketball or prepare to play baseball or run track later in the spring.

Senior Darion Foster was planning on giving wrestling another try. When he was a sophomore, after finishing up his season on the tenth grade squad, Foster moved up to the junior varsity wrestling team, where he had what he described as a "decent" year.

Then following his junior season of football, which consisted of only two games because of a pair of injuries, Foster wasn't able to wrestle. Unfortunately, he had broken his forearm in the last JV game of the fall.

So as he planned another try at wrestling, Foster didn't know what to expect. Neither did his live-in uncle, Chris Fisher, who told the team's wrestling coach that Foster might be "OK," but not to expect much, considering the two-year layoff.

After Foster's first practice, Fisher got a call from Plano's head wrestling coach.

"Um, I thought you told me he was going to be OK."

"Oh no, what happened?" responded Fisher. "Was Darion awful? What?"

"No, Coach. Darion wasn't awful. This kid is really good. He pinned the best wrestler we've got. He's better than OK."

A relieved Fisher raised his eyebrows in surprise, eager to hear about his nephew's first practice. As it turned out, Foster had gotten much stronger in the last two years, filling out his body with wider shoulders and a stouter torso. Plus, being an undersized defensive tackle, Foster had to learn how to use his hands to fight off blocks against bigger, stronger offensive linemen.

In doing so, he had picked up a thing or two about leverage, meaning when he got on the mat, Foster was now quite a force in the 220-pound class.

Not only did he hold his own in practice against some of Plano's top wrestlers, but Foster then stood out in some of the school's early meets, winning his share of matches.

"My coach took a big interest in me right from the start," Foster said. "He just saw me as a big kid, and more of a project. I didn't have great form, but I just tried to keep my intensity. Just like in football where you have to bring it every play. After a few practices, he told me I had the chance to be great, so that gave me a lot of confidence."

However, no matter if athletes such as Foster switch from a helmet and shoulder pads to a wrestling singlet, their roles as students are supposed to remain unchanged.

But that wasn't the case for Foster, who was normally an A and B student with the occasional C. His Senior English class was giving him problems. In fact, there was a final exam essay that Foster didn't turn in, which jeopardized his chances to not only pass the class, but also participate in wrestling moving forward.

Undoubtedly, that didn't sit well at home, where Coach Fisher became a rather upset "Uncle Chris."

Oftentimes when a player struggles in a particular class, the head coach will get the first call. So it was Jaydon McCullough who initially got word of Foster's struggles in the English class. He then asked Fisher if he could meet with Darion.

"I know Chris was upset with him, and sometimes as a parent it's not easy to get through to your own kids," McCullough said. "I know it was that way with my kids. We had coaches on the staff who could talk to my son. Sometimes they just need a different voice. I just told Darion that I knew he could do better and that he was a good kid. So I just said, get what needs to be done. Simple as that."

Foster was able to compete in a tournament in Oklahoma, and as soon as he got back, he retyped his essay, turned it in, apologized to his teacher, and assured her that such a lapse wouldn't happen again. While it might seem like a missed assignment or a poor grade to some, it's not the same for kids like Foster, whose father figure is one of the coaches. He knows he's viewed differently and he embraces that fact. So when he makes a mistake, Foster feels it more than the average student might.

"I felt terrible that I let my uncle and aunt down," Foster said. "My Uncle Chris is like my dad, and it hurts to disappoint him and Coach McCullough and everyone who has helped me. They're not really like coaches, but more like family. I've grown up with them. They're all like father figures to me. I don't want to let them down."

Even when football season is over, the coaching—and teaching—never stops.

Saturday

When *Dave Campbell's Texas Football* magazine hit the stands in July, the cover of the annual football "bible" for the entire state focused on a lost rivalry. Texas and Texas A&M no longer played each other every season after the Aggies moved to the SEC, and it didn't seem as if either school had a strong interest in renewing the series through its non-conference schedule. Therefore, one of the state's longest and most intense rivalries was suspended for now.

On the top right corner of the magazine, though, was a small picture that featured Bears and Horned Frogs players with the title "Best in Texas" and a tagline below that read "TCU/Baylor fight for supremacy in the Big 12 and the state." Just like that, Baylor and TCU, the two private schools that at one time were perhaps the least competitive football programs in the state, had now become the best rivalry in Texas.

The 2014 matchup certainly didn't do anything to diminish the notion, providing one of college football's best games of the year. In a battle of two top-ten teams, Baylor trailed by twenty-one early in the fourth quarter before rallying for the final twenty-four points, winning the game, 61–58, on a last-second field goal. Even though Baylor was slightly favored, the dramatic comeback caused the students and fans to rush the field in excitement.

The wild scene also saw Bears safety Orion Stewart approach TCU head coach Gary Patterson and give him a few choice words that stemmed from the previous year when Patterson used his postgame press conference following a 41–38 loss to Baylor to vent about many things, including his dislike for the way Baylor handled safety Ahmad Dixon, who was ejected from that game for targeting. Briles and Patterson actually exchanged some words during and following that 2013 meeting as well. Briles went to midfield during the game when Patterson was yelling at Dixon following a helmet-to-helmet hit on Horned Frogs wide receiver Trevone Boykin.

Afterward, Briles told Patterson to "leave it on the field" and "shake it off," which didn't sit well with the TCU coach, who went on an epic rant moments later in his press conference, citing that "Gary Patterson lives in Fort Worth" and his team "won't take a backseat to anyone."

He also mentioned Dixon and referenced that he "beat a guy up in the off-season," although TCU played that game with a quarterback who had been in drug rehab earlier in the year.

Needless to say, most programs have their share of incidents and typically refrain from discussing other teams' issues.

So Stewart said his 2014 postgame remarks to Patterson were sparked by the year before. But the aftermath of that victory was felt on both campuses throughout the year. After the Bears lost to West Virginia, TCU eventually jumped Baylor in the first-ever College Football Playoff rankings, despite the two having the same record.

When ESPN's *College Football GameDay* went to Waco at the end of the year for a game against Kansas State, nearly every one of the handmade signs from the fans had the score "61–58" written on it. Baylor wanted everyone to know which team had won the game and should be deserving of the higher ranking.

As it turned out, both Baylor and TCU were excluded from the four-team playoff, a scenario that many felt occurred because the Big 12 conference and its commissioner, Bob Bowlsby, said the league would consider both teams as co-champions and would not designate one of the schools above the other to the committee. That was somewhat laughable considering the Big 12's slogan is "One True Champion," but without a conference title game at the end of the season, Baylor and TCU remained tied at 11–1 and were consequently left out of national playoff consideration.

But the rivalry between TCU and Baylor continued all throughout the summer and into the 2015 season. And whether it was merely a coincidence or not, when the Bears' preseason team photo had two offensive linemen, Jarell Broxton (61) and Spencer Drango (58), standing side by side, TCU got the message loud and clear.

In October, Baylor students went to class one morning to find Robert Griffin III's statue outside of McLane Stadium had been spray-painted purple. The next day, a brick wall on TCU's campus in Fort Worth was spray-painted green with the score, 61–58, and another wall had a green

"BU" plastered on it. Even in October during a WWE wrestling match in Dallas, where makeshift signs were just as popular as they are on *GameDay*, one read "61–58." The rivalry was everywhere.

Some of the comments Patterson made throughout the season suggested that beating Baylor was his top priority, including his postgame conversation with West Virginia's head coach, Dana Holgorsen, a month before TCU would face the Bears. Patterson also held out Trevone Boykin from the team's game against Oklahoma six days before the Horned Frogs were to face Baylor, his star quarterback having twisted his right ankle the week before. Patterson wanted to make sure Boykin was healthy.

Against the Sooners, TCU rallied from eighteen down to get to within a point, but opted for a two-point conversion in the final seconds instead of sending the game into overtime. Afterward, Patterson pointed out to the second-guessing reporters, "We have a ballgame next Friday, so if you go to three overtimes, you've got no chance to win that game next week."

Now it must be pointed out that Patterson did have a history of going for two-point conversions on the road, beating West Virginia that way in 2012 and Boise State in 2011. But make no mistake, this decision and his comments later were yet more proof of what was becoming obvious.

Patterson wanted to beat Baylor, plain and simple. But Briles and the Bears certainly wanted to beat TCU as well.

This was pegged as the matchup of the year in the Big 12, expected to be for the conference title. With one loss, Baylor still had a shot at claiming a share of the crown. Needless to say, though, this wasn't as high-profile a matchup on the national level. Still, it was a huge game in Texas.

So big that Mother Nature didn't want to miss it. In fact, she made sure she played a major role from start to finish.

Briles knew rain was in the forecast for most of the day. And that was nothing new for Baylor, the team having played in downpours already during the season against Iowa State and Oklahoma. But this proved to be unlike anything they had seen before.

The torrential downpour never let up—at all—and was combined with temperatures in the low thirties that even dipped below freezing later in the evening. A couple of lightning sightings during pregame warm-ups delayed the kickoff for forty-five minutes, making everyone wait just a tad longer for the drama-filled contest to begin.

When Briles ran out on the field for the start of the game, one thing immediately came to his mind.

"I don't have enough layers of clothes on," he said to one of his assistants.

He later found a raincoat to go over his sweatshirt, but he could sense this was going to be problematic for everyone, both those playing and even those standing around. For added warmth, some of the assistant coaches and support staff found trash bags during the lightning delay and wrapped them around their feet before then putting on their socks and shoes.

Despite the cold, when the game started the Baylor offense looked hot enough. With Chris Johnson making his first career start behind center, he led the Bears to a quick touchdown, extending their streak of reaching the end zone on their opening offensive possession to a nation-leading eleven games.

TCU came right back, though, behind Boykin, tying the game before the Bears answered as well, mixing up some runs and passes to grab a 14–7 lead midway through the first quarter.

The driving rainstorm seemingly was having little effect on Baylor after two drives, both of which resulted in touchdowns. But while the rain never stopped, the scoring did.

As the conditions continued to get wetter, the grass field at Amon G. Carter Stadium made it more difficult for either team to get their footing and sustain a drive. The Horned Frogs tied things up when Johnson's fumble was returned for a touchdown, knotting the game at halftime, 14–14.

Neither team would score again, although Baylor had plenty of chances. Johnson had a wide-open KD Cannon in the end zone early in the fourth quarter, but the ball was stripped out of his hands just before he threw it, resulting in a turnover.

Later in the fourth, running back Devin Chafin picked up a first down as he crossed midfield, but also lost a fumble. The Bears' bruising back, who was the team's short-yardage specialist, came to the sideline infuriated and ripped off his bright neon gloves, tossing them to the ground.

The Baylor equipment staffers ran toward him and offered him a different pair, but he shrugged them off.

"If we get the ball back, I'm not using anything," he said. "Just my hands."

Baylor did get the ball back after the defense made yet another key stop, but neither team could add to the scoreboard. Sixty minutes wouldn't decide this waterlogged affair, which hadn't seen a point since the first half. That was quite a contrast from the 2014 classic, when Baylor totaled twenty-four points in the final eleven minutes of the fourth quarter with the two teams combining for 119 points.

To TCU's credit, the student section might have all gotten sick in the process, but few people left throughout the game. And the fans were just as hyped as ever as the two teams headed into overtime.

Baylor, however, scored first, when Johnson, who had not completed a single pass in the second half, lofted a throw to Chafin, of all people, who snagged the ball—with no gloves—in the end zone for his first career touchdown catch.

"I really thought we had it," Briles said. "In overtime, I kept thinking our defense would make one more stop and we were going to get out of this mess with a win."

Baylor had TCU on the ropes and nearly picked off a pass in the end zone that would've ended the game, but a pass interference call gave the Frogs new life. TCU instead tied the score, and then crossed the goal line again in the second overtime, putting the Bears on their heels and trailing for the first time all night, 28–21.

Facing fourth-and-inches at the TCU 16-yard line, Baylor went to

Chafin one more time, but a blitzing cornerback off the edge stuffed him in the backfield for a loss. Before the running back could even get off the ground, TCU fans stormed the field, just as the Bears' faithful had done a year earlier.

Stunned, freezing, numb, and heartbroken, Briles made his way to the center of the field, looking for Patterson and the customary handshake. But he never found the TCU coach, who was swarmed first by fans and players, and then ESPN's sideline reporter for an interview.

Briles found a few TCU fans instead, one even telling him to "Get fucked!" with another getting in his face before a state trooper pushed him aside.

Walking across the field and into the tunnel, the Bears were devastated, but some handled it better than others. Cannon was hearing it from a few TCU fans as he headed to the locker room and he fired back, exchanging some heated words before his teammates grabbed him.

"You can't do that KD," said one of the backup linemen, trying to calm the situation.

"I'm hurt, man. I'm hurt. I hate losing to them. I'm hurt!" Cannon said with his head down and a couple of his teammates hugging him on their way into the locker room.

All year long, the players had come together before each game and then broken the huddle by saying "Big 12 Champs."

And now, for the first time since the members of this senior class were freshmen, they realized it wasn't going to happen.

The visiting locker room at TCU isn't the biggest, forcing the training tables to be outside the doors in a busy hallway. As the teary-eyed players listened to Briles and the coaches discuss the game, two sat outside the locker room, staring at the ground but not saying a word.

Injured quarterbacks Seth Russell and Jarrett Stidham could only sit there in disbelief. Russell was wearing a heavy neck brace following surgery back in October while Stidham was leaning on crutches after suffering a broken foot just six days earlier at Oklahoma State.

Both of them wondered what could've been. Sure, the rain would've been problematic for either of them, but they figured they could've completed a few passes in the second half and sustained a few more drives. In this game, just one field goal in the second half would've sent the Bears to 10–1, leaving them one home win away, against Texas the next week, from clinching a third straight title. Instead, Baylor lost the most intense rivalry game on its schedule.

Briles called it the worst weather conditions he'd ever played in during his thirty-seven years of coaching. His son, Kendal, could only think of a seventh-grade football game he played against Lancaster, back when the family lived in Stephenville.

"It sleeted the whole game and it was a muddy field," Kendal recalled. "We got beat, 6–2, and I can remember standing in my garage naked because I had to take off all of my clothes before I could go in and shower. It was the coldest I had ever been in my life. But that was nothing compared to the relentless weather we had in Fort Worth."

But Kendal admits the TCU game, and even that one against Lancaster when he was 13 years old, would've been more gratifying had his team come out victorious.

On the other side of the stadium, reporters filled the TCU press conference room, wondering just what Patterson might say after this amazing, emotional night. But those who were waiting, maybe hoping for some explosive comments this time around would be disappointed. Patterson had nothing but praise for his rivals.

"Well, first off, Baylor has a great football season, period, end of story," Patterson said. "It's hard for them. They had to play without their quarterback. If it's been difficult for them, they've hung tough and haven't made excuses. I know you guys think it's a rivalry, but it's a good Baylor football team. Very well coached. But it was very good for TCU tonight. We found a way to win."

As the Baylor players left the stadium, they were met by, what else, more rain, which drenched them again as they scurried into the coach buses that were fired up and ready to head back to Waco.

With spirits and clothes dampened, the only thing that wasn't was

Baylor's chances of landing a New Year's Eve bowl game. Word started to trickle through the buses that a win next week against the Longhorns could still land them in the Sugar Bowl.

But first, they had to get over the sting from the fact that this game, and a chance to three-peat as conference champions, had just slipped away.

Sunday

In their previous forty seasons, the Dallas Cowboys had hoisted the Vince Lombardi Trophy as the best team in the NFL five different times. They'd made eight Super Bowls and won eighteen NFC East titles.

In that span, they'd also been one of the NFL's worst teams in selected years, including a 1–15 mark in 1989, which followed a 3–13 campaign in 1988.

There had been ups and downs, but one thing had remained rather constant—at least since 1966: come 3 p.m. on Thanksgiving Day, the Cowboys were always on television, always playing at home, and always taking center stage, just like America's Team should for one of America's most prestigious holidays.

The tailgating scene outside the stadium has a different smell on Thanksgiving Day. Sure, there might be some of the standard bratwurst and Texas barbecue going around, but many families, especially the ones who make this game a yearly tradition, go all the way with a complete Thanksgiving feast. The deep fryers come out, giving everyone a chance to share the flavor.

Something about having fried turkey, combined with the general festive spirit on Thanksgiving, will prompt tailgaters to occasionally pass out samples to their fellow fans—wearing Cowboys jerseys, of course—who are making their way up to the game.

For the majority of the country, families sit around the dining room table and enjoy a special dinner in the comfy confines of their homes. To thousands of Cowboys fans, Thanksgiving Day consists of portable chairs, paper plates, plastic forks, and tinfoil pans of mashed potatoes, casseroles, cranberries, and all of the other Turkey Day treats.

But inside the stadium, the atmosphere is just as electric. No matter the record, no matter the opponent, Thanksgiving Day always energizes the game. That was the case at the old Texas Stadium in Irving, and it hasn't changed since the Cowboys moved over to their plush AT&T Stadium home in 2009.

This year, there was a little more buzz in the air, but it had less to do with the Panthers coming to town with an unscathed 10–0 record. The excitement centered on the Cowboys, despite the team's dismal 3–7 mark. There was hope, and it rested on the shoulders of their quarterback. Tony Romo's return from an eight-week layoff due to a broken collarbone stopped the team's seven-game losing skid the Sunday before in Miami.

The only concern was how Romo would respond coming off a short week, having played just four days earlier. A year ago, Romo had wisely managed his surgically repaired back by taking off Wednesdays each week to rest his body. However, his worst game of the 2014 season occurred on Thanksgiving, when rest was not an option. Now, there was even less wiggle room for error.

Donning new uniforms for this week's game, as part of the NFL's Color Rush campaign, the Cowboys sported white jerseys and white pants, an outfit that seemed to be popular among the players. In a huddle of defensive backs just before kickoff, one of the players shouted, "We look good. We might as well play good!"

As it turned out, the Cowboys only looked good.

From the very start, the team's worry over Romo's rustiness was justified. He threw an interception on the first drive, which was returned for a touchdown. As disheartening as the pick-six was for the Cowboys, seeing wide receiver Dez Bryant fail to chase after Carolina's Kurt Coleman might have been even worse. Bryant got locked up with the Panthers' star cornerback, Josh Norman, on his route, and even though he saw the ball intercepted by Coleman, Bryant continued to jaw with Norman in front of Carolina's bench, never attempting to make the tackle; and it could have been a possibility, considering Coleman raced back over to Bryant's side of the field en route to the end zone.

Bryant and Norman would battle all day, with Norman getting the best of the matchup, holding Bryant to just two catches on eight targets. After the game he told reporters, "Hey, they need to get Dez's seventy mil back," referring to Bryant's five-year, $70 million contract that he had signed before the season.

But it wasn't just Bryant who struggled on offense. Romo threw another pick-six to Carolina's Luke Kuechly, as the Panthers raced out to a 23–3 halftime advantage.

And even though the Cowboys actually cut into the Panthers' lead, the second half got extremely worse. On the final play of the third quarter, blitzed by the still-attacking Panthers defense, Romo was hit by Carolina's Thomas Davis, who drove the quarterback and his left shoulder into the ground.

Instantly, Romo knew. This third time was no charm, as the quarterback heard and felt the same thing as before. His left collarbone, the same one he had broken in 2010 against the Giants and the same one he broke in Week 2 at Philadelphia, was again the source of excruciating pain.

"Not again?" Romo thought to himself. "This can't be happening."

But while he optimistically told reporters after the game that it was too early to speculate until an X-ray and CT scan were performed, Romo knew his season was likely over. And with that, it meant the Cowboys' season was all but done as well.

Following the 33–14 loss, Romo stood with his left arm in a sling at the press conference podium and talked less about the injury and more about the first three quarters, where he admitted he "didn't give our team a chance to win today. They depend on me to go out there and perform on a certain level. I cost our team today. And I have to live with that."

After the game, Romo got a ride back home where his wife, Candice, their two sons, and other family members gathered around and ate . . . pizza. Of course.

The Romo household created its own tradition on Thursday nights after the Thanksgiving Day game, ordering pizza to keep things simple for Romo, who really just wanted to come home and re-watch the game he just played, win or lose. On Fridays is when the family does a more traditional Thanksgiving Day meal with the entire family.

Despite the loss, Romo stuck with tradition and cued up the tape yet again. But considering he threw three interceptions, two of which were returned for scores, his team lost by nineteen, and he was knocked out of the game for what was probably a season-ending injury to his left collarbone, nothing could get the bad taste out of his mouth.

Not even pizza.

Chapter 15

SURPRISE, SURPRISE

Friday

Every day that Jaydon McCullough walks down a rather quiet hallway to get to the coaching wing where his office resides, he is reminded of his school's history.

And it's not just the finer moments, the trophies that sit in a glass case marking the seven state championships, but also the numerous other hardware from playoff wins in the Regional and Area rounds.

Team accomplishments are the ultimate goal, but nothing happens without the individuals who have lost blood, sweat, and even tears for the Plano program. Because of that, the kids are honored in their own way as hundreds of framed 8×10 photos of each player McCullough and his staff have coached hang on both sides of the hallways.

If a player earns a varsity letter, he goes up on the wall. That includes standouts such as Rex Burkhead, whom McCullough considers the best player he's ever coached in his twenty years at Plano. Burkhead is one of two Wildcats, along with lineman Alan Reuber, who has made it to the NFL since the 1970s.

But even the players who barely sniff the field during their time at Plano will get a picture on the wall. It's just another way the coaches pay tribute to those who have put in the time, effort, and dedication for the maroon and white.

Now three weeks removed from the end of Plano's schedule, McCullough was already looking ahead to the 2016 campaign. His 4–6 record kept him up at night and would likely do so until next season rolled around.

But even though his eyes were fixated on the future, McCullough hadn't forgotten the present or the past. In every interview he did with the media, the head coach typically found a way to shift the focus from football or specific plays and steer the conversation toward the bigger picture.

"We're trying to get these kids to be honorable men and to do things the right way when they leave here," McCullough said. "Most of them aren't going to play football after they're done. We know that. They know that. Everything they do is a reflection of us, and I think that's why we get into coaching. So we can help these young men grow into the best football players they can be, but more important, the best young men they can be."

That's why he talked to all of them about the importance of going to college. If they had the ability, opportunity, and desire to play football at the next level, that was a bonus.

Obviously, running back Brandon Stephens had been one of the highest recruits the Wildcats had ever had. His press conference back in early September saw him announce his intention to sign with Stanford, but there were rumblings starting that he might be wavering on that decision.

In the hallway, Stephens would tell his inquisitive classmates that Stanford was the choice, but quietly, and privately, he was pondering other options. The phone calls and the letters certainly didn't stop, as schools such as Texas A&M, Alabama, UCLA, and Oklahoma, to which he actually had made an unofficial visit after the season, were creeping back into the picture.

When college coaches called to speak to McCullough or one of his assistants, the high school coaches would oftentimes turn into salesmen, trying desperately to convince their collegiate counterparts to accept their players, knowing the more kids they put on college rosters, the better it would look for the Wildcats program.

But McCullough didn't have to sell any team on Stephens, or even offensive lineman Kadarius Smith, who had committed to SMU several weeks back. Some of his other seniors, though, were a different story. McCullough fielded a few calls from lower-level colleges asking about Isaiah Williams, a talented offensive lineman who suffered a season-ending knee injury back in August and never played a down. Defensive end Byron Tate, a running back in his junior year, was another player on the radar of a couple of Division III schools in Texas.

"You want your kids to get that opportunity," McCullough said, "but you also have to be honest with the schools. They can see the tape, but they want to know about them, how they practice, what kind of kids they are, what kind of students they are."

Ultimately, McCullough and his staff were going to do what they could to put their players in college, but once that happened, they were far from forgotten. As the college football schedule came to a close for 2015, several of the assistants continued to communicate with former Wildcats who were wrapping up their seasons at the next level.

Chris Fisher rarely missed a chance to reach out to players he once coached such as David Griffith, a linebacker who had gone on to the University of Louisiana-Monroe. Griffith was one of Plano's best players in 2013, and he came back for a game against Allen during Monroe's bye week in September.

During the 2015 season, Plano had ten former players in college uniforms, including Sam Tecklenburg, whom McCullough has said ranks among the top "two or three" players he's coached at Plano. Tecklenburg was a redshirt freshman at Baylor, where he practiced all year as a tight end.

Several of the Plano coaches kept up with his progress during the year, as they did with other redshirting freshman, including Beau Hott (New Mexico) and Neema Behbahani (Texas A&M-Commerce). Both players made it back for Plano games in 2015.

Even though they may be a few years removed, the Wildcats staff will always be their "coaches." When wide receiver Anthony Antwine, who graduated from Plano in 2013, made his first career start for Arkansas during the season against Ole Miss on national television, the Plano coaches quickly texted each other to spread the word.

And when former Plano quarterback Richard Lagow finished up his junior college stint at Cisco College and decided to transfer to the University of Indiana, Plano offensive coordinator, Joey Stone, was one of the first to know.

The coaches checked up on the injury status of former kicker John Cummings, who played at West Texas A&M, as well as linebacker Sam Morell after he suffered a knee injury at BYU. Although he was five years removed from the Plano program, when Kobie Douglas was named senior captain at Incarnate Word in San Antonio, word reached the Wildcats staff in a hurry.

And it went further than the kids who were playing football. Coach Fisher traded texts with Brooks Panhans during the season, checking in with the former Plano quarterback who was then a student at Cornell University, and with Mitch Hansen, who had decided to focus on baseball during his final year and was eventually a second-round pick of the Los Angeles Dodgers.

The players who come through Plano are immediate members of the school's family. They all come and go, but they are never forgotten.

There's a big hallway full of pictures to make sure of that.

Saturday

In professional baseball, every team wants to beat the New York Yankees. In the NBA, beating the Los Angeles Lakers or New York Knicks holds the same sway. And in the world of professional football, of course, the Dallas Cowboys always get everyone's best shot.

It goes with the territory of being among the most prestigious, rich-in-history franchises. Along the way, they've developed both love and hatred among fans. Even in down seasons for those storied teams, the thrill of beating them never seems to get old for their opponents.

In college football, especially in the Lone Star State, that team is the Texas Longhorns. For so many years, the Longhorns ruled the state when it came to football. In some regards, they still are viewed as the premier football program in Texas, despite a few struggling seasons that have failed to meet the always sky-high expectations for the school's fan base.

Before Art Briles arrived on campus in 2008, Baylor fans had to go back to the Grant Teaff–coached days of the 1970s and 1980s to recall some of their favorite moments. Ask a team historian to name a few memorable games, and a 50–7 win in 1989 always comes to mind. Or the 1978 tilt when Teaff inspired his players with a pregame speech that included his putting a live worm in his mouth to get their attention. The Baylor players exploded out of the locker room and won the game, 38–14.

And you guessed it, both of those victories occurred against Texas.

In 2015, the Longhorns were not going to a bowl, sitting with just a 4–7 record as they entered their final contest of the season. For Texas, traveling to Waco, which is just an hour north of Austin, was the closest the team would get to a real bowl game.

Meanwhile Baylor, coming off the heartbreaking loss to TCU in one of the rainiest college football games of all time, now had no shot of winning the Big 12 title. But because of tiebreakers, the Bears could still be the Big 12's representative in the Sugar Bowl, assuming of course that they took care of business at home and beat Texas.

In the history books, the Longhorns have dominated the series, owning a 74–26–4 record that once included sixteen consecutive wins from 1958 to 1973 and another twelve straight from 1998 to 2009.

But the tables had turned in recent years, with Baylor winning four of its last five games against Texas, only dropping a 56–50 shootout in Austin during the 2012 season. Seemingly, the biggest win Baylor had over the Longhorns, however, occurred at the end of the 2013 season when

Briles told Texas he would stay at Baylor, choosing not to be interviewed for the Longhorns' head-coaching position.

As the 2015 regular season came to an end, the Bears were about to make their sixth-straight bowl appearance. And if they could beat Texas, it would be the school's first trip to the Sugar Bowl in fifty-nine years. That would be quite a birthday present for Briles, who had just turned sixty two days earlier on December 3.

In fact, he wasn't aware that his family had organized a surprise birthday party for him following the Texas game at one of his favorite Mexican restaurants close to the stadium. The rather small group of invitees were told to be there around 4 p.m., a good five hours after the 11 a.m. kickoff. But there was one rather strong contingency: if the final outcome of the game didn't correlate to a festive party atmosphere, then the party was likely going to be called off.

But lose to Texas? With a Sugar Bowl on the line? It didn't seem realistic, especially considering the clear skies above McLane Stadium, something of which the Bears hadn't seen much throughout the year. With better weather, Baylor was hoping, expecting, and counting on seeing the Chris Johnson who came off the bench two weeks earlier to shock Oklahoma State with three touchdowns, and not the one who turned the ball over twice and didn't complete a single pass in the second half during the loss to TCU.

Before the game even started, one of the lingering questions surrounding the program was seemingly answered—and it wasn't good news for the perceptive fans in the stands. The last home game was senior day with the Bears introducing all of the players who were appearing in their final game at McLane Stadium. Each senior was announced, standing next to Briles, who gave them a quick hug and a personalized one-liner before sending them through the "Baylor Line," the freshman students who run onto the field before the game, one of the school's most recognized traditions.

The big surprise, though, was seeing wide receiver Corey Coleman in the line, considering he was just a junior. Sure, there were questions about whether Coleman, a finalist for the Biletnikoff Award as the nation's top receiver, was going to bolt for the NFL after the season, but no one figured the answer would be revealed like this, on "senior" day.

Briles and Coleman both confirmed to reporters in the postgame press conference that he would skip his final year and go pro. Briles pointed out that since Coleman redshirted his freshman season in 2012, and had already spent four years in the program; they decided to let him be honored by the crowd one last time.

But despite a decorated career that saw him rewrite some of Baylor's record books, catching more touchdown passes than any player in school history, Coleman's final game would be unlike anything he had seen in his previous four years.

From the start, Baylor should've known things would be different, as the offense was held without a touchdown on the opening series for the first time all year. Then on the Bears' fourth offensive series, still without a point, Johnson was blasted by two Texas defenders during a run, fumbling the ball away for yet another turnover. But more importantly, the quarterback took a huge blow to the head and was diagnosed with a concussion, ending his day midway through the first quarter.

Coaches, players, trainers, support staff, former players, and everyone else on the sidelines all just looked on in disbelief.

Really? This is really happening again? The top three quarterbacks are all injured now? Who's next?

The answer was no one. Baylor did not have a fourth quarterback on its roster behind Seth Russell, Jarrett Stidham, and now Johnson, who was woozy as he was helped off the field.

While he did get some practice reps during the week, wide receiver Lynx Hawthorne was never really expecting to play quarterback. The team's punt returner and slot receiver, he hadn't played quarterback since his high school days in Refugio, Texas, where he was used more as an option runner to take advantage of his cat-like speed.

But his arm? Well, Hawthorne really couldn't throw the ball more than thirty-five yards down the field and even those passes were wobbly and off target. He was not a quarterback by any means, but at this point, he was the best Baylor had. Perhaps unsurprisingly, Hawthorne's first pass of the day was intercepted, and after a couple of short throws on Baylor's next drive, he was picked off again in an attempt to get the ball down the field.

Nothing was working for the Bears. Even when they did mount some kind of offensive movement, kicker Chris Callahan, who had been inconsistent all year, then missed two field goals to keep Baylor off the scoreboard.

To make matters worse, another brewing problem was happening on the other side as Texas was racking up points, building a 20–0 lead as the two teams went into the locker room for halftime.

Stunned at how the first two quarters had played out, Briles heard some of his players and coaches trying to rally the team with motivational words such as "we're all right, we've got this" and "there's a lot of football left to go."

But he wasn't sure his team was all right.

"I don't know if we can get a first down," he said to one of his offensive assistants walking into the locker room. "We've got to do something."

Halftime in college football is typically around twenty minutes. To the Baylor coaches on this day, it probably felt like two. Not only did they need to regroup, but they also were about to restructure their entire offense—and all in one halftime.

Kendal Briles recalled that offensive assistant coach Joe John Finley, who was a tight end at Oklahoma before spending four years in the NFL, was the first one to speak up with the idea.

"We got in there, we were just trying to settle down and figure out what was going on. We needed to make yards and first downs," Kendal said. "Joe John Finley said we could expand the package and just snap it to the running back. We had two plays [in the game plan] for that week, so we could take some pressure off Chris, so we just expanded that, and that was our halftime adjustment."

But as the offensive assistants were trying to figure out how to run these new plays, more issues were popping up. Not only was Baylor down three quarterbacks, but the top two running backs—Shock Linwood and Devin Chafin—were both now banged up as well and weren't available for the second half.

"It was chaotic for a little bit," recalled Jeff Lebby, who had just lost his top two backs for what was now going to be a running offense. "We had guys up on the chalkboard drawing plays, and we're trying to get Johnny [Jefferson] and 'T-Dub' [Terence Williams] ready to go."

Somehow, amidst all the confusion, the Bears were able to come out in the second half looking like a brand-new team.

Baylor got the ball and immediately pounded it right down Texas' throat, using a combination of Jefferson and Williams, who were both primarily taking direct snaps from the center. Hawthorne was still in the mix and actually took a snap and handed it to Jefferson on the Bears' first touchdown.

The next drive produced a field goal and the third offensive possession resulted in Hawthorne running to the outside, where he extended the ball to the pylon, scoring a dramatic touchdown that pulled Baylor to within 20–17 early in the fourth quarter.

Yes, it was very effective, but the Bears were used to scoring fast, having put up at least fourteen points in one quarter twenty-one different times. In this game by the time the offense got to seventeen points total, there was only 9:40 to play.

Once a quiet, stunned crowd at McLane Stadium, the fans were now alive, almost willing the Bears back into the game. Texas had yet to score a point in the second half and the momentum was clearly in Baylor's favor. Just one more stop on defense, and it seemed probable the home team would complete the improbable comeback.

Texas wouldn't roll over, driving for a field goal of its own, but the Bears were in striking distance, down just 23–17.

"Let's go win the game," Art Briles said to Hawthorne as he walked back on to the field. "We're in great shape. Let's go win."

Unfortunately, on a fourth-down play from the Baylor 31-yard line,

Jefferson picked up the first down, but lost a fumble in the process. The Longhorns recovered and then chewed up valuable minutes.

Baylor did have one last-ditch effort, moving to the Texas 47-yard line with just four seconds left. Knowing that Hawthorne couldn't throw the ball to the end zone, they inserted Jefferson as the true quarterback. While he had a nice throw with a tight spiral, Jefferson probably threw it a tad early and didn't give his receivers—Coleman, KD Cannon, and Jay Lee—a chance to run under it for a "Hail Mary" completion. The ball was picked off at the goal line with the Texas players then running onto the field to celebrate their fifth win of the season.

The Bears were certainly not stunned by the outcome. Down 20–0 at the half without a true quarterback in uniform, there wasn't much faith that Baylor would be throwing the ball into the end zone for a chance to win.

But that didn't make the pain go away. In fact, while all the players and coaches wanted to run inside to the locker room and rid themselves of the moment, they couldn't. The Baylor video department had produced a memorable tribute to the seniors in their final game. So there they stood, watching the video board and a montage of highlights to the song "Brother" by the group NEEDTOBREATHE.

Some of the seniors could barely watch. Shawn Oakman, who was featured halfway through the two-and-a-half-minute video, could barely lift his head up, staring straight into the ground. All-America tackle Spencer Drango had his arms draped around some fellow linemen and couldn't hold back the tears as he watched his "brothers" up on the screen, knowing they would never play another game in this stadium.

Even more gut-wrenching was losing out on a chance to play in the Sugar Bowl in New Orleans, likely against Ole Miss. Instead, Baylor was now projected to play in late December in the Russell Athletic Bowl in Orlando.

"We just have to try to salvage our season by going to our bowl game and winning," a dejected Briles said in the postgame press conference. "That's really all we can do at this point. But we're extremely disappointed for sure."

It was a strange feeling of mixed emotions for Briles, who knew how important a trip to the Sugar Bowl would've been for his program. But trailing 20–0 and without a true quarterback, yet still coming back and giving themselves a chance to win, was "inspiring" to the head coach.

"We had eight different guys take a snap in the game," Briles said. "That's not good. But we found a way to rally to where it was like, 'Hey we may have five bullets in it, but that sixth one missed. We're still alive, and we're still good.' "

But it was not good enough to party. After the game, Briles wasn't even told of the birthday event, and like usual, went home with his family and waited for the official word on where his team would be headed next.

Sunday

The younger generation of football fans, the millennials, might have a different opinion from their elders about the NFL's top game of the week. They also might have different answers when asked about the Cowboys' biggest rival.

But for the fans who watched Roger Staubach and Bob Lilly and respected Tom Landry and his stoic facial expressions and consistent, classic wardrobe, they still reflect back to what they call the good ol' days. And back then, no game was ever bigger than the Dallas Cowboys and Washington Redskins, especially on *Monday Night Football*.

Whether it was the real-life version of Cowboys and Indians, or just a bitter rivalry between two teams that couldn't stand each other, Dallas and Washington have always provided fireworks and memorable moments.

Even though ESPN's Monday night matchup now has secondary status, the NFL having since made *Sunday Night Football* its premier showcase, it's still the final game of the week. And when the Cowboys and Redskins met for a December 7 showdown, it marked the seventeenth matchup on Monday night between the two teams, tying the Oakland Raiders–Denver Broncos rivalry for the most meetings on *MNF*.

In the pregame warm-ups, Rolando McClain, who wasn't the most vocal leader on the team and rarely gave rah-rah speeches, jumped in the middle of the Cowboys' linebacker huddle before kickoff.

"Man, ya'll remember when we were back in high school . . . and the Friday night lights?" McClain asked, referencing the title of what became a best-selling book, movie, and then TV series depicting a high school football team in Odessa, Texas. "Man, it don't get any better than this. Let's have fun, play for each other, and leave it all out there."

If ESPN had a choice, the Cowboys would've entered the game with a better mark than 3–8, and Tony Romo would also have been in uniform. Then again, after twelve games, it was rather clear that the Cowboys' record and Romo's health went hand in hand.

The Cowboys decided not to place Romo on injured reserve as long as they were mathematically alive for the playoffs. Dallas still had a shot to win the NFC East, and if that could happen, Romo would at least have a chance to return, assuming he didn't have surgery to repair his damaged left clavicle.

Romo held off on the surgery and traveled with the team, serving as another set of experienced eyes for backup Matt Cassel and anyone else who needed it. Romo would occasionally go to the defensive huddle and offer up his take on alignments as well as tendencies he saw from the opposing quarterback.

On this night, Romo had a front-row seat for history, although he would've rather been the one throwing the ball. But Jason Witten, who came into the league with Romo back in 2003, became just the tenth player, and second tight end, in NFL history to record 1,000 catches. His seven-yard reception from Cassel didn't go unnoticed on the Cowboys' sideline as seemingly every player on the team went over to Witten at the next change of possession to offer up his praise.

"You're the best," Romo said to Witten in a subtle, quick way, knowing the tight end didn't like to get caught up in individual achievements, especially in the middle of a game. The Cowboys' equipment staff made sure to retrieve the ball and lock it up in one of their storage cases, so they could paint it up and deliver it back to Witten for a keepsake.

While his teammates were congratulatory, there was a different problem brewing on the Cowboys' sideline, one that wasn't an issue on the opposite side. Today's NFL has made huge strides in game management, thanks to technology. Every team in the league uses electronic tablets to get real-time pictures of each player and the pre-snap alignments. It has become a vital part of coaches' sideline adjustments, especially since the photos and video are usually available for viewing by the time the players get back to the bench.

However, in the second quarter, the tablets did not function for the Cowboys during two straight series. When Jason Garrett was informed of the issue, he went straight to referee Walt Anderson, figuring this was similar to when the headsets go out on one sideline.

NFL rules state that one team cannot use its headsets to radio from the sideline to the assistant coaches upstairs in the booth if the other team cannot. Anderson told Garrett he would make sure the Redskins stopped using their tablets.

A few plays later, though, the Cowboys coaches realized the problem hadn't been fixed. And to make matters worse, Dallas couldn't even go back to its "old-school" way of printing the photos because the sideline printer was also not powering up.

Garrett again called Anderson over. "Walt, we can see what's happening over there. Ours aren't working. And they're using theirs. So, do something. Stop the game or something."

Anderson eventually had to get clarification on the rule from the NFL office, and relayed the message that the tablets were not under the same rules. Therefore, the Redskins didn't have to stop using them. Garrett was beside himself, but all of this was happening in between series, and sometimes even between plays.

With the Cowboys chalking it up as yet another "home-field advantage," the situation never got fixed. Cassel, a 10-year veteran, said it was the first time he'd ever gone through a game without looking at some kind of overhead pictures.

Perhaps the malfunction was one reason the Cowboys had a hard time getting Dez Bryant open, but trailing 9–6 midway through the fourth, Cassel finally delivered a strike to the star receiver for a 42-yard catch, his first of the game. After Dallas failed to take the lead with a touchdown, another Dan Bailey field goal tied the score.

But that would be the start of a *special* fourth quarter that saw the Cowboys' special teams take over. A forced fumble on Washington's DeSean Jackson during a punt return, one that saw him backtrack thirty yards to try to get around the corner, was recovered by punter Chris Jones with 1:26 to play.

Oddly enough, the Cowboys hadn't scored a touchdown all game, but when they finally did, it wasn't exactly what the coaches wanted. From the sidelines, Garrett had wanted the offense to pick up some yards, chew off the final seconds of the clock, and then let Bailey win the game with another field goal. But Darren McFadden ran out of bounds on first down, and then scored on the next snap, giving Dallas a 16–9 lead, but with too much time on the clock.

Jackson then tied the game for the Redskins with a 28-yard catch, but once again, with forty-four seconds left to play, there was enough time for the Cowboys.

"Go win the game, Lucky!" Romo said to rookie return man, Lucky Whitehead, as he trotted back for the ensuing kickoff.

Whitehead didn't win it there, but his 46-yard return gave the Cowboys a chance. Cassel then hooked up with Bryant for two passes before Bailey drilled his fourth field goal, this one from fifty-four yards out to give the Cowboys a 19–16 victory.

For the first time all season, the Cowboys had earned a victory without Romo in uniform.

The players' celebration didn't reflect a four-win squad. Then again, this 4–8 team was only one game back from its three rivals in the NFC East, who were all at 5–7. Better yet, the Cowboys were 3–2 in division play, giving them a tiebreaker edge if they could pull even in the standings.

After a few minutes of jubilation in the locker room, a stone-faced Garrett interrupted the commotion to address the team.

"Guys, it wasn't perfect on offense. It wasn't perfect on defense. It wasn't perfect in the kicking game. But what was all over that, what was all over that for sixty minutes was fight. At different times in the game, there was an opportunity to look for an escape hatch. Over and over again, an opportunity to say, 'pretty good fight, but it's their night tonight.' We didn't do that.

"Don't ever lose sight on what happened tonight. We're going to build on this. When you have courage enough to put it all out there, and take advantage of an opportunity, you get another opportunity. And it's waiting for us Sunday in Green Bay."

Somehow, the Cowboys were still alive. And heading back to the place where their season died just eleven months earlier.

Chapter 16

WINTER WONDERLAND

Friday

The phone calls started about 8 a.m. on most mornings. There were sporadic calls throughout the afternoon, and then they picked up again in the evenings.

This was the household of Brandon Stephens, one of the best running backs in the state of Texas, who had just finished his senior season, wrapping up a four-year career at the varsity level. If it wasn't recruiting coordinators or college coaches calling to get a piece of him, it was the countless number of reporters from recruiting websites trying to get the latest scoop on the eighteen-year-old and where he intended to play football at the next level.

Stephens had heard stories about the intense recruitment of other players, and even some teammates, but wasn't expecting anything like this. And to think, what if he *wasn't* already committed to Stanford? Had Stephens not committed to the Pac-12 school back in September, he knew the calls and text messages would've been over the top, probably something he couldn't have handled.

"It was pretty crazy after the season," Stephens said. "I thought it would die down, and it did a little, but there were a lot of schools that just kept calling."

There was one particular university in Texas, an institution Stephens chose not to reveal, who went a little too far.

"I really had no interest at all in their school," Stephens said. "But they never stopped calling and messaging. Finally, I had to just be upfront with them and tell this guy to chill out. There wasn't any interest in that school. At times, I really got tired of the whole thing."

As of mid-December, Stephens was holding strong with his commitment to Stanford, which finished its college season on a high note, winning the Pac-12 championship thanks to the legs of do-it-all running back, Christian McCaffrey. Whether it was running the ball, catching passes, or returning kicks, McCaffrey quickly took the college football world by storm. He finished second in the Heisman Trophy voting behind Alabama's Derrick Henry, but did win National Player of the Year honors as voted on by the Associated Press.

While Stephens would get asked by friends if he still felt strongly about Stanford, especially considering McCaffrey's presence, the Plano senior always had the same answer.

"No, I loved watching him play," Stephens said. "Playing with Christian was an exciting part of going there. But I never really looked at the guys on the team like that. It wasn't about the players. It was more about the school being a good fit for me."

As Stephens headed into the Christmas break, Stanford indeed seemed the right fit.

Meanwhile, Darion Foster was still deciding on his college of choice. He had applied to Sam Houston State University in Huntsville, Texas, mainly for its prestigious criminal justice program.

Foster had always had an interest in Midwestern State University in Wichita Falls as well. Living with his uncle and aunt, he had been to several MSU sporting events, considering both Chris and Janna were graduates of the school. The two-hour distance from Plano was also appealing, giving him enough space and freedom to be on his own, but also close enough to get back home for holidays, birthdays, and maybe just to get his laundry done on the weekend.

But before he could focus on his next career move, Foster was focused on his wrestling moves, which were improving with each tournament.

At a tri-state meet at Lake Highlands High School in Richardson, a suburb of Dallas, Foster advanced to the final round and was not only ahead on points, but had also been controlling the entire match. Unfortunately, just a couple of minutes away from winning his first meet, Foster, exhausted and still a bit raw with his technique, got caught off balance and was pinned, finishing second.

In the stands, his uncle couldn't contain his disappointment. After the match and before Foster got back on the team bus, he chatted with his aunt and uncle, and while Fisher didn't say much, Foster knew "he was pissed off. I could feel it."

Had Fisher been told a few weeks earlier that Foster would place second in any tournament, he would've been ecstatic and shocked. But watching him control a match and find a way to lose was hard for him to take.

At home, it was Janna who had to remind her husband that Foster did finish second, and that he shouldn't overlook that accomplishment.

A few weeks later in Arlington, Foster finally got his victory, winning three matches over a two-day span in the 220-pound weight class, to claim his first-ever tournament medal. Immediately after the match, Foster found his phone and texted the news to Fisher, who wasn't able to make the meet. Needless to say, it was one of the best text messages Fisher had ever received.

If that text was among Fisher's favorites, the phone call he received the Friday before Christmas will also go down as an all-timer. At home watching the Class 4A state championship game between La Vega and Argyle, he got a call from Amarillo's 806 area code, which is common considering the dozens of his family members who live there.

But this wasn't someone from his family. Instead, Amarillo ISD Athletic Director Brad Thiessen was on the line to inform the coach that he had been selected as one of five final candidates for the head-coaching position at his alma mater, Palo Duro High School. The two had a quick chat, and Fisher agreed to be up there for a January 4 interview when he would meet with several school and district officials.

Now, this call to interview for a spot as a head coach was one he had received before, but never at a place that meant so much to him and his family. This wasn't just any job. It was the one that inspired him to get into coaching. He knew when he interviewed for the position that his passion and desire would be evident for the simple reason that this job was different.

And now, Fisher could only hope the outcome of the upcoming interview would be different as well.

Saturday

In college football, there are two easy ways to determine a team's success each year: either it played in a bowl game or did not.

Sure, there are different levels of expectations for all programs. Some are eyeing a national championship and nothing short of that is acceptable, while there are others that are ecstatic about just reaching a bowl game, giving their players and fans one last chance to celebrate a hopeful victory.

Art Briles is somewhat greedy. He wants both feelings to continue at his school. Yes, he wants a program ranked at the top each year, knowing the prestige of being considered one of the best in the nation will also bring in the best in the nation in terms of recruits.

But he always wants his players, coaches, and most certainly the fan base to remember where this program was not long ago. There was a time when the only reference to the postseason in Waco was the high school playoff games played at Baylor's old Floyd Casey Stadium.

Now, the Bears were considered mainstays in the bowl picture—only this year was still a letdown. The failed chance to make the Sugar Bowl in New Orleans stuck with the team for a few days, but Briles did his best to quickly change the attitude and mindset.

Baylor accepted the invitation from the Russell Athletic Bowl to face

North Carolina on December 29 in Orlando. And even though the pay-out for this bowl game was in the range of $2.2 million, a steep plunge from the expected $4 million the Bears would've received if they had gone to the Sugar Bowl, Baylor athletic director Ian McCaw said he was "honored" to have his team play in the game.

Considering North Carolina had recently lost to Clemson in the Atlantic Coast Conference Championship Game, keeping the Tar Heels out of the four-team national playoff, Baylor had the chance to face a quality squad, which would hopefully appease some of the critics who had blasted Baylor's non-conference schedule for its lack of high-caliber opponents.

Unbeknownst to many, at the end of the 2014 season, Baylor had agreed on a two-year contract with the University of Tennessee, where both teams would get one home game in the series. But the Southeastern Conference office stepped in and denied the game for unspecified reasons. Baylor was scheduled to buy out SMU from its 2015 opener in order to play the Volunteers before the game was overruled.

Whether as part of their regular-season schedule or in a bowl game, the country seemingly wanted the Bears to face better competition, especially after they finished 11–1 the last two years, only to lose to Central Florida in the Fiesta Bowl and then to Michigan State in the Cotton Bowl.

After falling to the Longhorns the previous Saturday, Briles sat and watched the UNC-Clemson game from his couch that night, knowing the Tar Heels would likely be his opponent if they lost as well. Right away, he saw a good team that he knew would be a tough opponent, even more so considering the uncertainty that surrounded his offense.

But the feeling of inspiration he felt after the Texas loss was starting to grow inside of Briles and rub off on his coaching staff.

"I think we felt like what we did, just drawing up plays at halftime, showed us that it could really be effective," Briles said. "We knew if we had a couple of weeks of good practice with the offense, we might have something to work with."

Those were intra-office conversations not meant for the public or media. While the national perception was that either Jarrett Stidham would be healthy in time for the bowl game and/or Chris Johnson would recover from his concussion and return to the starting lineup to play quarterback, the Bears were actually planning on running the "Wildcat" offense, or as they conveniently renamed it, the "WildBear."

During the two extra practice weeks, Baylor worked extensively on the timing of this new offense, which called for the center to snap the ball directly to a running back, receiver, or whoever lined up back there.

"You guys aren't quarterbacks out here," offensive coordinator Kendal Briles said during a practice huddle one cool, but sunny December day. "You guys are snap-catchers. You never know who is going to get the snap."

And hopefully North Carolina wouldn't either. So all along, Baylor announced Johnson as the starter because, in truth, he would play and catch most of the snaps. But they were also prepared to use tailbacks Johnny Jefferson, Devin Chafin, and Terence Williams, and run motion plays often for receivers Lynx Hawthorne and KD Cannon to swing around on reverses.

One player missing from the equation was Corey Coleman, the nation's leader in touchdown catches with twenty. Since the Oklahoma game four weeks earlier, when he suffered an injury during practice while playing defense in an attempt to surprise the Sooners by putting the ultra-quick receiver against OU's Sterling Shepherd on occasional snaps, Coleman had been nursing a groin issue that was only getting worse.

Surprisingly enough, the twenty scores occurred in the first eight games as Coleman didn't find the end zone once in the last four weeks. Some of that was due to the fact that Baylor was losing quarterbacks, some of it was the weather, and some of it was Coleman just not being his explosive self.

Art Briles is notorious for giving everyone around him a nickname or three. Players, coaches, support staff, media, friends, daughters—everyone he cares about seems to have a nickname from the coach. For Coleman, he was showing exactly why Briles had called him "Pretty Tough" for the last couple of years.

The double meaning referred to Coleman's always-fashionable attire, his charming smile, and his all-around efforts to keep up with his appearance. Football players are supposed to be rough and rugged, but Coleman's teammates have always called him "pretty." Yet, when it was time to work and get dirty, Coleman had never had a problem putting in the effort, evident by his chiseled physique that looked nothing like the scrawny freshman receiver who arrived in Waco in 2012.

And Coleman's ability to grind through a nagging groin injury that had developed into a sports hernia showed a toughness that few outside the Baylor organization knew he possessed.

While Coleman was leaning toward sitting out the bowl game to undergo surgery, he held off until after he got back from Atlanta, the site of the College Football Awards show where Coleman was one of three finalists for the Biletnikoff Award, given to the country's best wide receiver in honor of NFL Hall of Famer Fred Biletnikoff.

He had already earned All-America and All–Big 12 honors, but this one was different for Coleman. This represented not only him, but also those at Baylor before him who helped create "Wide Receiver U," the self-proclaimed nickname the school used to promote the successful pass-catchers who have transitioned to the NFL: players such as Kendall Wright, Terrance Williams, and even Josh Gordon, who starred at Baylor before drug issues ended his time in Waco. Sadly, failed drug tests in the NFL had also likely prevented Gordon from being one of the league's most dominating receivers.

Still, the wideouts at Baylor are a fraternity as well as a family. So when Coleman heard his name called as the winner, beating out TCU's Josh Doctson and Ole Miss standout Laquan Treadwell, he immediately thought of his "big brothers" who showed him the ropes. Coleman credited Williams and Wright, but also guys like Antwan Goodley, Tevin Reese, and Levi Norwood.

"Words can't really describe how I feel right now," Coleman said.

"This is for the guys like 'T-Dub,' Kendall, and all the guys with Wide Receiver U. It goes for all the receivers that helped me get it and accomplish this. I'm just blessed to win the award."

With Art Briles, Kendal Briles, and offensive line coach, Randy Clements, among those on hand in Atlanta, they thought they might get two awards during the evening's festivities. But All-America left tackle Spencer Drango, one of three finalists for the Outland Trophy as the nation's best lineman, came up short to Stanford's Joshua Garnett.

While Drango still had one more chance to show off his blocking ability, the award show proved to be the final event for Coleman, who decided to undergo surgery for the sports hernia and miss the bowl game. Top running back Shock Linwood needed surgery as well for a fractured foot; Stidham was never cleared to practice because of his foot injury; and, obviously, Seth Russell had been out with a neck injury since October.

The top two quarterbacks, the leading rusher, and the nation's best receiver were all planning to miss Baylor's bowl game against North Carolina. Still, when the Bears boarded their charter plane on December 23 for Orlando, there was plenty of reason for excitement and hope.

Unlike other road trips, the entire coaching staff was allowed to bring their families on the trip. While New Orleans might have provided a more prestigious bowl game for the team, there wasn't a better location for the families than Orlando, which features Disney World and Universal Studios. All four of Briles' grandchildren, who ranged in age from one to six, were on the trip, and he expected them to have plenty of memorable moments throughout their seven-day stay.

But his focus on the task at hand never wavered. Sure, there were team functions that saw the players visit local hospitals, something the head coach called "humbling and inspiring," and there was even a kickoff luncheon in a giant ballroom that welcomed players from both teams.

At one point during the event, which primarily honors many of the executives of the bowl game's numerous sponsors, one of the prize giveaways called for both quarterbacks to stand up and throw a football to a random table of sponsors. North Carolina's Marquise Williams drew a rather close table and tossed the ball a few yards to a man in a suit.

But Johnson wasn't so lucky. He was asked to throw the ball some forty yards to table 72 in the back corner of the room. Trying not to break any dishes along the way, he heaved the ball, which fell incomplete to a sea of hands trying to either catch it or protect themselves from this rifling football that was hard to see in the middle of a dimly lit ballroom.

Most of the audience chuckled, mainly at the sight of a football hurtling through the crowd. To the Baylor coaches, it was more ironic than humorous.

Because for what they had planned for Monday night's game, that very well could've been the longest pass Johnson would attempt all week.

Sunday

For the past eleven months, Dez Bryant had not been able to escape it. Sometimes he didn't really want to, but on other occasions he had no choice but to be reminded about a haunting experience that hadn't exactly improved over time.

Bryant knew he caught the ball back in January against the Packers in the NFC Divisional Round of the playoffs. He knew he made the catch, switched the ball to his left hand, extended that hand to the goal line, and made three steps in the process. Whether or not the ball hit the ground was irrelevant to Bryant, as well as thousands of Cowboys fans, because to him, he had secured the catch long before he went to the ground.

For a moment, the NFL officials agreed with him, ruling it a catch on the field. But after a Packers' challenge, the play, which came on fourth down, was overturned. The Cowboys never got the ball back again and instead of taking the lead with about four minutes remaining, their season came to an end right there on a chilly, but not freezing, Lambeau Field.

Everywhere he had gone since that play, Bryant said he was reminded about it "at least a couple of times." It could have been at a restaurant or grocery store, from a valet attendant, or just some random person he ran into; but make no mistake, they all seemed to chime in with some sort of "it was a catch" or "you got robbed" comment.

On Twitter, the hashtag #dezcaughtit had been used more than 70,000 times by Cowboys fans who just couldn't get over the moment that prevented them from advancing to the NFC Championship Game, where they would've faced a Seattle team they had already defeated back in October of that season.

For a guy who was reminded of the play daily, Bryant said the "catch" in Green Bay still "felt like yesterday" to him.

But that was lifetimes ago compared to the situation in which the Cowboys now found themselves. At just 4–8 and likely needing to run the table and win out for any chance at the playoffs, Dallas trekked back up to Green Bay and once again caught somewhat of a break in the weather. In December, the Wisconsin town is typically an icebox with snow or sleet, but on this Sunday afternoon, the Cowboys were met with some rather cold rain, but nothing that resembled the usual "frozen tundra."

When Bryant went out for pregame warm-ups, he instantly heard a chant of "Dez caught the ball! Dez caught the ball!" which made him chuckle as he pointed up to a patch of Cowboys fans, showing his approval.

But determined to stand out and prove last year was a fluke, Bryant appeared to be pressing once the game started. He dropped a couple of passes that he usually hauls in, including one in the end zone that bounced off his hands, resulting in an early interception.

Later in the first half, Bryant made what looked like another highlight-reel catch, reminiscent of the one from the playoffs. While this one was ruled a catch as well, the replay officials again reviewed the play and overturned the call.

Bryant wasn't just in shock. For the first time in his six-year career, he seemed as if he was losing confidence. Maybe it was the weather, which included a steady rainfall, but Bryant switched gloves three times during the game. Nothing was working, as he finished with just one catch for nine yards.

The star receiver wasn't alone, though, in his troubles. The Cowboys' defense hung around for a while, keeping the game close at 14–7 before the bottom dropped out. Poor tackling in the fourth quarter allowed Green Bay to pour it on with two late touchdowns, pushing the final score to 28–7.

The Cowboys sunk to 4–9, but still they weren't out of playoff contention just yet. If they could manage to win the next three games and finish with a 7–9 record, there was a shot they would win the NFC East.

But for a team that was having trouble gaining positive yards on three straight plays, winning three straight games seemed implausible, if not impossible.

However, those narrow playoff chances were the reason why the Cowboys refused to make personnel changes that would've given them more options to compete. For one, Tony Romo continued to stay on the active roster, although with his left arm in a sling, it was rather obvious he wasn't coming back to action. The word around Valley Ranch was that if the Cowboys snuck into the playoffs, somehow managed to win their first playoff game, and then advanced to the divisional round, which would've been a four-game winning streak with Matt Cassel running the show, Romo might have a chance to come back. And thus, the Cowboys saved his roster spot until the playoffs were no longer an option.

Secondly, Bryant was not healthy. His foot was good enough for him to play in games, but not exactly healthy enough for him to practice each week. In fact, one of the funnier moments of the season—yes, there were a few—occurred when members of the training and equipment staffs were working on a specialized shoe that Bryant could wear in practice.

As a member of the Nike Jordan brand, Bryant gets dozens of shoes each month, and his locker is filled with different pairs that he wears in practice. Returning from this fractured foot injury wasn't easy, and finding a shoe that fit just right was a challenge.

Bryant wanted to switch out the soles of one pair of shoes and put them inside another. But the sole was double-sided taped so well that no one could get it out. Assistant equipment manager Bucky Buchanan, associate trainer Britt Brown, and two other interns from both staffs were all working on this one shoe and trying to rip out the sole. At one point, eight different hands were holding, tugging, or ripping at the sole—and none of them belonged to Bryant, who was barely standing on two feet as he found the scene utterly amusing.

"I wish I had my phone so I could take a picture of ya'll," Bryant said, which was met with a playful cuss word or three.

But jokes aside, dealing with Bryant's foot was a season-long issue, just like Atlanta receivers Roddy White and Julio Jones claimed it would be back in Week 3. Just before the Cowboys and Falcons played, the Atlanta duo chimed in on Bryant's attempt to return from the fractured foot, with White saying it wouldn't get back to 100 percent all year, based off his experience of watching Jones deal with the same issue the previous season.

Just like the Cowboys were keeping Romo on the roster, the same went for Bryant, who emphatically told reporters one day in the locker room that he was "not shutting it down until the season is over," meaning he was not going to go on injured reserve if and when the Cowboys were eliminated from the playoffs.

While it didn't seem possible that anyone other than Romo or Bryant could occupy the headlines, another storyline was forming as the Cowboys prepared to face the New York Jets in a rare Saturday night tilt at AT&T Stadium.

While Cassel was the only backup quarterback to win a game for Dallas during the year, his record of 1–5 as a starter didn't sit well with the ever-frustrated fan base or even some on the coaching staff. Actually, the assistants were somewhat split down the middle heading into the Jets game about sticking with Cassel or moving to their fourth quarterback of the season, Kellen Moore.

Without a doubt, if Moore hadn't been so short at 5–10, not even close to the six feet the Cowboys listed him as on the official roster, he probably would've been inserted into the lineup sooner. With a baby-faced, clean-shaven, and unassuming look, Moore was anything but a prototypical NFL quarterback. Nor did he resemble a college passer, even though he had been a pretty good one.

At Boise State, Moore was the first Division I quarterback to win fifty career games, owning a 50–3 record as a four-year starter for the Broncos. The two-time All-American went undrafted, but spent three years with the Lions, mostly on the practice squad. In Detroit, he spent two seasons with then-Lions offensive coordinator, Scott Linehan, who moved on to Dallas, where he became a major voice in bringing Moore to the Cowboys. Now, Linehan was one of the coaches in the young quarterback's camp again, wanting to give him a shot.

After the Packers loss, Garrett told the media, "We believe in Matt Cassel," which might have been true. But that didn't mean they were above making a change. After a horribly thrown interception early in the Jets game, Cassel was pulled in favor of Moore, who was told by Linehan on the sideline, "You're up."

Moore got quite an ovation from the crowd, which turned into a roar when he beat an all-out New York blitz to find Bryant, who did the rest, giving Moore his first career touchdown pass.

On the sideline, the players nearly decapitated Moore, pounding his helmet with congratulatory slaps. The celebration was led by Garrett, who obviously could relate to his new quarterback, having been mostly a backup during his own career. The head coach knew firsthand the challenges of staying ready despite limited practice reps.

The touchdown gave the Cowboys the lead, and better yet, a chance to knock off a Jets team fighting for a playoff spot. But just like Moore showed flashes of preparation and poise, he also displayed a few other moments that revealed his lack of experience. Moore threw three interceptions, including one in the end zone and another on a desperation heave in the final minutes, as the Cowboys dropped yet another game, 19–16.

Moral victories might exist in other NFL cities, but never in Dallas, especially for home games. Many of the Cowboys walked off the field with their faces pointed downward, their record falling to a dismal 1–6 at AT&T Stadium for the season. When Romo rallied the team to a dramatic comeback win over the Giants in early September, no one could've imagined that they would then lose six straight at home. Of course, not many could've thought three other quarterbacks would take snaps for this offense as well.

And with that, the Cowboys were officially dead. A team that began the year with so much promise and hope was now eliminated from the playoffs with a 4–10 record.

With two games to play, the season couldn't end fast enough.

Chapter 17
BOWL OF FUN

Friday

At the high school level, assistant coaches find themselves doing more than just giving instruction on fundamentals and running drills.

Not only do they teach classes, grade papers, and administer tests to their students during the day, but the assistants also are the ones who often break down the game film, do the laundry, issue the equipment, and fix things when they break. They drive the school buses to and from games and will order the food that is ready for the team when the game ends.

In college and the pros, there are individuals and even staffs that handle each of those duties.

So it only makes sense that many high school assistants aspire to move up the ranks and field their own program one day. That attitude certainly isn't confined to only coaches or sports. Getting a promotion usually means more money, and more money can lead to stability for a person and his family.

At Plano, Chris Fisher had been rather upfront about his desire to lead his own team. Having interviewed for five different head-coaching gigs in the past, in several different parts of the state, it was clear that Fisher wasn't too picky about where he got his shot. He just wanted one.

But this sixth job interview was going to be different. Fisher didn't just feel it; he knew it. He knew, once he returned to his old stomping grounds of Palo Duro High School in Amarillo and met with the super-intendent, the athletic director, the principal, and everyone else on the hiring committee, that he would convince them he was the right person for the job.

Out of nearly eighty applicants, Fisher was one of five final candidates. And while he wasn't sure who the other applicants were, he was convinced no one was better qualified for *this* job. And he expressed it wholeheartedly in the interview.

"I truly believe all of the other jobs I interviewed for led me to that moment," Fisher said. "When it was time to talk football, we talked X's and O's and I knew some of the people in the room were getting me. When it was time to talk about the kids, I had no problem doing that, mainly because I was one of those kids. I've walked through those hall-ways. Some of those teachers now were *my* teachers back then.

"I told them about the community, having grown up in the Northside [of Amarillo], and that I understood what this school and this football team means to the people there. Those people are my family, literally, so I better know this community."

Lastly, Fisher recalled a moment that made the school's principal come to tears.

"I just told them about my journey as a coach: There might be other candidates who have won playoff games like we did. There might be some other candidates who have stood on that [Cowboys'] star at Texas Stadium. But the ones who have done that, haven't worn the blue and white. They don't know what it means to be a Palo Duro Don. I've lived in other places, but Amarillo has always been home. I've been a Palo Duro Don since I was a little kid coming to Dick Bivins Stadium. And I'm a Palo Duro Don right here as I sit before you. This is home. And I want nothing more than to come home."

Three weeks later, Fisher was announced as the next head coach of the Palo Duro Dons.

In his introductory press conference, which included nearly thirty of Fisher's family members standing in the back, he once again brought his passion, showing the Amarillo faithful that this former kid who sold programs at the Palo Duro games, who then played and starred for the Dons, was ready for the challenge of taking over the team, but still wasn't afraid to ask for help.

"I need one Northside family and that's what I've been sent here to do," Fisher said to those in attendance. "That's my job. I need one Northside family from grades K through 12 with one single mission. And that's preparing kids for life after high school. Whether it's college or whatever they choose to do. We need to raise better young men and women. We need to instill them with that character it takes to be successful. We need to hold them accountable, and that's what we plan to do. It's not going to be an easy fix. It's not going to be a quick fix. But, we can do it together."

The word "family" was mentioned two other times in his press conference, but when he spoke of his own family, including his wife and three daughters who were all in attendance, the joyful, upbeat press conference took an emotional turn.

Said Fisher to his daughters, Alyssa, Jaylen, and Aynslee, "Last, but not least, girls, you know the deal. We spend a lot of time away from each other. I spend a lot of time with other peoples' kids. But you guys, you never ever questioned it. Every second that we have together is precious. And all I want to do is be a good man for you. We are going to do this, and we are going to be successful. I have to say thank you. I'm not here without you, and everything I do is for you."

One person who couldn't be on hand was also a big part of Fisher's family. But Darion Foster, who had lived with his Uncle Chris for the last eight years, was back in Plano for the wrestling team's senior night. Luckily, his mother, Heather, was able to get down to the Dallas area and be there for her son.

But unlike the football season, where senior night represented the final game of the year, Foster was fortunate enough to advance to the district tournament, where he finished third, good enough to then move on to the regional tournament in nearby Allen. Foster won his first match rather quickly, but was eventually knocked out by the state's top wrestler, Patrick Bryan, who gave Foster quite the compliment afterward.

"He came up to me and said, 'In all honesty, you were my hardest match I've had in Texas this year,' " Foster recalled. "That was pretty neat, especially considering where I started from. So I didn't like to lose, but I couldn't feel that bad about it."

But the biggest news surrounding the Plano football program wasn't the fact that a longtime assistant was leaving to take a head-coaching job. And it wasn't that a few seniors had moved on too, such as Foster with his wrestling or quarterback Matt Keys' starring in the school play, *Legally Blonde.*

A story that became national news centered on star running back Brandon Stephens, who had been firmly committed to Stanford for nearly four months. However, just a few weeks before National Signing Day, when students across the country sign their letter of intent to the college where they will play football and other fall sports, Stephens had decided to re-open the recruitment.

He loved Stanford. He loved being there on the beautiful campus in Palo Alto, California, but something just didn't feel right.

"I just wasn't sure it was the right fit anymore," Stephens said. "Nothing really happened with them to change my mind. They didn't do anything. I just had to pull back and see where my heart was. And it really wasn't there with them at that time."

So with one phone call to a recruiting coordinator who had spent several months calling and texting the running back, Stephens informed Stanford of his decision to look elsewhere.

"They were disappointed, but they understood," Stephens recalled. "After that call, it was a huge relief for me. I knew I didn't have a lot of time, but there were some other places I wanted to visit. I just knew I wanted something different."

But nothing too drastic. All of the things he loved about Stanford—the rich tradition, being far from home, living on the West Coast, the wide-open style of football in the Pac 12—were considerations Stephens still coveted.

And ultimately, he would find those at another school. Only this time, he would keep it a secret until the end.

Saturday

There are many fans, media critics, and perhaps even some coaches who believe college football has too many bowl games.

The 2015–2016 schedule rolled out forty such contests, meaning 80 of the 128 teams in the Division I Football Bowl Subdivision played in the postseason. There's also a growing belief by some that other than the two semifinal games in the College Football Playoff, and then the National Championship Game, none of the others really mean anything.

People who share those sentiments weren't on any of the nine buses that rolled out of the luxurious Hilton Orlando hotel and trekked over to the Citrus Bowl for a Monday night matchup against North Carolina on December 29.

Among the most prestigious bowl games in college football, the Russell Athletic Bowl might rank somewhere in the middle, but it was by far the biggest and most important game Baylor was going to play all year. At least that's what Art Briles and his staff made their players believe all week in practice as they prepared for a Tar Heels team that had just seen its 11-game winning streak come to an end against Clemson, the number-one team in the country.

Ironically enough, Clemson and Oklahoma were meeting in one of the national semifinal games on January 1, but it was actually a rematch of a bowl game the two programs had played a year earlier in, yes, the Russell Athletic Bowl.

And don't think some of the coaches weren't reminding their players of that fact, especially some of the younger guys who were coming back the next year. No, this wasn't where the Bears thought they would end up, but if Clemson and Oklahoma could take the leap from this bowl game to the playoffs in one season, Baylor was convinced it could do the same.

But first, they had to put on a show, something most national pundits didn't think could happen, especially with Baylor missing its top two quarterbacks in Seth Russell and Jarrett Stidham, its leading rusher, Shock Linwood, and the nation's best receiver in Corey Coleman. Baylor went from a 3-point favorite initially to a 3-point underdog by most Las Vegas oddsmakers. A 6-point swing is rare for point spreads, but as key players for Baylor kept dropping like flies, the team's chances to win appeared to be going down at a similar rate.

In the lobby of the hotel, the players had to make a long walk from the elevators to the buses. Surrounded by fans and supporters on both sides, many were loose, wearing big smiles, just excited to play this final game in what had been a grueling season.

One player who wasn't all smiles, though, was running back Johnny Jefferson. And that was quite a change for the sophomore, who rarely walked around without a smile on his face. But his focus was at an all-time high even a few hours before kickoff.

Earlier in the week, Jefferson addressed the entire team, apologizing for his costly fumble in the Texas game that wiped out a chance to complete a second-half comeback. He promised his fellow players that he would make up for the "big mistake." But as confident as he was, and as anxious as he was to redeem himself, not even Jefferson could foresee what was about to happen.

The game began just as the prognosticators predicted. With Chris Johnson taking most of the snaps, Baylor had trouble sustaining its first drive, failing to score on its first possession for now the second straight game after starting the season with eleven consecutive opening-series touchdowns. On the flip side, North Carolina used four third-down conversions to find the end zone and take an early 7–0 lead.

But on the next series, Johnson did something that seemingly changed the entire course of the game: he overthrew a wide-open KD Cannon about forty-five yards down the field.

Yes, an incomplete deep pass, which was actually his second of the game after also overthrowing a receiver on the first series. Usually, passes that don't connect are considered wasted opportunities, but in this case they were highly effective.

Even though Johnson didn't hit Cannon streaking down the right sideline, the play showed everyone, including North Carolina's defensive coaches, that Johnson had an arm and Cannon had the speed. It made the Tar Heels stay back for most of the game, which opened a crack in the door that Baylor needed.

Another key moment occurred on a fourth-down play during that same drive when Baylor needed three yards. With Jefferson back as the only "snap-catcher," he surprisingly got to throw it, winging a pass out to the left flat for Ishmael Zamora, who picked up the first down. That drive saw Johnson, Jefferson, Cannon, Devin Chafin, Terence Williams, and Lynx Hawthorne all take snaps, with Hawthorne tying the game on a short run.

There were sweeps to the left, pitches to the right, smash runs up the middle, delay counters, and draws—and North Carolina wasn't prepared for any of it.

"After that first drive, I think we knew we had something," said Jeff Lebby. "We were confident all week that we could get it rolling. But not until you get out there do you really know if it's going to work."

It worked. It worked all night long, and it was mainly Jefferson doing the damage.

In the second quarter, Baylor broke open a 14–10 game with two rushing touchdowns by Jefferson, who was simply running through gaping holes provided by the offensive line. Led by four seniors, including left tackle Spencer Drango, Baylor's big men wore out the Tar Heels.

Chafin and Williams provided some of the dirty runs up the middle, but it was Jefferson's slashing that did most of the damage, as he finished off two straight drives with scores to build a 28–10 lead.

But a late first-half touchdown by the Tar Heels, which was aided by a penalty on defensive end Shawn Oakman for continuing to run after the quarterback despite losing his helmet, had Briles as agitated as he'd been at any point during the regular season.

"Helmets don't just come off!" he yelled at the side judge and any other official who could hear him. "It got ripped right off. How can you not see that? I've never seen a helmet just fly off."

Briles was upset for about five minutes, and his kicker missing a field-goal attempt just before halftime didn't improve the coach's mood any. It showed on his way off the field, as he had testy interviews with ESPN's sideline reporter and then Baylor's radio broadcast.

To the country watching, it was just another bowl game between a couple of teams ranked in the top twenty. To Briles and Baylor, these next thirty minutes of football were about to define their entire season.

But unlike the previous game against Texas, where Baylor coaches were scurrying to come up with their "WildBear" formation on the fly, this halftime was more about tweaking and polishing. Their plan was working, and nothing North Carolina could do defensively could stop it.

And so it continued in the second half, with the turning point occurring after Baylor pushed the lead to 35–24. North Carolina came right back and drove to the 5-yard line, but a forced fumble—one of the many great plays in the game by linebacker Aiavion Edwards—was recovered by the Bears in the end zone for a touchback.

On the next play, Jefferson then dropped the hammer on the Heels, busting loose for an 80-yard run that served as the backbreaker, extending the lead to 42–24. The only player who might have caught Jefferson on the play was Kendal Briles, who usually stands even with the line of scrimmage on the snap. He took off down his own sideline, cruising past the entire bench area and arriving down by the goal line at nearly the same time as Jefferson.

Kendal was one of the first to jump on Jefferson on the sideline as the Bears, now up eighteen points late in the third, started to sense the game was theirs. And that's when Kaz Kazadi gave them a flashback to 362 days ago.

"Don't forget about last year," Kazadi said, referring to the Bears' 20-point fourth-quarter lead in the Cotton Bowl that vanished, leading to Michigan State's stunning 42–41 win on New Year's Day. "That's not happening again. We won't let up."

The intensity on the field was extreme, but the trash talking in the stands was rather "suite" as well. The head coach of each team is given a luxury suite for the game, filled with food and beverages for their families. But the indoor suites also have an outside patio that overlooks the field. Just a four-foot barrier separated the two suites, which just so happened to have some frustrated UNC fans in one who were going back and forth with Briles' family in the other.

No two individuals are more into a Baylor game than Briles' two daughters, Jancy and Staley. Both in their thirties, the two sisters rarely miss anything that occurs on the field, whether it's a penalty that wasn't called or an injury to one of the players. And when it comes to voicing both pleasure and disdain, the two rarely have much voice left after each game.

The verbal jabs had been going back and forth with one UNC fan in particular throughout the night, and after the Tar Heels scored to make it 42–31, Jancy and Staley started to hear more chirping from the nearby suite.

"Just throw the ball one time, I dare you," the man said, referring to Baylor's run-oriented offense that was having so much success. "You don't even have a quarterback to throw it."

A few plays later, Baylor was back in the end zone, thanks to a 13-play drive that saw eleven runs, including rushes on the final seven snaps. Williams powered the ball over the goal line for a 49–31 lead, prompting Jancy, who is usually the more conservative one of the two, to simply lose it.

Standing up, with her veins about to pop out of her neck, the now red-faced oldest daughter shouted back:

"You don't have to pass it . . . when you can . . . run it up your ass!!!"

That comment even shocked some of her own family members, who at this point were trying to calm her down and remind her of the 18-point lead.

But her intensity was just another example how much this game meant to Baylor. She was a proud daughter who would cringe when she heard comments about her dad's 2–6 record in bowl games. This matchup didn't just mean a lot to Baylor. It was perhaps even more important to the Briles household—a fact some poor UNC fan had to experience the hard way.

In the fourth quarter, Jefferson more than kept his promise to his teammates. With a Baylor school record 299 rushing yards, he was able to finish the year with an even 1,000 yards, which along with Linwood's 1,329 yards gave the Bears two 1,000-yard rushers in a season for the first time in school history.

As the final seconds ticked off, Briles was trying to seek out North Carolina head coach, Larry Fedora, for the postgame handshake when his life suddenly turned cold. A Gatorade bucket of ice water drenched his backside, but Briles didn't mind. He grabbed the culprit, fifth-year senior Jay Lee, and gave him a big hug. It was the best worst feeling Briles had ever felt.

The team celebrated on the field like they had just advanced to the championship. Briles kissed the trophy up on the stage, and many players posed with the hardware or just with each other, sporting their Russell Athletic Bowl–winning T-shirts.

Inside the locker room afterward was an even wilder scene, as Briles awarded the game ball to offensive line coach, Randy Clements, announcing to the players that Baylor had just set an NCAA bowl record with 645 rushing yards in the game. That was followed by Briles' ever-popular "Whose house?" chant that turned into a raucous, water-tossing mosh pit that was so loud and over the top that it interrupted North Carolina's postgame press conference, which was being held on the other side of the locker room wall.

But this was Baylor's time to rejoice. After everything that had occurred before the season with the investigation, followed by injury after injury after injury, the Bears got to go out in style, finishing on the highest of high notes.

No quarterback, no backup, no starting tailback, and no superstar receiver—absolutely no problem for Briles and his staff. The game plan was downright wizardry, starting from two weeks earlier when he had declared Johnson the starting quarterback. But Baylor was able to keep its plan quiet, knowing all along that they were going to build off the second-half success against Texas, polish up the "WildBear" formation, and then proceed to run right over and through North Carolina's defense.

One player who didn't want the party to end was fifth-year senior Trevor Clemons-Valdez, who had started the season as a coaching intern but later suited up as a tight end. Now, he sat there in the locker room and just watched the entire scene before him.

"I was getting calls and texts from my family waiting on me," he said, "but I just sat there and didn't want to take my uniform off. I knew once I did, I probably wouldn't wear another football uniform again, so I just wanted to soak it all in. I was probably the last guy to take off my jersey that night."

Briles decided not to do his postgame press conference, sending Kendal to take his place. He did remind his son to mention that Baylor had now won fifty games in five years. But he didn't have to remind any of the coaches of the streak, as it was something the entire staff was pointing out with each hug and high-five.

"Fifty wins in five years," Lebby said. "How about that? Unreal."

For a program that had never earned more than thirty-six wins in a five-year period before Briles arrived in Waco, getting to fifty was proof that Baylor football was indeed higher than it had ever been.

And to think, this 10–3 season was actually a *down year.*

But while it appeared Baylor had finally pulled the season out of the ditch and was able to finish the season on a positive note, they had no clue what was waiting for them in the ensuing off-season—something that would completely turn the program upside down.

Sunday

There's an old saying in football, and it holds true at virtually all levels:

If you've got two quarterbacks, you've got none.

Obviously, there are exceptions to the rule, but normally, if one guy hasn't separated himself from the other, then it's likely that neither is good enough to make much of a difference in the game.

If that's the case with two, then it's certainly worse with three quarterbacks—and the Cowboys were now preparing to use their fourth.

But with the team sitting at 4–10 after a loss to the Jets, and preparing to head up to Buffalo to face the Bills two days after Christmas, there really wasn't much more to lose. Jason Garrett had said over and over how much he respected Matt Cassel and his experience and professionalism, but even he couldn't overlook Cassel's inability to get the job done. So it was time to turn the reins over to Kellen Moore as a starter.

The last time the Cowboys started four quarterbacks in one season came in 2001, when the quartet of Quincy Carter, Anthony Wright, Clint Stoerner, and Ryan Leaf produced a grand total of five wins. At this point in the 2015 season, the Cowboys would have gladly accepted a fifth victory and figured Moore had a good chance to get them there against the Bills, who were also out of playoff contention.

When it comes to routine, Garrett never likes big changes. Here's a guy who wears a navy blue long-sleeve shirt with either navy shorts or sweatpants, depending on the weather, every single day of the week.

To him, being eliminated from the playoffs meant very little when it came to preparation. The term "meaningless game" was laughable. That being said, the holiday season provided some exceptions. On Friday, which was Christmas Day, he allowed everyone to come in later, pushing back meetings and practice to allow his players, coaches, and staff the chance to spend their morning with family and friends or maybe just sleep in.

The team departed on Saturday for Buffalo, which could've been much worse weather-wise in late December. Temperatures in the single digits and below can be normal in upstate New York at that time of year, but the team arrived with temps in the thirty to forty range. But, of course, in keeping with the theme of the entire season in stops such as Miami, Green Bay, and somewhat in Washington, D.C., the Cowboys couldn't escape the rain, which ended up pouring all game long.

Although Moore was making his first start, he wasn't too unfamiliar with the Bills, having played against the team during the preseason when he was a member of the Detroit Lions. Buffalo head coach, Rex Ryan, said Moore "torched them," but also added that he was a "little bitty dude who throws with the wrong hand."

Actually, the southpaw, who would become the first left-handed quarterback to start a game for Dallas, was hoping to avoid the nightmarish beginning the last Cowboys passer had in Ralph Wilson Stadium.

Although Tony Romo was able to rally his team to a dramatic 25–24 win over the Bills on *Monday Night Football* in 2007, he endured six turnovers, including five picks. Buffalo had returned both an interception and a kickoff for touchdowns on their way to taking a 24–13 lead before the Cowboys wrapped up their comeback by scoring nine points in the final twenty seconds, including a 53-yard winning field goal, to come out on top.

The funny part of that game occurred on the sidelines as Bucky Buchanan, one of the team's longtime equipment staffers, was tired of losing footballs when he traveled to road games, especially AFC teams such as Buffalo that rarely host the Cowboys.

In the NFL, the offense uses its own footballs, which are marked by the club's logo. Buchanan noticed that of the twenty-four balls he would bring for each game, he would only come back with a handful, as ball boys from the other team or anyone else on the sideline would snag one for a keepsake.

So for this 2007 game, Buchanan brought only twelve, the minimum required by the NFL. As it turned out, balls from all of Romo's turnovers were taken to the Bills' sideline by the players. The kickoff return for a score was also kept, and there was a field goal that went over the net and into the stands that wasn't retrieved.

By the end of the game, as the Cowboys were driving for the final score, they only had one football remaining—the one being used. So every incomplete pass down the field had to be retrieved and thrown back to the huddle, instead of using another ball from the sideline to speed up the process. Buchanan wasn't sure what the penalty was for not having enough footballs, but fortunately he didn't have to find out, as Dallas was able to finish the game with that last remaining ball and come out with the win.

Needless to say, Buchanan has packed twenty-four footballs for every road game since, including this next stop in Buffalo.

While Moore didn't turn the ball over as much as Romo did in 2007, he also wasn't very effective down in the red zone, a problem that had plagued the team all year, regardless of who was under center. The Cowboys managed a couple of field goals and for a while that was enough to keep the score close.

Dallas, playing without Dez Bryant who was held out of action with the recurring foot problems, trailed 9–6, but had the Bills pinned deep in their own territory midway through the fourth quarter. And that's when it happened. Again. Playing so well for most of the game, the defense gave up a huge play late, just as the unit had done throughout the season. The Cowboys couldn't corral quarterback Tyrod Taylor for a near safety in the end zone and let him scramble for a first down. Moments later, Bills running back Mike Gillislee dashed around the end for a 50-yard touchdown to put the game away.

The Cowboys, soaked and nearly frozen from the constant rain, headed toward the warm locker room knowing there was just one more game left to play in their dismal season, where nothing seemed to work, especially at the quarterback position.

Moore completed 13 of his 31 attempts for 186 passing yards and an interception. Nothing to get excited about, although considering the weather conditions and the game being his first start, it appeared he would probably be behind center in the season finale back home against the Washington Redskins.

Ironically enough, Cassel thought he would've been playing in this game when he was traded by the Bills to the Cowboys earlier in the season. As it turned out, he won the same amount of games for Buffalo as he did with Dallas—one.

To make this carousel even stranger, the one quarterback who wasn't with the team anymore, Brandon Weeden, had been picked up and signed by the Houston Texans, a team that was dealing with its own quarterback issues. Weeden not only started that weekend's game, but also led Houston to a 34–6 win over Tennessee. That put them one step closer to the AFC South title, which they claimed the following Sunday.

And if that wasn't enough, on the Cowboys' flight back to Buffalo, which is typically more than three hours anyway, bad storms in the Dallas area closed the DFW Airport temporarily, causing the charter to circle around for nearly forty-five minutes before the decision was made to fly elsewhere and refuel.

The destination turned out to be Houston, and before too long, the joke going around the plane was that Weeden himself would be there to greet the team. It was just a quick stop to refuel before the Cowboys made it back to Dallas, making the trip about a six-hour journey.

An hour for each point scored in the game.

Before the season finale against Washington, the biggest question being asked by both fans and reporters was whether or not Garrett was planning on using younger players and resting starters since the game meant very little to the Cowboys or even the Redskins, who had already clinched first place in the NFC East. Garrett scoffed at the notion.

In his final meeting with the team on the Saturday night before the game, he showed the players a video he had the Cowboys' television department put together that recapped the final game and at-bat for New York Yankees great, Derek Jeter. The future Hall-of-Fame shortstop had announced his retirement, and with his club eliminated from the playoffs, the regular-season home finale would indeed be his last in venerable Yankees Stadium.

Garrett showed a highlight of the game, and how Jeter was able to drive in the winning RBI with a hit. His teammates mobbed him at first base, happy that he could go out in style in front of the home fans.

"People said that game didn't matter," Garrett stated to his team. "Well, it mattered to someone. It mattered to Derek Jeter. We're privileged to play this game. We only get sixteen of them. I can promise you, every game matters. You might not know why it matters at the time, but they all count for a reason."

One person who absolutely got the message was wide receiver Terrance Williams, who thought about telling Garrett after the meeting how much he enjoyed it before changing his mind.

"I just thought I would show him on the field," Williams said. "There wasn't any need to talk about it. Just go do it."

With Bryant again sitting out the last game, Williams had a career-high 173 yards receiving on eight receptions, easily putting together the best game of his career. He was a steady target for Moore, who kept slinging the ball around despite the Cowboys falling behind 24–0 in the second quarter.

When the dust settled, Moore had at least made the score more respectable, the Cowboys eventually losing, 34–23. The quarterback finished with 435 yards passing, the seventh-highest single-game total in Cowboys history.

But while the 400-yard club was a nice ending for Moore, the number that overshadowed his effort was simply four, as the team stumbled to the finish line with a 4–12 record. The four-win season for the Cowboys was one of the worst in franchise history, and the worst for Jerry Jones since they went 1–15 back in 1989, his first year as owner.

Who could've dreamed the Cowboys would be mentioned with that inept squad? This was supposed to be a Super Bowl year, a year that would put Tony Romo, Jason Garrett, and the Cowboys back on top.

Instead, it was a painful journey that provided more twists, turns, dips, and spins than any rollercoaster that their Arlington neighbors, Six Flags over Texas, could ever create.

But finally, as the Cowboys walked off the AT&T Stadium field after another disappointing defeat, the ride was over. And that was the best news the team had heard in months.

Chapter 18

CHANGING COLORS

Friday

While some things will change over time, others will always stay the same.

In many cases, that's the story of high school football teams in Texas, especially when it comes to schedules and rivalries. No matter how tough a district might be for a school, particularly in Plano's case given how loaded it was with competitive teams, every head coach in Texas knows things can and usually do change every two years.

The University Interscholastic League (UIL) is the governing board of Texas high school athletics and gets together every other year to restructure the districts in an attempt to even the playing field for all schools, along with having every new district make geographic sense.

While Jaydon McCullough always expected some change, this year's realignment was welcomed, considering the Wildcats had found themselves in the only nine-team district in Texas for the last two years. At the same time, even when there was change, he knew the three local schools—Plano Senior, Plano West, and Plano East—would always be together and most likely combined with Allen, one of the state's perennial powerhouses.

McCullough, some of his assistant coaches, and Plano ISD athletic director, Gerald Brence, attended the annual Dallas-area realignment announcement, which turned into somewhat of a coaches convention as teams immediately try to not only figure out their new district mates, but also rapidly scurry to find non-district opponents.

More than five hundred coaches and athletic directors jammed into a giant room at an athletic complex in North Richland Hills, where McCullough learned his Wildcats were moving down to a traditional eight-team district and only keeping the two other Plano schools, Allen, and McKinney Boyd. Moving out of his district were Lewisville, Hebron, Flower Mound, and Flower Mound Marcus. They were replaced by Wylie, McKinney High School, and John H. Guyer High School in Denton, which was surprising and was met with mixed feelings. Denton was not only the farthest destination now for the Plano schools, but Guyer was traditionally quite competitive in all sports.

Still, getting back to eight teams was a plus and the switch was more of a wash for McCullough, who quickly picked up some non-district foes, including Hebron.

Adding opponents to the schedule was a bit easier than actually finding new coaches for the staff, though, particularly trying to replace departed defensive backs coach, Chris Fisher, who was dealing with his own realignment and scheduling about six hours north in Amarillo. During his first day on the job as the new head football coach at Palo Duro High School, Fisher used his realignment-day experience at Plano to help him quickly fill some scheduling gaps. He had planned to seek out a possible game against a school in Wichita Falls, where he went to college at Midwestern State; and as it turned out, Fisher was indeed able to schedule his Dons a game there against Rider High School, which also happened to be from where his wife, Janna, had graduated in 1994.

On a personal level, just being away from his family for the next few months would be a challenge in itself for Fisher, whose wife and daughters stayed in Plano to finish out the school year. Part of that decision included letting Darion Foster stay as well and graduate with his fellow seniors at Plano. While he decided against playing football, or even wrestling, at the collegiate level, Foster did make his aunt and uncle rather proud when he announced his decision to attend Midwestern State, where both of them had earned their degrees.

Likewise, quarterback Matt Keys knew he wasn't playing college football, which allowed him to pick the school of his choice. Keys was accepted by the Business program at the University of Texas and decided to spend his next four years in Austin.

"I always rooted for the Longhorns as a kid," Keys said, "so it's a great fit for me. They have a great business program there, and I'm looking forward to just having fun and being a student."

In fact, he was getting a head start on doing so in the spring. *Legally Blonde* was a success for Keys, who said starring as the quarterback in front of thousands of people every Friday night more than prepped him for the stage. The play sold out all three nights, but Keys wasn't done performing.

One of the thirteen finalists for the annual Mr. Plano award, which is a pageant-style contest where each organization in the school is represented, Keys was actually the representative for the Fellowship of Christian Athletes and not football. Still, his on-stage rap of Dr. Seuss' *Green Eggs and Ham* set him apart, as he was crowned the 2016 Mr. Plano.

But as January rolled into February, one of the best-kept secrets was about to be revealed as Plano prepared for National Signing Day, which had become a holiday of sorts for fans wanting to see what high school studs would be joining which college football programs.

Signing Day has become an event for nearly every high school across the country, giving student-athletes in all sports a press-conference type of setting to announce their college decisions in front of their families, friends, coaches, teammates, and peers.

At Plano, the speculation was building for weeks about what running back Brandon Stephens would do come Wednesday, February 3. After de-committing from Stanford a few weeks earlier, he had kept his decision quiet, not even informing many of his friends about the visits he was taking to other schools.

On the day of the event, Plano set up eleven different tables in the gymnasium, including five for football, along with some for signees in women's soccer, men's soccer, and men's golf. But the main attraction was Stephens, whose table wasn't like the other athletes who had their college of choice printed on a sign. His was covered up, creating even more drama for the occasion. His father, Tim, who had sported Stanford red throughout the season at home games, was wearing a red pullover, perhaps suggesting his son might be headed back to Stanford, or maybe Oklahoma.

The unveiling had to wait until the rest of the students were announced. Four of Stephens' teammates were headed to the next level as offensive tackle K'Darius Smith signed with SMU, while the trio of Byron Tate, Zach Wakefield, and Isaiah Williams, who missed the entire season with a knee injury, all signed with Southwestern College, a lower-level NAIA school in Kansas.

Finally, it was Stephens' turn to reveal his choice. With three local Dallas TV stations standing in front of him, cameras rolling, he walked to the podium and first thanked God, his parents, his coaches, his teammates, his classmates, and everyone else who helped him on his journey. He then motioned for Smith to bring him his backpack, which had the college cap he was about to wear, with his mother, Charlotte, quickly coming off of her bleacher seat to help uncover the sign at his table.

"At this time, I'm going to make an announcement that I'll be attending the University of California at Los Angeles," said Stephens as he pulled out a baby blue cap that had UCLA on the front. Charlotte then unzipped her jacket to sport her UCLA gear as well.

The crowd cheered, but several were stunned. UCLA never seemed to be on Stephens' radar, although the running back said they were firmly in the picture over the last six weeks.

"There was a lot to like about the place," Stephens said. "Once I decided that Stanford wasn't the best fit for me, I knew I wanted to stay out west. When I visited there, I just knew it was a good fit."

Local football fans had heard a similar announcement a year earlier when Plano West star tailback, Soso Jamabo, also signed with UCLA. Once on opposing teams, Stephens said he kept in touch with Jamabo throughout the past year.

"It's funny because at first I wasn't a big fan of him because he was my rival," Stephens said of Jamabo, who averaged 6.1 yards per carry, totaled 404 yards, and rushed for four touchdowns as a true freshman in 2015. "And now I'm going to be in the same backfield as him. We're both pretty excited about that."

Stephens signed his letter of intent, as did all of the student-athletes, and just like that, he was a UCLA Bruin. And for his parents, the process was finally over.

"We're so happy for Brandon and proud of him for being able to make his own decisions," Tim Stephens said. "I think going to a school that is a long distance away will be good for him. It's good for the soul.

"But, hopefully, we can get back to a little bit of normalcy."

A few steps away, McCullough looked on with pride, knowing Brandon Stephens was one of the most highly rated recruits Plano had ever enjoyed. Seeing him sign with a traditional power such as UCLA was great exposure for his program. But at the same time, McCullough was sad to see his star player go.

The coach stuck around to do a few interviews, but not for too long. McCullough shook hands, took some pictures, and told a few stories, but then said his goodbyes, citing a busy schedule on his plate for the rest of the morning.

The head coach walked back to his office, knowing he had assistant positions to fill, a quarterback to find, and a superstar running back to replace. There literally was no time to waste, as the 2016 season opener was only seven months away.

Saturday

Bowl games in the last week of December usually get forgotten by New Year's Day. A star-studded lineup of games on January 1, not to mention the College Football Playoffs and National Championship Game, almost always overshadow any team effort or individual performance that might have occurred just seven to ten days prior.

But the national buzz that Baylor created after dominating North Carolina without a true quarterback, the number-one receiver in the country, and the team's leading rusher, wasn't going away. National pundits were weighing in, offering up high praise to Art Briles and his staff, throwing out words such as "masterful" and "genius" for the way the Bears overcame all of their injuries and off-the-field distractions to manhandle a Tar Heels team that the experts thought was simply a better squad.

Football is a copycat business, and it's the same at all levels. Successful coaches get a chance to move up the proverbial ladder, which is how Briles got to this point in the first place, starting at tiny Sundown High School in West Texas and moving to Sweetwater, Georgetown, and then Stephenville High School, where he won four state titles, before moving up to Texas Tech as an assistant coach. That led him to head-coaching jobs at the University of Houston and now Baylor, where he had taken one of the worst college football programs in the country and made it a national power.

Because hiring Briles away from Baylor had somewhat turned into a lost cause over the last few years, most athletic directors knew Briles wasn't going anywhere, especially now that he had turned Baylor into an elite program. So if you can't get the head coach, at least try for his assistants. Or better yet, former assistants under Briles at other stops.

What the Russell Athletic Bowl showed was that Baylor could more than play the cards that were dealt. There's no better sign of a good coach than one who can make the best out of a seemingly bad situation—something Briles showed the minute he took the job.

A few weeks after the Bears' win, Briles wasn't thrilled to learn that Texas had hired a couple of his former assistant coaches, most notably Sterlin Gilbert to be the Longhorns' new offensive coordinator. Gilbert held the same title at Tulsa, a staff that was a who's who of Briles' former assistants, including head coach, Phillip Montgomery. He had been with Briles for eighteen years, at three different stops, before taking the Golden Hurricanes' job before the 2015 season.

Gilbert and Matt Mattox both got into coaching thanks to Briles, who hired them on his staff at Houston back in 2005. While Briles was certainly happy for any of his young coaches to get the chance to move up, he was halfway joking when he described the two hires as "identity theft," knowing both Gilbert and Mattox had a strong understanding of the offensive concepts Briles liked to use.

The uneasy feeling of seeing those moves would've been magnified by a thousand had his running backs coach and passing game coordinator, Jeff Lebby, also walked out the door. Keeping him on staff was beneficial to the team and his entire family, so when the University of Missouri called numerous times in an attempt to land Lebby as its co–offensive coordinator and offensive line coach, the possibility caused some nervous nights for the Briles family.

While Texas seemingly hired Gilbert to get an inside track on adopting Baylor's offensive system, that didn't appear to be Missouri's sole reason for its interest in Lebby, who had coached with the Tigers' new offensive coordinator, Josh Huepel, while at Oklahoma before coming to Baylor. Still, at the end of the day, Lebby passed on the job just like he had done a few years earlier when a spot on the San Francisco 49ers' staff had opened up. Baylor had a great thing going, and Lebby certainly wasn't ready to move himself and his family.

That decision was definitely a win-win-win for Briles, who also kept one of his best recruiters on the staff in Lebby as signing day approached. For months, Baylor's recruiting class was shaping up as perhaps the best in school history, with many highly recruited players committed to the Bears.

However, as all veteran coaches have experienced in the past, verbal commitments aren't always solid. Not until the signed letters of intent start rolling in on the fax will the coaches rest easy.

And as National Signing Day approached, Baylor was starting to feel a bit uneasy about some of its most-prized commits, such as offensive tackle Patrick Hudson. The Silsbee, Texas, native, rated by some national recruiting services as one of the top two offensive linemen in the country, had been solid in his commitment to the Bears throughout his senior year. But a few weeks before signing day, he had taken an official visit to Texas and pictures of him wearing a Longhorns jersey and flashing the "hook 'em" sign were surfacing on the Internet. Some of the recruiting reporters were even suggesting Hudson was on "flip watch," as a prominent player who could flip his decision to another school.

Briles, however, might have sweated Hudson's decision a little more had the player's mother not told him during the weekend that her son wasn't planning on making any changes. And sure enough, Hudson was one of the first to fax over his letter of intent come Wednesday morning.

In actuality, the Bears got a huge flip a few days earlier when Waco defensive back Parrish Cobb decided to change his commitment from Oklahoma to stay home and play for Baylor. When Briles and his staff first got to Waco, keeping local kids at home hadn't been a regular occurrence. Future NFL stars such as LaDainian Tomlinson (TCU) and Derrick Johnson (Texas) never truly considered playing for Baylor, and they weren't alone. Waco's high school standouts usually left for greener pastures.

Slowly but surely, though, the tide turned as Baylor started winning, with Ahmad Dixon deciding in 2010 to stay in Waco as one of the first big hometown wins. And Briles and Lebby both considered Cobb's last-minute change another huge recruiting swing for the program's 2016 class. And this one hit home, literally, for Lebby, who was next-door neighbors with Cobb and his family in 2009 and 2010 when he was just a graduate assistant on Baylor's staff.

"Parrish is born and raised in Waco, Waco to the core," Lebby said. "We've stayed in touch over the years. For him to flip and commit to us was a big deal. Just a huge, huge flip."

The other memorable last-minute change for Baylor since Briles took over came in 2013 with the signing of Andrew Billings, another Waco standout who was seemingly headed for Texas until he surprised the coaching staff, not with a phone call, but via fax. When his commitment rolled through the fax machine, it sent a roar throughout the hallways of the coaching offices. They knew getting a dominant defensive tackle such as Billings could be a game changer.

They couldn't have been more right about that after Billings naturally disappointed his coaches after the 2015 season by announcing he would forgo his senior year and jump to the NFL. Billings was one of three Baylor underclassmen to enter the NFL Draft, along with cornerback Xavien Howard and receiver Corey Coleman, who had made his own announcement back in early December after the Texas game.

"It's always a little bittersweet," Briles told reporters during Baylor's Pro Day on campus, where all draft-eligible players get the chance to conduct combine-like drills, tests, and on-field workouts in front of NFL personnel. "On one hand, you wish they would stay and play four years because they're just good. You want good players. But as a coach, it's great exposure for the program to have your players drafted. Plus, it's what all kids dream about. They dream about playing in the NFL and you want them to go catch their dreams."

Standing in Baylor's indoor facility during the middle of the Pro Day workout, he pointed up to the wall where colorful, giant banners of the school's recent first-round picks hung larger than life. Robert Griffin III and Kendall Wright were two of the five NFL first-rounders who suited up for Baylor since Briles arrived.

"We've got some room for a few more," he quipped. "I'm thinking we could have two, maybe even three this year."

Briles believed all three of his underclassmen had a chance to be first-round picks, especially after Coleman ran a blazing 4.35 in front of the scouts at the Pro Day. Howard and Billings would also have a chance to sneak into the first round, he figured.

One player who seemed likely to be a first-round pick had he come out a year earlier was defensive end Shawn Oakman, who decided to return to Baylor for the 2015 campaign, eyeing the chance to possibly be a top-ten pick. But over the course of the year, his play on the field didn't quite size up to his muscular, Adonis-like body.

While Oakman did become Baylor's all-time leader in sacks and flashed dominant plays throughout the season, his draft status instead declined. But Oakman's arrow started pointing up again when he recorded two sacks during the Senior Bowl—the most prestigious college all-star game—and then ran a 4.79 time in the 40-yard dash, which is quite fast for a 6–7, 290-pound athlete.

However, just two weeks before the draft, Oakman was arrested by Waco Police on a sexual assault charge that stemmed from an incident that occurred on April 3. While Oakman claimed the entire incident was consensual, his name was not cleared by the time that the NFL gathered for its yearly selection process on April 28. The once-presumed first-round pick, who had to watch his draft stock dip into the middle rounds, now wasn't expected to be drafted at all, or even signed by a pro team as an undrafted free agent.

For Baylor, it was yet another dark cloud on the matter of sexual assault, coming on the heels of the Sam Ukwuachu incident and the ongoing Pepper Hamilton investigation.

Oakman's incident marred what had been a rather pleasant off-season for Baylor, which had conducted another successful spring of practices. Sophomore quarterback Jarett Stidham was able to run most of the first-team reps, and Seth Russell was also cleared for contact after undergoing neck surgery back in October. For Briles, it was creating a good "problem" in that Stidham and Russell figured to have quite a competition for the starting job come August.

But before he could officially roll into the 2016 season, Briles had to put a bow on the previous year, which occurred in Chicago at the NFL Draft. Accompanied by his son, Kendal, Briles had a seat at Coleman's table in the Green Room, where about twenty-five projected first-round picks sit with their families and closest friends and/or coaches to await word on their next football destination.

After fourteen picks came off the board, Coleman's cell phone rang, prompting every bystander within earshot to perk up in excitement to hear who was on the other end.

But those who were within earshot of Coleman only heard him say, "What's up?" and "I'm ready, Coach" and "Yes, sir."

Coleman hung up the phone and said, "I'm going to Cleveland, baby!" which brought an eruption of cheers and hugs from his biggest supporters, including his mom, Cassandra Jones, who couldn't control her emotions as she emphatically hugged her son.

On the other end of the phone, Coleman was talking with Browns' executive vice president, Sashi Brown, and head coach, Hue Jackson. Brown asked him if he was "ready to catch some touchdowns?"

Moments later, Coleman was announced as the fifteenth overall pick, becoming the first wide receiver taken off the board, ahead of both Josh Doctson of TCU and Ole Miss' Laquon Treadwell, the two receivers he also had beaten out to win the Biletnikoff Award in December.

"First receiver off the board!" Briles said to Kendal, knowing their self-proclaimed moniker as "Wide Receiver U" had just received an extra jolt of ammunition. The Briles duo also had a few "Go Cleveland!" chants, knowing they would be paying even closer attention to the Browns now with Coleman joining Griffin, who had signed a free-agent deal with Cleveland in March. Griffin, the 2011 Heisman Trophy winner, never played with Coleman while at Baylor, but made several trips back to Waco to work out and support the program, creating a bond with many of the receivers, including Coleman.

A Richardson, Texas, native who starred at J.J. Pearce High School, Coleman dreamed of one day playing for the Dallas Cowboys. But as the catches turned into touchdowns during his time at Baylor and reality set in that the NFL was no longer a dream but his destiny, his allegiance shifted instantly to his new team.

"I'm just so excited about getting drafted and going to Cleveland," Coleman said. "This is a dream come true for me."

For Briles, that was music to his ears, considering he always tells his players to "catch your dreams." In fact, throughout the draft weekend, with every congratulatory tweet he sent out regarding his players, he used the hashtag "#dreamscaught."

While only Coleman went in the first round, Howard went high in the second (thirty-ninth overall) to the Miami Dolphins, while Billings surprisingly slipped into the fourth round, taken by the Cincinnati Bengals. Spencer Drango joined Coleman and Griffin in Cleveland as a fifth-round pick and long-snapper, Jimmy Landes, was the only player at his position to get drafted, going to the Detroit Lions in the sixth round.

Baylor basketball player Rico Gathers, who hadn't played football since junior high but had decided to take his skills and power-forward body to the gridiron, was drafted by the Cowboys in the sixth round. Baylor then had five more players sign free-agent deals with teams following the draft.

"It's an exciting time for these players, and it's an exciting time for Baylor," Briles said. "They grow up with a dream of playing in the NFL. To watch them live out their dreams is really what it's all about."

However, the dream for some was a nightmare for Oakman, who never heard his name called during the draft weekend. In fact, no NFL team even inquired with Briles to get further information on the situation and perhaps sign him at a later point if his name was cleared.

But as it would turn out, the Oakman incident was merely the start of what would become a monumental twist to the Baylor football program that had been under an increasing amount of scrutiny since the previous August. Even though Oakman had graduated and was not technically on the football team anymore, his incident seemed to demonstrate that the cases of Sam Ukwuachu and Tevin Elliot before his were not isolated events. And this time, national media outlets weren't so forgiving. An ESPN *Outside the Lines* report listed more details on previous incidents going back several years, including Tevin Elliott. *Outside the Lines* also revealed an alleged 2013 sexual assault involving Oakman that was never reported to authorities, which led to his one-game suspension for the SMU game at the start of the 2015 season.

Baylor coaches and officials refuted some of the claims of the *Outside the Lines* report, as did the Waco Police Department, which was criticized for shielding some of the incidents involving football players from the media and public record. From the Oakman situation, to the Uk-wuachu trial that went to an appeal hearing, to many of the incidents in the report, most of them were either unsettled by the courts, still pending, or had never gone to a trial.

Still, the number of occurrences had starting to become overwhelming. And Baylor's reputation—from that of President Ken Starr to Athletic Director Ian McCall to Art Briles and his staff—started to receive unruly media attention, with most of them suggesting those three, and more, be removed from their positions.

Ironically enough, on the morning of May 15, about three miles from the Baylor campus, blasts of dynamite could be heard throughout town. The historic Floyd Casey Stadium, the home for Baylor football from 1950 to 2013, was demolished, taking about five seconds to crumble to the ground.

The stadium, while archaic and outdated over the years, was a symbol of history—where the program had been for more than sixty years. One of Briles' early visions when taking over the program was winning enough games to create a culture that would not only warrant a new stadium, but also lead the heavy-pocketed to support it. All of that had taken place as Baylor had completed two seasons in the plush McLane Stadium.

By blowing up Floyd Casey Stadium, it was like Baylor was saying it was blowing up a part of the school's past. But no one could've ever predicted an even bigger explosion on the horizon that would undoubtedly shake up the present and, perhaps, the future of the program as well.

Sunday

While there are a plethora of differences between the high school, college, and NFL levels, one of the biggest involves the addition of players to a roster.

For the most part, high schools are limited to the players who live within the district lines. Colleges spend countless hours, even two to three years in advance, to recruit players, jumping through all sorts of hoops and toeing the line within the NCAA rules to land the best players.

While the phrase "the rich get richer" applies mostly to college programs, it's not the case for the NFL. The teams that struggle the most get first crack at getting the best players in the draft, and after a disappointing, yet shocking 4–12 season, the Cowboys found themselves right at the top of the draft order, owning the fourth overall pick, their highest position since 1991, when they traded up to get the number-one selection.

While the Cowboys learned of their draft order immediately following the regular season, there was still nearly four months before the NFL Draft and several key moments and obstacles that stood before them.

The first of them was the Senior Bowl, the annual all-star game for college seniors wanting to showcase their skills on the field through a week full of practices as well as the actual game. The event has continued to grow over the years, as all thirty-two teams now flock to Mobile, Alabama, sending scouts, coaches, and front-office personnel to mingle with each other, oftentimes using that opportunity to interview potential coaching assistants for vacant spots. In fact, unemployed coaches and staff members seeking NFL employment make it a point to show up during Senior Bowl week.

This year would see the Cowboys send more than just coaches and scouts. Because of their poor record, they were picked by the NFL to serve as one of the coaching staffs of the game, meaning their entire football staff of equipment managers, trainers, and video staffers also made the trip.

Some called it "Week 18" of the NFL season, although the level of intensity of the on-field coaching and the meetings during the week weren't exactly equal to the regular season. Still, Jason Garrett saw it as a chance to get a close-up look at many of the players who would be in the draft, including a possible quarterback candidate in Carson Wentz, an intriguing prospect from North Dakota State. The 6-5, 237-pound quarterback came from a small school, but a program that knows how to win. Wentz helped his team capture two straight national championships on the second-tier FCS level of college football, and he held a 20–3 record as a starter.

Placed on the North squad, Wentz was coached by the Cowboys, giving them a front-row seat to evaluate his arm strength, his mechanics, his command of the huddle, and how he prepared off the field.

At the end of one practice, Jerry Jones was in the middle of a media session with a few reporters when he noticed Wentz walking off the field. Jones excused himself quickly, knowing what he was about to do would create quite a buzz.

He stopped Wentz to introduce himself, catching the quarterback by surprise, before carrying on for a quick chat.

"Is it hard breathing up there," Jones said, referring to Wentz' towering height. The rookie-to-be laughed it off and then shook hands with the Cowboys owner, who then went back to the reporters, although most of them had followed Jones to hear the conversation.

Just like that, it was as if Jones and the Cowboys had launched a draft-sized grenade at the rest of the league.

Message delivered.

Don't think for a second that Jones couldn't have met with Wentz at any time during his two-day visit to Mobile, but he wanted it out there for the world to see. He got the chance to buy the Cowboys because he was a smart businessman who knew how to play the game.

That one meeting put the Cowboys in the quarterback market, whether it was actually true or not. But with Tony Romo having battled a back injury for the last two years, and now broken his clavicle three times since 2010, not to mention his turning thirty-six in April, the writing seemed to be on the wall that the Cowboys would be entertaining the thought of taking a quarterback—at least at some point in this draft, and perhaps with the number-four pick.

As for Romo, who had been debating on whether or not to undergo surgery on his left clavicle, he finally decided to have what was called a Mumford procedure on March 8. The surgery included shaving off the bone to create more space between the shoulder joints. The timetable for his return was just six to eight weeks, giving him ample time to be ready for the off-season workouts and, of course, training camp.

Publicly, Jones and the Cowboys were standing fully behind Romo, as the owner said several times through the media that his quarterback still had "four or five more years left in him." Behind closed doors, however, there were rumblings around Valley Ranch that this was indeed the time to draft a signal-caller for the future.

Romo started four games in 2015, with the Cowboys going 3–1. In the twelve games without him, their record was a dismal 1–11. Clearly, this team had no shot of winning games, much less competing for division titles, without him.

But it also caused quite a debate within places such as the scouting War Room and the coaches' meeting rooms.

Should the Cowboys try to draft some help for Romo? Or try to find his replacement?

Perhaps, they could find a way to do both. But after a 4–12 effort, Dallas had more problem areas than just quarterback, including one spot that was getting worse.

When the season ended, defensive end seemed like a position that might have a couple of young cornerstones for the future. By the end of April, both of those players had been suspended by the NFL. Randy Gregory's four-game setback wasn't a huge surprise, considering he failed his first drug test at the Scouting Combine back in 2015, which caused him to drop from being a potential top-ten pick to where the Cowboys took him in the second round with the sixtieth overall selection. Despite the team's issuing a personal handler to live with him during his rookie season and help him get to places and events on time, Gregory still failed three more drug tests and was eventually suspended for the first four games of the 2016 season.

Along with him was DeMarcus Lawrence, who led the Cowboys in sacks with eight-and-a-half in 2015, including seven in the last eight games. But Lawrence was also hit with a four-game suspension for violating the league's substance abuse policy.

In need of defensive end help, the Cowboys could've turned to unrestricted free agent Greg Hardy, who had not been re-signed by Dallas or any team. His one season with the Cowboys provided more off-the-field headaches than his six sacks were worth. However, every time either Jerry Jones or Stephen Jones fielded any question by the media regarding Hardy, they chose not to address the situation. They never sounded too open to bring Hardy back, but for some reason the book was never closed. One theory, and something the Jones family has done in the past with other free agents, is that publicly dismissing the notion of re-signing Hardy would potentially have a negative impact on his signing with another team. Maybe they knew emphatically they didn't want Hardy's services again, but they didn't want to create a potential blackball situation for the defensive end around the league.

So for whatever the reason, defensive end was quietly becoming a top priority as well, which linked the Cowboys to Ohio State's Joey Bosa, a pass-rushing specialist who figured to be on the board when Dallas went on the clock.

Florida State's Jalen Ramsey, a playmaking defensive back, was also a name that was frequently linked to the Cowboys. The problem with Ramsey was that many thought he was more of a safety than a cornerback, and taking that position so high in the draft was simply too rich.

During one of the pre-draft meetings to talk specifically about Ramsey, coaches and scouts in the War Room got another playmaking defensive back from Florida State on the phone to get his opinion about Ramsey.

Surely, FSU legend Deion Sanders would give a glowing report of a player billed to be the greatest to come out of Tallahassee since "Prime Time" himself. However, Sanders is a straight shooter, which makes him one of the more popular football analysts on NFL Network these days. And he told the Cowboys he thought Ramsey was a better fit to play safety, citing that his hip movement needed work, and he expressed his concerns about whether the young Seminole could be a shutdown cornerback.

Meanwhile, the quarterback situation was taking care of itself. Jared Goff and Wentz elevated themselves to the top two picks. Before the draft even began, it was clear that the best two passers wouldn't even be around for the Cowboys at number four after the Rams traded up to number one and the Eagles made a trade to get the second pick.

So with quarterback no longer a viable option, the defensive back they really liked coming with concerns about his ability to play cornerback, and not everyone in the War Room convinced that Bosa was a real difference maker, there was one name that just kept resurfacing each and every day as the draft got closer.

Ezekiel Elliott.

But could the Cowboys really pull the trigger on a running back, a position that the team proved over the last two years could function without the investment of a high draft pick? DeMarco Murray broke Emmitt Smith's franchise single-season rushing record in 2014 with a 1,845-yard effort. And even after the Cowboys chose not to shell out big bucks in free agency, prompting Murray to sign a whopping five-year, $42 million deal with the Philadelphia Eagles, the Cowboys still got a 1,089-yard campaign out of eight-year veteran Darren McFadden. Of course, that was after the team's failed experiment with Joseph Randle, who couldn't stay out of trouble and was eventually cut halfway through the year.

The Cowboys found out early in 2015 that passing on the opportunity to bring Murray back was the right call. Whether he was just a one-year wonder in Dallas or a wrong fit in Philly, he struggled in his first, and only, year with the Eagles, who traded him to the Titans in March after he rushed for just 702 yards and six touchdowns.

The writing was on the wall that taking a running back later in the draft was the smart move. Yet, the Cowboys couldn't get over Elliott, the everyday bruiser with speed who first caught Garrett's eye in the

2014 National Championship Game at AT&T Stadium when the Buckeye rushed for 246 yards and three touchdowns to help Ohio State beat Oregon.

By the time draft day hit, it looked like a two-man race between Ramsey and Elliott, who were both actually available when the Cowboys picked. The War Room was rather split on the two players, but after a few more minutes of debate, there was one ringing statement, brought up by an unbiased scout in the room, that seemingly sealed the deal.

"We're pretty sure Ramsey can help us at some point. We know Elliott makes us better tomorrow."

Moments later, Jones was handed the phone with Elliott on the other end of the line.

"Hello, Dallas Cowboy, this is Jerry Jones!" the owner and general manager said to Elliott, who was sitting in the Green Room at the NFL Draft in Chicago.

"How you doing, Jerry?" Elliott said, as he was getting hugged by his parents and family.

Both parties had trouble hearing the other because of the cheering and commotion occurring around them. While the Cowboys War Room always gets excited after each pick, the selection of "Zeke" was the type of splash that would instantly pump excitement back into a franchise that had hit roadblock after roadblock the previous season.

The Cowboys then nearly pulled off yet another monstrous move later that evening as they desperately tried to trade back into the first round in order to take Memphis quarterback Paxton Lynch. Ultimately, the Seattle Seahawks took Denver's trade instead of the Cowboys' offer and Lynch went to the Broncos. Even two days later, Jones admitted he "lost sleep" over not overpaying for what could've been the team's much-needed quarterback of the future.

The Cowboys eventually landed a passer in the fourth round in Mississippi State's Dak Prescott, and made some other eye-opening picks by taking Jaylon Smith in the second round, the injured linebacker not likely suiting up at all in 2016, and the aforementioned Baylor basketball player, Rico Gathers, who hadn't played organized football since he was thirteen.

Clearly, the Cowboys were making splashy headlines with their draft picks, starting from the first round all the way to the sixth. But Jones managed to create more buzz in a different way following Thursday's first round. When chatting with reporters about several topics, Jones was stopped by a veteran writer just before walking back into the War Room.

The question was blunt and rather simple.

"Is bringing back Greg Hardy completely off the table?"

Without much hesitation this time, Jones nodded and said, "Yes," and emphatically walked back into the scouting department area.

Just like that, the Hardy era was over in just one season.

Even that kind of news didn't exactly deflect the attention away from drafting Elliott, who was already drawing comparisons to some of the greatest running backs in club history, including the Hall of Famer Smith. And Zeke was embracing it.

Riding in Jones' private jet from Chicago to Dallas the day after the draft, Elliott brought up to some team employees if he should ask to wear Smith's 22 jersey, which has been unofficially retired since the day he left the team.

Elliott smartly didn't press the matter, picking 21 instead. Ironically enough, that was the jersey number Randle had worn with the hope that he would be able to carry the team back to the playoffs again.

Needless to say, the Cowboys weren't messing around now. They knew Romo's window was closing and what better way to help a quarterback than to give him a dynamic running back who could take the pressure off.

Then again, that's more like an oxymoron in Dallas. The pressure is never off for the starting quarterback, or the entire franchise for that matter.

When the Cowboys finish a season 12–4, the expectation the following year is to make the Super Bowl. And when they finish 4–12 and play four different quarterbacks, the expectation the following year is to . . . make the Super Bowl.

Globally recognized around the world, and still referenced as America's Team within the United States, the Cowboys will always rule Texas.

Hundreds of high school teams compete against each other every year to be called state champions. Dozens of college teams battle it out to be conference and perhaps even national champions.

But the undeniable "champion" of Texas is the Dallas Cowboys.

As Garrett and his staff began the process of building a team for 2016, they knew the goal, regardless of how realistic it may or may not be, was to get back to the Super Bowl.

Nothing less is expected. Nothing less is accepted.

EPILOGUE

In Texas the football season never really ends. Things may go a bit quiet, the headlines on the sports page may have a bit less drama, but Friday, Saturday, and Sunday happen every week—even in the off-season.

Still, some off-seasons are more eventful than most, and following the 2016 NFL draft, the Baylor Bears began one of the most controversial and difficult off-seasons in recent memory. Only this time the drama wasn't about recruits or practices. It wasn't about who would be the program's starting quarterback. It was about something much bigger that would leave the school and its football team forever changed.

More than eight months after the university hired the law firm of Pepper Hamilton to conduct an independent investigation on how the school, and specifically the football program, handled sexual assault claims, the firm was ready to reveal its findings to Baylor's Board of Regents. Interestingly, there was no official report of the law firm's findings, at least not anything written or printed out. Instead, the agency sent its investigators in front of the Board of Regents to orally describe what they had learned over the last eight months. There were no documents. No pieces of evidence. No emails or phone records that had been obtained were shared. Just a lecture-style speech from the investigators, in an attempt to paint the most appropriate picture they could.

As a result, the full details of Pepper Hamilton's actual findings were never made public simply because they couldn't be—no report actually existed from the firm. And while a 13-page report was later printed and sent out regarding some of the suggestions Pepper Hamilton made to improve sexual assault issues on campus, this document was created and distributed by Baylor based on Pepper Hamilton's presentation and was not made by the law firm itself. In the university's own document, the school shared some of the law firm's findings:

- Baylor's student conduct processes were wholly inadequate to consistently provide a prompt and equitable response under Title IX. Baylor failed to take action to identify and eliminate a potential hostile environment.
- University administrators directly discouraged some complainants from reporting or participating in student conduct processes and in one instance constituted retaliation against a complainant for reporting sexual assault.
- In addition to broader University failings, Pepper found specific failings within both the football program and Athletics Department leadership, including a failure to identify and respond to a pattern of sexual violence by a football player and to a report of dating violence.
- There are significant concerns about the tone and culture within Baylor's football program as it relates to accountability for all forms of student-athlete misconduct.
- Over the course of their review, Pepper investigated the University's response to reports of a sexual assault involving multiple football players. The football program and Athletics Department leadership failed to take appropriate action in response to these reports.

While no specific names were mentioned in the report, it's unknown whether or not the oral review mentioned some of the administrators by name. But one thing was clear, the football program was consistently mentioned throughout the report.

In the aftermath of the presentation, on the morning of May 26, 2016, the Board of Regents at Baylor had apparently seen enough and certainly heard enough from the now relentless national media that continued to air its displeasure over the reports of alleged sexual assaults and the suspected mishandling from the administrators at Baylor. Sure, some of the columnists with the louder voices suggested that Baylor get rid of all of the higher-ups, starting with the president and athletic director. But this is Texas, where football presides over everything. Getting rid of the president, even one with the name appeal of Ken Starr, wouldn't move the needle and satisfy those looking for retribution. No, to see any kind of change would mean Baylor had to remove the one person solely responsible for all of the football program—including its success.

And that's what Baylor ultimately decided, dismissing head coach Art Briles, a move that sent shockwaves throughout the country. It had been just a few days earlier that a report out of Austin suggested that the school was leaning toward firing only Starr and keeping Briles. That's when the media barked even louder, accusing Baylor of turning its back on societal issues and even academics and focusing only on football. Whether it was because of this criticism or not, Baylor decided to let go of Briles, who was informed by phone early on the morning of May 26 that he was being "suspended with intent to terminate." Regardless of the linguistic semantics, Briles was fired. He was immediately moved out of his office, his name was taken off the door, his access codes to the football complex were deactivated, and more importantly, a search committee was formed at Baylor to land a new coach.

While Baylor's initial statement only included Briles' dismissal, the university eventually fired both Starr and athletic director Ian McCaw.

One of the more recognizable school presidents in the country, a highly successful athletic director, and of course, a head coach that had been a proven winner at many stops, all took a backseat, as Baylor shifted its focus to the victims and, perhaps, future victims at either Baylor or other schools that needed a voice.

Within three days, Baylor had announced that it had hired veteran coach Jim Grobe, who had last been at Wake Forest, which like Baylor was a private school that struggled for years to stay competitive. Grobe did guide the Demon Deacons to some success in the late 2000s, but retired in 2013 with a career record of 110–115–1. Ironically enough, Grobe replaced Briles, whose first game as head coach of the Bears back in 2008 was actually against Grobe and his Wake Forest squad.

While Briles was removed, the rest of the assistants stayed on the staff, including his son Kendal Briles and son-in-law Jeff Lebby.

Even with Briles suspended, it was clear Baylor had moved on and it was only a matter of time before the official firing took place. One of the criticisms Briles received in the days after Baylor's announcement was over his decision not to reveal his side of the story, causing many to believe he indeed had something to hide. However, with him technically remaining under contract, both Baylor and Briles' lawyers advised him not to make any public comments as the two sides were still trying to negotiate a settlement.

Briles did issue a statement on June 2, exactly a week after his dismissal as head coach, directing the attention back toward the university.

Baylor Nation,

My heart goes out to the victims for the pain that they have endured. Sexual assault has no place on our campus or in our society. As a father of two daughters, a grandfather, and a husband, my prayers are with the victims of this type of abuse, wherever they are. After 38 years of coaching, I have certainly made mistakes and, in hindsight, I would have done certain things differently. I always strive to be a better coach, a better father and husband, and a better person.

Keep in mind, the complete scope of what happened here has not been disclosed and unfortunately at this time I am contractually obligated to remain silent on the matter. The report prepared by Pepper Hamilton, the law firm hired and paid for by Baylor's Board of Regents, has not been shared with me directly,

*despite my full cooperation with the investigation. I can only
assume that the report, which is not independent, supports the
conclusions that the Board has already drawn. I hope to share with
you what I was aware of as soon as I can so Baylor Nation can
begin the healing process.*

    *I have the utmost admiration for Baylor University, its
community, and its important mission. I am truly grateful for
having had the chance to coach hundreds of young student
athletes at this University. I am deeply humbled for having had the
opportunity to be a part of Baylor Nation.*

    Coach Art Briles

While Briles and his PR team felt the need to end his silence and release the statement, it wasn't an easy process considering he was still not
fully aware of the reasons for his firing. More than five weeks after his
removal, Briles had never been informed by any member of the Board of
Regents why the decision was made to fire him.

Through secondhand sources, Briles was once told the reason
stemmed from the "aggregate number" of domestic violence and sexual
assault charges against his players since he became the coach in 2008.
In that time, Tevin Elliott and Sam Ukwuachu had been convicted, and
Shawn Oakman, although he graduated in December of 2015 and was
living off campus, had been accused of an assault in April of 2016, just a
few weeks before Briles was fired.

Nationally, there was a wide range of speculation that Baylor made
the decision on Briles because of a "cover up" in the handling of sexual
assault matters. To the coach's knowledge, considering he was never informed directly by the powers that be, the decision was made only on the
number of incidents. As for any cover-up theory, Briles told the Board of
Regents during his only meeting with them two days before the decision
that he had never once encountered an alleged victim or her parents with
a face-to-face meeting or even a phone call. There had never been a conversation between Briles and any of the alleged victims.

Baylor's official statement of the personnel changes pointed to "a lack of strong institutional management and control on a number of levels. The Board's actions reflect a focus on the points at which the most significant levels of accountability and obligation should have been exercised."

Acting chair of the Board of Regents Richard Willis was the only spokesperson in the school's release.

"We have made these decisions, because, above all, we must safeguard our students and our campus," said Richard Willis, the acting chair of the Board of Regents. "We must set a new course to ensure the leaders of the University place a premium on responding effectively and with sensitivity to those impacted by the tragedy of interpersonal violence."

But there were other factors occurring that puzzled the Briles' camp and his supporters. For starters, the university took three years to comply with a policy enacted in 2011 by the U.S. Department of Education's Office for Civil Rights. Baylor did not hire a full-time Title IX coordinator until 2014. All of the sexual assault complaints against Bears football players occurred in those three years, leaving some to question what kind of procedures and protocols were even in place for Baylor administrators to follow during that time.

Secondly, the timing of these decisions fell in the middle of some scheduled turnovers on the Board of Regents. Willis, who was considered one of the major proponents in removing Briles, ended his term as BOR Chair on June 1, just six days after making the decision, one of about 10 board members who ended their terms. Was this just a mere coincidence that such a significant decision was coming down at the end of these regents' term? Or perhaps, could the decision to remove all of the higher-ups at Baylor be an easier call for those who wouldn't have to experience any of the aftermath of this decision? Also, another prominent Board of Regent, who remained on the board after June 1, told two Baylor assistant coaches in early June that he "doesn't care if Baylor ever wins another football game."

In the span of a few days, Baylor University had been turned upside down. The next few weeks after the decision was a rollercoaster of events that saw some of the school's biggest donors even try to strong-arm the Regents with threats of ending their gift-giving unless Briles was reinserted as head coach. While there were media reports that suggested that possibility, it was never a legitimate scenario to bring Briles back, and it was never a given that he would've accepted a return unless the terms were of his liking.

With nearly $40 million left on a contract that extended through the 2023 season, Briles wasn't going away quietly without a fair settlement. He eventually filed a lawsuit against Baylor on June 16, citing wrongful termination. That seemed to get the school's attention and a settlement was officially agreed upon less than 24 hours later. It took about a week for the official documents to be signed and sealed, and though the terms were not disclosed, Briles was awarded a rather hefty payment.

But Briles' firing was only the start. Not only did Baylor lose its highly successful coach, but it also lost most of its highly ranked recruiting class, as 11 incoming freshmen were granted their scholarship releases, making them free to sign with other programs. To no one's surprise, the University of Texas corralled four of them, including lineman Patrick Hudson and receiver Devin Duvernay. Baylor coaches figured the Longhorns would pounce on their former recruits, considering they were told by several players that, back in February, UT coaches sent out text messages with a link to an ESPN *Outside the Lines* story that had not aired yet, detailing some of the accusations of the Baylor saga. The Bears staff figured the Texas ties to the Longhorn Network, which is owned by ESPN, was a reason why the rival school's assistants were able to obtain the story in an attempt to flip some of the recruits before Signing Day. While that didn't occur then, Texas was able to capitalize on this new opportunity, as did other schools such as Auburn and Oklahoma.

Other schools were gaining ground thanks to Baylor's colossal loss—at least on the football field.

Even some of the current players decided to part ways with Baylor, including quarterback Jarrett Stidham, who chose to join a local community college and sit out a season from football. While Stidham never publicly announced his plans, those close to the football program believe the quarterback wanted to keep three years of eligibility left and possibly join Briles and/or some of the Baylor assistants that might take another job in 2017.

In the end, the decision-makers at Baylor chose to overlook the success garnered by the football program and focus on rehabilitating its reputation as an institution of higher learning. Briles was in charge of a football program, from top to bottom, that was deemed out of control by its own Board of Regents. And despite all of the success he created for the football program, Baylor opted for a change in leadership.

Because for all of the gray area that surrounded this situation—from what the coaches actually knew about these cases, to the role that Title IX should've played, to the way the Board of Regents received this report and the manner in which they made their changes—one thing was very black and white here: there were victims of sexual assault on the campus of Baylor. The actual number is unclear and some of the cases may still be pending. Regardless, one victim is one too many, and tragically there were even more than that. The fact that many of them occurred in a rather short period of time suggests it was sadly part of the culture on the campus of Baylor, especially within the athletic department, which in this state, always starts and ends with football.

And just like that, Baylor showed the country that while football was big in Texas, it wasn't big enough to outrun the problems that have followed it around the country.

This point was echoed just up the road in Dallas, where the Cowboys faced a similar tough decision with Greg Hardy, whose season had shown him to be a true talent on the football field. In fact, the team had plenty of reasons to re-sign Hardy in 2016, considering its lack of depth along the defensive line. But Hardy could never escape his off-the-field issues. His problems became the Cowboys' problems, the team forced to defend his actions to fans, sponsors, and even its own players. At the end of the day, despite the need to acquire the best talent at the most important positions, the Cowboys couldn't justify bringing Hardy back for another year, given his behavior, his past, and what he'd come to represent.

As different and nearly impossible to compare as the two situations were, both demonstrated in their own way that increasingly, even in Texas, football doesn't always win. Yes, pigskin is king in the Lone Star State. But if this one season proved anything, it's that there are limits to every king's rule. In many ways this is a change that the sport is going through around the country, as fans, teams, coaches, and players at all levels of the game must confront difficult questions about the game they love. In Texas the fans might make football king, but they also look to their teams to produce seasons and people that are worthy of their adoration. Simply loving the sport is no longer enough. The reality of Texas football has grown more complicated.

THE BEAUTY OF FOOTBALL is that typically, teams get to start over with a clean slate each season. No matter how good or bad the previous year was, the next season is a new chapter.

As I write this today, Plano High School is holding their summer practices, and Coach McCullough is there, walking them through the five-man sleds, barking at his players, trying to find a new starting quarterback and someone to replace a star running back who is off to UCLA. There is no time to rest as fall practices are just a few weeks away.

Meanwhile NFL camps are in full swing. The Cowboys are looking to move on from their injury plagued season to find something more positive. And whereas in previous years Tony Romo had long been the speculative punching bag for the team's hopes and dreams, having suffered through the 2015 campaign, fans and the press alike are turning toward him with a sense of optimism, knowing all too well what his absence from the team means. The Cowboys are also hoping a change of scenery might help their fortunes as they move away from their Valley Ranch headquarters into a brand-new, state-of-the-art complex in Frisco, Texas. However, the only change Cowboys fans really care about is getting the team back into the playoffs.

But getting past the 2015–16 season will likely take much longer for Baylor. Without a doubt, the incidents that transpired during, and mainly after, that season will have a lasting effect for years. The summer included more talk about lawsuits, settlements, and consequential transfers than the customary position battles and rival opponents.

But nothing is more resilient than football. Even at a place such as Baylor that wants no part of its struggling past that haunted them for many years. A new football season could be the first step in the healing process of what has been a long, difficult off-season for all parties involved.

Saturdays in Waco may not look the same for a while, but Baylor will have no choice but to bounce back. And while the circumstances are much different, Plano will look to do the same on Fridays, just like the Cowboys will be seeking a redemption season on Sundays.

The dates on the calendar always change. The players, and even the coaches, eventually revolve as well. But whether it's a Friday, Saturday, or Sunday in the fall, the passion of football never stops.

Especially in Texas.

ACKNOWLEDGMENTS

While I originally planned on writing this book based on the 2014 season, I never found the right publishing options that I deemed suitable for this project. But when HarperCollins came on board, we mutually decided to roll with the 2015 season, a decision that proved to be the right one, in more ways than one.

Let's start the thanking process right there with HarperCollins and Matt Harper, who not only shared a vision for this book, but brought different aspects and angles to the project that I had never realized. Working with him and his team at HarperCollins was an absolute pleasure. They're the best of the best, so it was an honor to be associated with their brand.

While I've written two other books before, this was by far the most challenging project I'd ever endured. Then again, it should be. I realized several times why no other writer had attempted something like this before.

But I couldn't have done without the love and support of my family, friends, and undoubtedly my coworkers, who made more sacrifices than they even realize.

I want to thank the Cowboys organization for allowing me the opportunity and access to write this book. Special thanks to Matt O'Neil, but mainly my boss, Derek Eagleton, who has always taken pride in my success, and once again, was extremely instrumental in giving me both support and encouragement throughout this journey. My team members at the Cowboys often picked me up on days where energy was low. I hope guys like David Helman and Rob Phillips know how much I appreciate them for their ability to pick up the slack. But the entire team of Bryan Broaddus, Kent Garrison, Shannon Gross, Taylor Stern, Ambar Garcia, and Claudia Castillo helped inspire me along the way, just by a simple acknowledgment here and there. On more than one occasion, a coworker would ask me if this or that would be included in the book; and I would respond with a "yes, of course," even though I actually forgot about that and was so happy for the reminder.

Many other coaches, players, and staff members at the Cowboys were able to help me with some of the stories and insights. They know who they are, and I want to thank all of them for their contributions.

Moving on to Baylor, I made a promise that I would always include Art Briles in the acknowledgments of any book I ever wrote, simply for the fact that he opened the door for me back in 2013, allowing me to write his biography, *Looking Up*. It was an honor to write that book, and I'm sure I wouldn't have just finished a third book had he not given me that chance. But I actually need to thank him again for this book for giving me more than enough of his time to help this process. His entire family, including oldest daughter, Jancy Briles, was extremely gracious with their time and insight.

Special thanks to many Baylor support staff members, most notably Diane McPheeters, who has a zillion things on her plate, but still made time to help.

At Plano, head coach, Jaydon McCullough, granted me the access I needed to get a front-row view of his team, not only this year but in recent seasons as well. I want to thank him and his staff for their hospitality. Some of the coaches were very helpful, but none more so than Chris Fisher. Without a doubt, of all the subjects I've written about in my three books, telling his story and his journey is by far the most gratifying and inspiring.

The students at Plano who gave me their time—Matt Keys, Darion

Foster, and Brandon Stephens—were all amazing kids to work with. I look forward to watching their progress in life, in whatever field—football, business, or anything else—they choose to take.

I also want to acknowledge Colin Brence and Sam Tecklenburg, along with their families. Because the timeline was pushed back, their stories weren't as prominent, but I do appreciate the time and generosity that were given to me.

I can't go on any further without mentioning my personal editor, Kurt Daniels, who is much more than that. He not only serves as an unbiased proofreader and fact-checker, but he's helped open some doors for me with all three of my books, so that has made him a huge part of my own success. I hope he knows just how much I value his opinion, not to mention the time he's spent reviewing my work.

Saving the best for last, my family is as supportive a group as you'll ever find. My mother, Camille, is one of the best proofreaders I know, and she and her husband, Robb, couldn't wait to get their hands on this manuscript. My dad, Tim, is saving a spot on his bookshelf for this one, which is probably the only time I'll ever share a spot next to Tom Clancy or James Patterson.

My daughter, Olivia, told me she can't wait until she gets older so she can not only read the books I write, but understand them, too. I hope she knows that a statement like that from a nine-year-old is worth more than ever cracking a book. Her mother, Josie, has always been understanding when it comes to shuffling schedules around.

My stepdaughter, Marisa, had to grow up fast this past year by helping out around the house when I wasn't there, especially on the weekends when I was covering three games in three days.

But the true hero in this entire process was my beautiful wife, Julie. We welcomed our son, Jacob, to the family in June of 2015, and she spent many days and nights tending to him while I was on the road. Dividing time was a big challenge, but Julie never lost sight of the ultimate goal. At her own job, she loves to show people my books, and I have no doubt she will take great pride in showing off this one as well.

Of course, I might beat her to the punch on that one. Although trying to stay humble, I don't mind admitting the pride I have in completing this project. I knew it was something that hadn't been done before, and I pushed myself to limits I didn't know I had.

Overall, these past two seasons have been quite a journey. Moving the book from 2014 to 2015 turned out to be a blessing in disguise. Sure, there were a few more losses this time around, but it made me realize that there is more to Texas football than just winning.

Sure this state loves a winner, but more than anything, this state just loves football.

Something you can see rather clearly, whether it's Friday, Saturday, or Sunday.